Massimo Cappon

ROCK AND ICE CLIMBING

ORBIS PUBLISHING·London

Photographs by Massimo Cappon

Other photographs supplied by: Roberto Ive, Centro di Documentazione Mondadori, Archivio Ghedina (Cortina), Istituto Vittorio Sella (Biella), Archivio Zanichelli

The author would like to thank the following for allowing themselves to be photographed for this book: the ice climbers Ivan Negro, Francesco Della Beffa, Adriano Lora Tonet, the rock climbers Mario Lacedelli and Sandro Zardini, the guide Franco Garda, the director of the Alpine Mountain Rescue Services from the Valle d'Aosta and the director of the CNSA, Bruno Toniolo. Particular thanks go to Roberto Ive for his help and collaboration.

Editor: Enzo de Michele
Illustrations: Sergio Quaranta
Designer: Giuseppe Villa

First published in Great Britain by
Orbis Publishing Limited, London 1983

© Arnoldo Mondadori Editore 1981, 1983

Printed in Italy by Mondadori

ISBN 0-85613-475-9

Contents

Introduction

The world of mountains has dimensions all of its own. Those familiar concepts of time and space take on a quite different meaning. And the relationship between the various forces at play and the proportions in question is invariably conspicuously imbalanced.

A man decides to climb to the heights. From the terrace at the refuge the summit is no more than a faraway tip of colour, lost in the eloquent architecture of rock and snow. The climber's body arches into the void. All his senses are focused on the movements he has to make. His hands intuitively sense which holds are safe. The tips of his boots seek out the slightest projections in the rock-face. If everything goes without a hitch, within a few minutes, or hours, or maybe after a whole day, all those tensions will dissolve at the top of the climb – that idyllic place where all the contours of the mountain magically converge, and where the climber's equilibrium will reassume its habitual horizontal dimension. But it may well happen, during the ascent, that something snaps or breaks, without a moment's warning, and when that happens the climber is no more than a puppet, dangling over the abyss. Or it may be the deadly cold of a snowstorm which breaks the rhythm of the descent. At times like that the mere amateur will find himself spontaneously asking himself: 'Why am I doing this?'

The simplest reply to this question was uttered in 1924 by the Englishman George L. Mallory, before he set off on his last legendary ascent, never to be seen again: 'Why do I want to climb Everest? Because it's there.' One of the oldest motivations is the myth of the 'Sacred Mountain'. The loftiest peaks, nudged by clouds and enveloped by an aura of awestruck fear, are the home of the gods – the magic bridge between heaven and earth. Olympus, Parnassus, Sinai, Kailas, Ama Dablam, Fuji – all religions have identified, in the form of some mountain-top, man's anxiety over the divine. All religions have turned mountain-tops into a symbol of man's supreme aspirations. Early forms of mountaineering were undoubtedly stimulated by pilgrimages, sacrificial ceremonies and other rites. A mummy dating back to Inca times has been found on the summit of Cerro del Toro, which soars to 6300 metres (20,700 ft). On Mount Taishan, in Shantung province, the rulers of the ancient Chinese dynasties asked the gods to confirm their commands. And in the world of modern mountaineering there also seems to be an ascetic stimulus, though possibly less consciously. In the lyrical definition of Ruskin, mountains are 'the Earth's great cathedrals, with their doors of rock, their altars of snow and their vaults glittering with stars'. And many an account of experiences lived in the Himalaya, in the 'death zone' – at 8000 metres (26,300 ft) – is laced with mysticism.

'The purest of sports' (as Mummery described it) is the most individualistic of individualistic sports, and the mountain itself is a mirror of this. On the rock-face, regardless of a mountaineer's motivations, he will also find himself – find out who he is. Mountaineering consists of a sense of struggle and an affirmation of a person's own determination. Mountaineering has to do with a personal and moral statement – it is only possible to demonstrate one's courage by getting the better of the natural reaction of fear, and it is only possible to demonstrate one's generosity and friendship by getting the better of one's own selfishness – a taste for discovery and adventure (and every ascent, great and small, is an adventure), a quest for primitive, raw emotions and sensations in a direct confrontation with nature, and the satisfaction of an objective achieved after a great deal of commitment and hard work. In a word, every major ascent is an existential fable. In the words of Goethe: 'Only those who set out, day by day, to conquer freedom and life are worthy of these things.'

For the Italian climber Walter Bonatti, one of the legendary names in the history of mountaineering, this sport is 'struggle, adventure, romanticism, escapism and ... sport'. But it is also, and most importantly, 'a way of approaching nature, via mountains, in order to savour once again that forgotten contact, and to heed the lesson of simplicity and severity which is still so valid in this day and age'. For Reinhold Messner, that outstanding climber from the Alto Adige (Upper Adige), who has twice climbed Everest without oxygen, the stimulus, is in a state of permanent inner restlessness, in which there is no possibility of complete

gratification. For Messner there is a state of 'being continually beaten without ever being able to win'. He explains:

One day I discovered a new mountain on the horizon. I looked at the pure lines of its ridges and crests and faces, and straightaway I felt that I had to climb it, that I had to turn the dream into reality. Something snapped inside me, and I knew that I would only be able to regain my equilibrium on the top of that mountain. But I also know that joy is a mirage. Once I had come down to earth the magic was no longer there and I would have to make that ascent all over again.

When it comes to tackling an ascent, the mountaineer feels an aesthetic sensation, together with a physical and almost sensual pleasure in the act of climbing in a world of vertical geometry, thus dominating gravity. People will climb a mountain out of a taste for the new or the unknown. Others will do it because of the mountain's own history. A climber may take the same route several times over (and every time he will have a different experience), or he may try to tackle different problems at every ascent. But on the whole mountaineering is lived and experienced as an inner proof of oneself. Says Messner:

The mountains tell you, quite ruthlessly, who you are, and what you are. Mountaineering is a game where you can't cheat. When you're on a long climb, what counts is not your heart or your lungs or your fitness or your technique so much as your inner motivation, your ability to withstand the cold, tiredness and solitude; more than that, what's important is your determination, cool nerves, and knowing how to make the right choices.

The fascination of the risk element (which is always there even when you try to reduce it as much as possible) is an important ingredient of mountaineering too. As we read in Preuss's journal:

We know only too well that fate can turn you from winners into losers. Only people who don't grasp this will treat their own life lightly. People who clearly understand that this is the nature of the game, and even say so, should not be demeaned. In the mountains there are victories worthy of the highest rung.

But it would nevertheless be wrong to identify, *a priori*, the acceptance of the risk element with some self-destructive urge. On the contrary, the mountaineer is an affirmation of life, in all its fullness. The climber climbs mountains *to live*, 'to deliver, constantly, his own life from the claws of death' (Messner). And it is his clear moral duty to measure up to the situation at all times. Anyone who has had mountaineering experience has known those magic moments when, as a result of a series of favourable circumstances, everything seems possible. This 'state of grace' implies an absolute mastery of one's own capabilities, but it is above all a mental state of total harmony, of being 'at one'.

Mountaineering is also, and first and foremost, a form of freedom, a yearning for space, and an intolerance of all types of conditioning. It is also freedom from the rhetoric of 'Titanism', from the 'conquest' of the 'woman-mountain', and from the sense of 'aggression' towards the mountain seen as an object. It is freedom from the gratuitous identification of mountaineering with something that is by definition noble, heroic and unselfish, practised in a 'sacred' space where everything is pure and beautiful. You can venture into the mountains with the most negative and dangerous of motivations as well – for reasons of ambition, out of frustration, or revenge, or with a competitive or nationalistic spirit. You can reveal yourself as somebody selfish and mean, just as you can in any other situation – but the risk is greater when climbing mountains... In a word, mountaineering can be transformed into a dry, athletic exercise, or a club activity, without instilling any other values into it. Whether 'conquerors of the futile' (Lionel Terray) or *Bergvagabunden* (mountain vagabonds), mountaineers nevertheless adhere to one principal ancestral summons: the same summons which drove the first people inhabiting the African savanna to clamber over a range of low hills merely 'to see further'.

Previous page: the joy of climbing on the compact granite of Mont Blanc. In the background looms the summit of the Aiguille Blanche. Above: emerging on the summit ridge after an ice climb. Left: dawn on Mont Maudit, in the Mont Blanc group, with the first climbers already starting up the north face of the Tour Ronde.

The nature of mountains

Pinnacles, peaks and glaciers ... from time immemorial a symbol of solemn, motionless eternity ... But mountains are quite the opposite: the result of tremendous forces which are continually moulding the face of our planet. If you imagine running through the history of the earth in a film lasting a couple of hours, this history would appear as something living, something assailed by great spasms and movements. We would see vast mountain chains emerging in what used once to be seas or plains; we would see rivers blazing their trails by hewing out deep canyons; we would see glaciers retreating or advancing, forming huge wedges in narrow valleys and leaving behind them accumulations of moraine; we would see reliefs tapering upwards to form dizzy summits and then vanishing forever; and we would see volcanoes growing and towering over plateaux, and then flooding them with their lava. The external forces of erosion, wind, ice, water and the chemical activities of the atmosphere, all attack rocks, reducing them to dust, slowly demolishing them, changing them in many different ways. When water finds its way into cracks and fissures and freezes, it acts like a wedge: thousands and millions of chisel blows, light or hard, working away at every pinnacle, and every rock-face. And the landslides and sedimentary deposits that slither down mountain-sides eventually fill valleys and lakes.

To all appearances, the mountainous environment is chaotic. To the eyes of a geologist, on the other hand, it represents an open book which tells him about the past history of the planet. In the sixties, after the discoveries made in the course of the 'International Geophysical Year', the theory of plate tectonics (which has a precursor in A. Wegener's theory of 1912) was finally in a position to explain all the major geological phenomena jointly: volcanic activity, seismic activity, continental drift, and the origins of the world's great mountain ranges. The earth has experienced six or seven major orogenetic cycles. The 'recent' phase started about 200 million years ago with the re-emergence of volcanic material which gave rise to the splitting-up of the super-continent known as Pangaea into six principal plates, and their subsequent movement in different directions. These plates, which, broadly speaking, correspond to the continents as we know them today, are part of the lithosphere – the outermost and most brittle part of the earth.

The Alpine-Himalayan system started to take shape 50 million years ago with the closing-off of a large inland sea called Tethys, in which sedimentary and igneous rocks had accumulated above an oceanic trench. The collision between the African plate and the Euro-Asiatic plate gave rise to the overlapping of various geological strata and the compression of a portion of crust which was originally 1000 km (620 miles) across to less than 100 km (62 miles) across. As India drew near to the rest of Asia, this caused the formation of the mighty Himalayan peaks. The orogenetic thrust is still active today and is set against the leaching action caused by erosion (0.4-0.5 mm a year on the slopes of the Swiss Alps). The major glacial cycles that occurred during the Quaternary period brought about profound changes to the shape of the mountains and valleys affected. The most conspicuous hallmark left by glaciation is the 'chiselling' effect on the four sides of the Matterhorn, which has given it its unmistakable shape, like an undaunted, solitary pyramid.

The various types of rocks are also associated with one another as a result of a continuous cycle of destruction and regeneration. The major groups are the sedimentary rocks (limestones), rocks of volcanic origin (basalts and granites), and metamorphic rocks (schists and gneisses). The white limestone rock-faces of the Austrian Alps, the southern 'ramparts' of the Marmolada and the Gran Sasso are what remain from the erosion and transformation wrought by the various atmospheric agents on the deposits of calcareous shells which once covered the bed of the Tethys. A similar structure occurs in dolomite rock – calcium and magnesium carbonate. At one time, the three Peaks of Lavaredo, and the Sella, the Sassolungo, the Brenta, and the Pale di San Martino, all formed coral atolls and reefs. The Dolomites are considered to be the rock-climber's paradise. The starting-points of the various climbs are almost invariably close to refuges, the rock-faces soar upwards over woodland and pastures, and the rock itself, which has been hewn and chiselled by the various atmospheric agents, offers plenty of hand- and footholds. This is an elegant form of climbing, taking vertical lines, making the

Mountains which are of interest to mountaineers must have certain specific features: a well-defined structure, good-quality rock, or sufficient altitude to be covered in snow and ice. In the Alps, the most characteristic environment is the Dolomite region, with its calcareous rock; another one is the Western Alps where there is a predominance of glacial conditions and solid granite rocks. Right: climbers on the Via Rossi of the First Sella Tower. Above: a party of climbers near the summit of the Piaz in the Vajolet region. The Dolomites are known as the 'rock-climber's paradise' because of the vertical nature and aerial elegance of the pinnacles, ridges and rock-faces. Top: on the Rochefort ridge, at 4000 metres (13,100 ft), in the Mont Blanc massif.

The Alps started to form 50 million years ago as a result of the closing-off of a large inland sea (called Tethys) and the compression of a portion of the earth's crust from 1000 km across (620 miles) to just 100 km (62 miles). Below: strata of the Triassic period as seen when following the Astaldi path, below the Tofane. The variation in environments creates different conditions for the mountaineer as well. Right above: the Ortles glacier. At high altitudes the weather is one of the basic variable elements which climbers must always keep their eye on. Right centre: a spring snow-field in the Pale di San Martino. Far right: a mushroom-shaped ice formation on the Khumbu moraine in the Himalaya, caused by the action of the sun. The boulder has kept the column beneath in the shade while the level all round dropped.

most of the smallest of holds and grips, and exploiting natural pillars and fissures. The ridges and crests of the Dolomites offer some of the most exciting climbing possible – with an airy flavour and always surrounded by wonderful views. The colour of the rock supplies the mountaineer with useful hints: grey-pink indicates the most solid and compact rock, yellow indicates crumbling, friable rock, and black striations indicate wet rock.

Granite is different and less consistent in conformation than limestone. It is a crystalline rock which originated from the cooling of a melted magma of silica and aluminium. Its typical structure is one of large overlaid plates, often extremely smooth and compact, or vertical monoliths (jagged rocks) fashioned into blocks with clear-cut and sharp edges, as if by some gigantic axe. Famous examples are the granite of the Masino Valley in the Central Alps, the red protogine of Mont Blanc, and that found in Yosemite, the cradle of modern rock climbing in the United States. Climbing on granite involves special techniques, using friction which requires good judgement of the slope of the rock, or following a progression of definite fissures and chimneys which split it. This involves the use of recesses, torsion, opposition, athletic movements and carefully planned manoeuvres. This type of climbing is perhaps less elegant than limestone climbing, and it is certainly more taxing. Because of the width of the cracks, it is often difficult to use pitons for aid or protection. The usual solution is to use 'bongs' or small chocks of metal

wedged in cracks. Highly recommended is the use of special lightweight climbing boots (sometimes called 'PA's') – which are flexible and smooth-soled – for routes where friction technique is required.

Unlike granite, schists and gneisses form horizontally stratified structures, and the rock is very often unstable and dangerous.

All mountaineers must obviously keep an eye on the general environment in which they are climbing. The clear difference between the environment of the Eastern Alps and that of the high mountains typical of the Western Alps (or the mighty Himalaya or Andes) has given rise to a far too rigid and 'historical' discrimination between the mountaineers of the two schools. In limestone environments, 'pure' rock-climbing technique is the most used, often in the most favourable weather conditions. In the Western Alps the mountaineer must bear in mind various other factors (snow conditions, the weather and the temperature, the major objective dangers, and the time it takes to reach the various routes); he must be tougher and fitter; he must carry heavier equipment, and he must have more advanced technical knowledge of what he is tackling. The major high-altitude routes, on ice or mixed terrain (rock and ice) require an even more painstaking logistical preparation, a good working knowledge of the descent route and possible escape routes, anticipation of all possible eventualities, and the judgement to give up the climb when conditions become too adverse.

Awareness of various objective dangers is the first requirement for anyone venturing into the mountains. Left: an avalanche caused by the slipping of a large slab of snow on the hazardous slopes of Mont Blanc du Tacul. Two mountaineers, who have unwisely strayed from the normal route, are having a narrow escape from hurtling blocks of ice. The risk of avalanches is highest during winter and spring. In summer there is a greater risk of being hit by falling seracs. Above: a hidden crevasse beneath a snow-bridge. On glaciers it is a good rule to be roped together at all times. Right: a descent by abseil from an overhang in the Dolomites, with bad weather looming. Summer storms are particularly feared for their violence and the risk of being struck by lightning.

In general, speed is safety in Alpine mountaineering. Climbers must start their routes early, often in darkness by the light of the head torch, so that the snow and the ice that they must cross on the glacier or climb on the route is still frozen. Early starts also give protection against the danger of séracs (ice cliffs) collapsing, something that happens as soon as the sun begins to thaw the ice and snow. Climbers must move carefully without frequent stops and keep up a steady pace. The longer a party takes on a route, the longer it is exposed to the danger of an accident.

The physical environment is influenced by the climate, by the latitude and by the altitude. It is well known that the temperature drops by 0.6°C every 100 metres (330 ft) the higher up you go. Beyond the summer limit of 0°C we are in the region of permanent snow and glaciers. In Greenland this limit is barely above sea-level; in the Alps it lies at about 3000 metres (9800 ft), and in the Himalaya and the Andes it is above 5000 metres (16,400 ft). The weather is directly associated with the various seasonal cycles: hence the winter snows in the Alps or the alternating monsoon phases in the Himalaya. The climate at high altitude is nevertheless characterized by drier air, marked temperature ranges, sudden cloud formations and more frequent precipitation. Bad weather is accompanied by a drop in temperature, snowfalls, lightning, and mist which can muddle a climber's sense of direction. On rock, which is dangerous enough even when it is merely wet, one can find an insidious and sometimes completely unnegotiable layer of black ice or verglas.

TWO
CENTURIES
OF CONQUEST

From the pioneers to modern times

Shrouded in superstition and legend, isolated in wild solitude, protected by apparently insuperable and fearsome natural obstacles (frost, avalanches, glaciers and giddy fortresses of rock), until the middle of the eighteenth century the peaks of the Alps (those *infames frigoribus Alpes*, in the words of Tacitus) seemed beyond the reach of men. And back in those days it seemed inconceivable that anyone could tackle the risks and hardships of an ascent, for the pure pleasure of doing it. In popular folklore the mountains were the uncontested realm of the devil and witches, and were inhabited by monstrous creatures. So entrenched were these beliefs that a Zurich scholar, J. Scheuchzer, saw fit in 1723 to dedicate a chapter of his learned tome on *Natural History* to Alpine dragons; and he even posed himself the question whether wingless dragons ought to be considered females, or a different species altogether.

Countless tales, in Italy, Austria and Switzerland, have been told of villages completely obliterated, along with all their inhabitants, by terrifying avalanches. It is no surprise to learn that at the end of the seventeenth century the Bishop of Annecy was summoned to solemnly exorcize the glaciers towering over Chamonix. The only people who ventured up to fairly high altitudes were hunters in search of chamois, or people looking for crystals. Legend has it that these latter would clamber up the steepest rock-faces barefoot, sometimes even cutting the soles of their feet with a knife to get a better grip with the sticky blood.

Mountaineering, in the modern sense of the term, has an 'official' starting date which relegates to the annals of prehistory those nonetheless remarkable ascents

made at an earlier date for religious or military purposes (such as the 'compulsory' ascent of Antoine de Ville de Beaupré, who, in 1492, on the orders of Charles VIII, reached the summit of Mont Aiguille – today this is one of the most popular grade III climbs on the Vercors), or isolated ascents like the one made by Bonifacio Rotario d'Asti on the Rocciamelone in 1358, or the one by Captain De Marchi on the Gran Sasso in 1573. In 1760, at the height of the Enlightenment, Horace Benedict de Saussure, a professor of philosophy and the natural sciences at Geneva, offered a prize to anyone who discovered a way up Mont Blanc, the highest peak in the Alps at 4810 metres (15,781 ft), where he wanted to undertake various scientific observations. This goal was reached on 8 August 1786, after many years of attempts and explorations, when Michel Gabriel Paccard and Jacques Balmat, respectively a doctor and a crystal prospector from Chamonix, equipped simply with an ironshod stick, without any ropes, ice-picks or crampons, were the first men to walk up that snow-covered ridge to the summit. As a result the first taboo was shattered, and the way upwards lay open.

The following year the same de Saussure, together with Jacques Balmat, Jean-Marie Couttet and fifteen other guides, reached the peak that he had dreamed about for so long, but was frustrated in the observations that he had planned to make with his armoury of equipment. But the account of his ascent reverberated loudly around Europe and attracted scholars, men of letters, poets, travellers and ordinary tourists to the Alps. Spurred on by a passion which one suspects went well beyond pure scientific interest, in 1788 de Saussure spent two weeks in a tent at the Col du Géant, a high pass not far from Mont Blanc, carrying out experiments and demonstrating (as had already been done by Balmat's solitary bivouac on one of his attempts on Mont Blanc) that it was possible to survive and become acclimatized even at high altitudes. In 1799, from the Col du Lys, he was one of the first to

First there was fear, then scientific interest, and finally the desire to conquer: the initial phases of the beginnings of mountaineering are illustrated on these pages. Left above: an early nineteenth-century print bears witness to the naive belief in 'Alpine dragons', here in the form of a glacier. Left below: the ascent made by the Geneva naturalist De Saussure to the top of Mont Blanc, in 1787, the year after the successful climb which marked the birth of modern mountaineering. Below: Napoleon III and the Empress Eugénie, with an army of guides and porters, among the séracs in the Mer de Glace, photographed in 1860 by the famous Bisson brothers.

Mountains as mysteries, a 'sacred' environment beyond the reach of man. The countless legends surrounding mountains have been dismantled little by little, not least by mountaineers themselves. Above: the 'three crosses' appeared to Whymper in 1865; in reality he witnessed a Brocken spectre or Brocken bow, an atmospheric phenomenon which is caused by the refraction of light in snow. Right: the victory and catastrophe of the Matterhorn, in two drawings by Doré. This lonely pyramid, soaring to 4478 metres (14,782 ft) on the border between Italy and Switzerland became, in the mid-nineteenth century, the symbol of nature's challenge to man's daring. The Matterhorn was conquered by that determined Englishman Edward Whymper on 14 July 1865, beating his rival, Carrel, who tackled the ascent from the Italian side, by three days. But disaster struck on the way down: four men, including the famous guide Michel Croz, fell to their death down the north face – the first major tragedy in the history of mountaineering.

describe 'the magnificent rock' of the Matterhorn. Between 1788 and 1827 there were a further thirteen successful ascents of Mont Blanc, and a woman – Marie Paradis, a chambermaid from Chamonix – also reached the summit. Over-confidence started to develop among would-be climbers of these lofty peaks. The total absence of even the most elementary climbing techniques and safety measures, coupled with a certain irresponsible optimism, led to a severe blow in 1820, when three guides of the Hamel club were killed by an avalanche on Mont Blanc. In 1827 the hazardous route known as the *Ancien passage*, which had been used up until then, was permanently abandoned in favour of the safer *Corridor* route, and subsequently for the present-day route along the Bosses Ridge.

In the first half of the nineteenth century mountaineering started to develop as a sport, and a clean break was made with the scientific and exploratory activities of the first pioneers. In the footsteps of the seven hunters from Macugnaga who, in 1778, had looked out from the Rocks of Discovery, on the Col du Lys, to confirm that the legend of the 'lost valley' was a reality, valley folk also started to look to the mountains. In 1854 the guides of Courmayeur, on their own, started explorations to find an Italian route to the top of Mont Blanc from the Col du Midi. At long last, on 13 August 1863, J.M. Perrod could boast from the top: '*Mes bougres de Chamoniards, cette fois nous n'avons plus besoin de vous pour arriver au sommet*' (You fellows of Chamonix, this time we don't need you to reach the summit).

The first half of the nineteenth century saw all the highest peaks in the Alps conquered one by one: the Grossglockner, the Jungfrau, the Ortles (climbed in 1804 by the chamois hunter Josef Pichler), the Bernina, Monte Rosa, the Grivola and, in the Dolomites, the Marmolada, the Civetta and the Pelmo. In the Dolomites in particular, it was difficult to verify the first successful ascents. Hunters from Cadore and Zoldano had surely reached the top of the Pelmo before the Englishman John Ball, who reached it in 1857. Matteo Ossi from Cadore had stood atop the Antelao before the Austrian Paul Grohmann; Simeone De Silvestro, nicknamed *Piovanèl*, had already climbed the Civetta before he accompanied Grohmann to the top; the ascent of the Marmolada (at 3343 metres/10,965 ft the highest point in the Dolomites), which was scaled in September 1864 by the same Grohmann with the guides Angelo and Fulgenzio Dimai, was made possible by the numerous earlier attempts that had been made. The first of these, which ended tragically with the death of the Agordo priest Giuseppe Terza, in fact marked the conventional birth of mountaineering in the Dolomites. In about 1860 nothing short of a competition developed in the Dolomites between English and German climbers, the former with guides from the Western Alps, the latter using local guides. The most spectacularly successful climbs were achieved by Paul Grohmann, who was also the first man to scale the Tofana di Roces (in 1864 with Lacedelli, A. Dimai and Santo Siorpaes), the Sassolungo, the Cima Grande di Lavaredo, the Sorapis and the Cristallo. The Cima Tosa, on the other hand, was first climbed on July 20, 1865 by Guiseppe Loss di Primiero and six companions.

In 1857 the *Alpine Club* was founded in London. The first president, John Ball, was a pioneer of mountaineering in the Dolomites. The aim of the club was to 'create understanding among mountaineers, to develop mountaineering and the explorations of mountains throughout the world, and to develop a deeper knowledge of mountains through literature, the sciences and the arts'. The club's gazette – the *Alpine Journal: A Record of Mountaineering, Adventure and Scientific Observation* – made decisive contributions to the development of this new sport. A few years later the Swiss Alpine Club came into being, followed by the Austrian (founded by Paul Grohmann) and Italian counterparts – the latter being founded by Quintino Sella in 1863.

Mountains became more accessible with the construction of refuges at high altitude (up until now the only refuge had been the eighteenth-century 'Temple of Nature' on the Montenvers, the base for the explorations made by Forbes and Tyndall), improvements in equipment and climbing techniques, and a deeper knowledge of the Alpine environment. The fashion for mountain-climbing won over many illustrious figures: in 1860 Napoleon III and the Empress Eugénie had photographic portraits made of themselves by the Bisson brothers as they clambered up the glaciers on Mont Blanc escorted by a veritable army of guides and porters. The small villages of Chamonix, Courmayeur, Zermatt, Grindelwald, Cortina and Innsbruck became the favourite holiday spots for high society and the

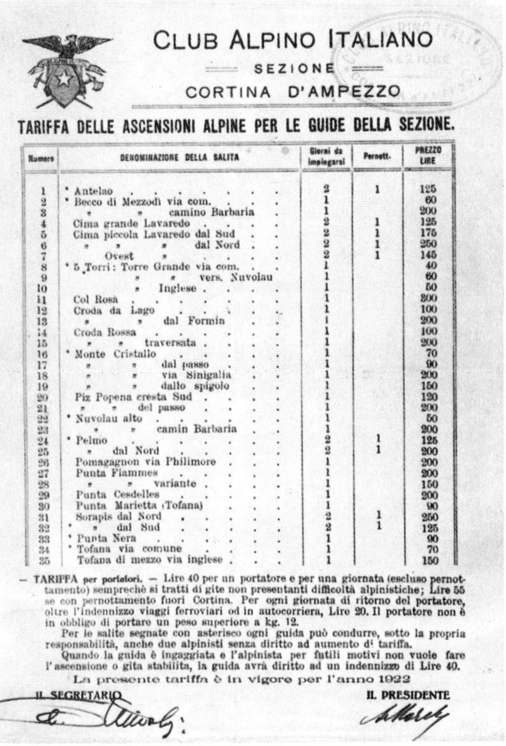

CLUB ALPINO ITALIANO

SEZIONE

CORTINA D'AMPEZZO

TARIFFA DELLE ASCENSIONI ALPINE PER LE GUIDE DELLA SEZIONE.

Numero	DENOMINAZIONE DELLA SALITA	Giorni da impiegarsi	Pernott.	PREZZO LIRE
1	* Antelao	2	1	125
2	* Becco di Mezzodì via com. .	1		60
3	" " camino Barbaria .	1		200
4	Cima grande Lavaredo . .	2	1	125
5	Cima piccola Lavaredo dal Sud .	2	1	175
6	" " dal Nord .	2	1	250
7	" Ovest . . .	2	1	145
8	* 5 Torri: Torre Grande via com. .	1		40
9	" " vers. Nuvolau .	1		60
10	" " Inglese . .	1		50
11	Col Rosa	1		200
12	Croda da Lago . . .	1		100
13	" " dal Formin .	1		200
14	Croda Rossa	1		100
15	" " traversata . .	1		70
16	* Monte Cristallo . . .	1		90
17	" " dal passo .	1		90
18	" " via Sinigalia .	1		200
19	" " dallo spigolo .	1		150
20	Piz Popena cresta Sud . .	1		120
21	" " del passo .	1		200
22	* Nuvolau alto . . .	1		50
23	" " camin Barbaria .	2	1	200
24	* Pelmo	2	1	125
25	" " dal Nord . .	2	1	200
26	Pomagagnon via Philimore .	1		200
27	Punta Fiammes . . .	1		200
28	" " variante . .	1		150
29	Punta Cesdelles . . .	1		250
30	Punta Marietta (Tofana) . .	1		90
31	Sorapis dal Nord . . .	1	1	250
32	" " dal Sud . .	2	1	125
33	* Punta Nera . . .	1		90
34	* Tofana via comune . .	1		70
35	Tofana di mezzo via inglese .	1		150

— TARIFFA per portatori. — Lire 40 per un portatore e per una giornata (escluso pernottamento) sempreché si tratti di gite non presentanti difficoltà alpinistiche; Lire 55 se con pernottamento fuori Cortina. Per ogni giornata di ritorno del portatore, oltre l'indennizzo viaggi ferroviari od in autocorriera, Lire 20. Il portatore non è in obbligo di portare un peso superiore a kg. 12.

Per le salite segnate con asterisco ogni guida può condurre, sotto la propria responsabilità, anche due alpinisti senza diritto ad aumento di tariffa.

Quando la guida è ingaggiata e l'alpinista per futili motivi non vuole fare l'ascensione o gita stabilita, la guida avrà diritto ad un indennizzo di Lire 40.

La presente tariffa è in vigore per l'anno 1922.

IL SEGRETARIO   IL PRESIDENTE

Mountaineering in the Dolomites started relatively late (to begin with interest was focused on the highest peaks), but it was in fact on these limestone rocks, from the end of the nineteenth century onwards, that climbing made its most spectacular advances. The pioneers of mountaineering in the Dolomites included English and Austrian climbers – 'collectors' of mountain-tops such as John Ball, Tuckett, Grohmann and Innerkoffler, but also many an 'unknown hero' – mountain-folk and chamois hunters – long since forgotten by history. Opposite page: some pages from the album of the famous guides of Ampezzo (shown below left). Above far left: mountaineering as a sport soon converted women as well. In 1874 the French Alpine Club was the first to admit lady members. Above left: Fulgenzio Dimai, who went with Grohmann up the Marmolada in 1864. Above: the various prices for guided ascents in the Cortina region in 1922.

urban middle-classes, and, to use the apt definition of the Englishman Leslie Stephen, the Alps became the 'playground of Europe'.

The enthusiastic books written by Alfred Wills (who climbed the Wetterhorn in 1854) revealed at that early date a spirit of adventure, and a sportsmanlike and unselfish passion for mountaineering which were no longer hidden behind culture and science. Way back in 1875 Leslie Stephen was bewailing the fact that 'the number of ascents to be made is so small that they can be counted on the fingers of one hand'. But mountaineering is self-perpetuating. The latter half of the nineteenth century and the early years of the twentieth – up until the First World War – represented the 'golden age', the heyday when climbers went out in search of difficulty, in search of ever more daring ascents, whether on major or lesser mountains. The pioneering days of mountaineering as a geographical and exploratory exercise came to an end once and for all in the Alps with the long travels made by Julius Kugy, a native of Trieste, in his Julian Alps in the early twentieth century.

The French have summed up the development of mountaineering in the Mont Blanc group like this: '*Après le Mont Blanc, la Verte; après la Verte, le Dru*' (After Mont Blanc, the Verte; after the Verte, the Dru). The Romantic attitudes of those days exalted the confrontation between men and mountains, between the ant and the giant. In the Central and Western Alps the Englishmen Coolidge, Stephen and Kennedy achieved remarkable successes, but the key figure in the world of mountaineering in the second half of the nineteenth century was undoubtedly Edward Whymper. Between 24 June and 14 July 1865, this pig-headed representative of Victorian England (the same England that produced Burton, Speke and Stanley) who was already well known for his determination and his exceptional climbing record (Meije, Barre des Ecrins, Mont Dolent, Aiguille de Trélatête, Aiguille d'Argentière) clinched three remarkable 'firsts': Les Grandes Jorasses, with Michel Croz, Christian Almer and Franz Biner, using a direct route from Courmayeur and in one day (from 1.35 am to 8.45 pm); La Verte, by the couloir which now bears his name, with Almer and Biner; and last of all, his greatest achievement, the Hörnli ridge of the Matterhorn, just a few days ahead of the ascent made by the two guides from Breuil – Jean-Antoine Carrel and Jean Bich – from the Italian side.

The conquest of the Matterhorn (lyrically defined by Ruskin as 'Europe's noblest crag') which, in those days, had become a symbol of nature's challenge to human daring, has a special place in the history of mountaineering, embodying as it does all the ups and down of an undertaking destined to become both a legend and a myth: the boldness of the very idea of it, the problems encountered, the race between two rival groups of climbers, the conquest, the tragedy, and the bitter controversy which followed the climb. In 1865, when Whymper climbed down to Zermatt from the Teodule, he had behind him some six attempts made from Breuil, including one made with the brave Jean-Antoine Carrel. This time too he would have liked to have Carrel with him. But Carrel was already committed, together with Felice Giordano, to an 'all-Italian' attempt on the Matterhorn. This is why Whymper chose to try the climb from the other side, along the Swiss Hörnli ridge, which, from below, was wrongly seen as the more difficult route. The faithful Almer turned down the invitation ('Anything, sir, but not the Matterhorn'). At Zermatt a motley group of men thus got together, consisting of Whymper, the valiant Michel Croz, two other guides – Peter Taugwalder the elder and his son – the English climbers Charles Hudson and Lord Francis Douglas, and the inexperienced Douglas Hadow.

The seven men set off at daybreak on 14 July from the Hörnli hut and made good going along the ridge. When they reached the spur which is the site of the present-day Solvay refuge, at 4270 metres (14,230 ft), they decided to make a slight detour on to the north face – 'the only really tricky part of the ascent'. Whymper records the climax of the climb as follows: 'At 1.40 pm the world lay at our feet, the Matterhorn had been conquered.' His first thought was to look out in the other direction, to see if there was any sign of Carrel and his fellow-climbers on their way up. 'I saw the group at once, on the ridge, a long way down. Our triumphant shouting must have dealt them a bitter blow. Of all the people who had tried to climb the Matterhorn, Carrel was the one who most deserved to reach the summit first, he was the first to believe that the climb was possible,' Whymper added with

It took a long time for mountaineers to develop a really efficient climbing technique, and to learn how to use ropes as a safety device. Below: a primitive belay system being used during the first ascent of the Dru in 1878. Bottom: the Englishman Albert Mummery hard at work in the famous Grépon crack, in 1881; this crack was considered 'the hardest climb in the Alps' at the time, and is assessed at grade IV.

typical generosity. On the way down tragedy struck with no warning: Hadow slipped, dragging Croz, Hudson and Douglas with him. They were all tied together by the same rope, but the rope linking them to the Taugwalders and Whymper snapped and the four of them vanished, without a sound, over the abyss of the north face. The epitaph penned by Whymper for Michel Croz reads: 'A courageous man, a loyal guide and a good friend'.

Despite the long controversy that raged over the dangers of mountain-climbing, this disaster did not halt its development. Proof lies in the bold ascents of the Brenva Spur on Mont Blanc in 1865 (Mathews, Moore, Walker, with Jacob and Melchior Anderegg), the Verte from the Argentière side (Cordier and Middlemore with Jacob Anderegg and Andreas Maurer in 1872), the Dufour from Macugnaga and the Nordend (tackled principally by the guide Ferdinand Imseng), and the south face of Mont Blanc from the Brouillard and Frêney glaciers (Eccles with Payot in 1877).

The first ascent of the Grand Dru, a great rock pinnacle close to the Verte, made by Dent and Hartley with Alexander Burgener and Karl Maurer in 1878, represented a new step forward, another technical and psychological barrier overcome. In 1881 the Englishman Albert Mummery, with Alexander Burgener and Benedict Venetz, negotiated a difficult crack (the first grade IV in the Mont Blanc group) and reached the summit of the Grépon from the Nantillons side. In the same year Mummery made an attempt on the Dent du Géant, which soars to just over 4000 metres (13,123 ft) on the ridge marking the border with Italy, and stopped at the foot of the Gran Placca. 'Absolutely impossible by fair means' he wrote on a scrap of paper which he left up there. Two years later, using questionable, even if rudimentary artificial equipment (a pole, ropes, 'metal spikes', and a hammer to make handholds in the rock), the guides Jean Joseph, Battista and Daniel Maquignaz led their clients – Alessandro, Alfonso, Corradino and Gaudenzio Sella – to the summit. That ascent, which caused an outcry because of the methods used, remained an isolated episode for many years, but it nevertheless heralded the age of 'artificial' climbing. The last glorious ascents of the nineteenth century in the Alps were the awesome ice routes taken by Minnigerode and Pinggera in the Central Alps (such as the north-east face of the Gran Zebrú in 1881), and the extremely long Peuterey ridge to summit of Mont Blanc, covered in three days in 1893 by Paul Güssfeldt, Emile Rey, Christian Klucker and Cesare Ollier.

The last years of the nineteenth century and the early years of the twentieth saw the arrival of the first true mountaineers in the modern sense of the word: they climbed largely without guides, or perhaps used the new generation of guides, and possessed the technical capabilities, passion and inventiveness capable of independently planning and achieving ascents of increasing difficulty. This period saw the emergence of crucial figures such as the brusque Alexander Burgener, Joseph Ravanel (known as 'The Red'), Emile Rey, Joseph Knubel (who accompanied Geoffrey Winthrop Young on the Mer de Glace face of the Grepon, on the Weisshorn, on the Brouillard ridge of Mont Blanc, and in the first exploratory descent of the Hirondelles ridge near the Jorasses), the Lochmatter brothers, who, with Ryan, conquered the south face of the Täschhorn in 1906, and undertook many successful climbs in the Chamonix Aiguilles. None of these great guides ever used pitons. Among the 'unguided' pioneers we also find the Englishman Albert Mummery in the second phase of his mountaineering career (before he disappeared in 1895 in a daring attempt on Nanga Parbat). But the field was more or less dominated by Germans and Austrians: Hermann von Barth, Emil Zsigmondy (who with his brother Otto in 1879 conquered the Feldkopf in the Zillertal Alps, the hardest climb of all in those days), Ludwig Purtscheller (with the east face of the Watzmann and some 1700 other peaks to his credit), and Eugen G. Lammer.

The obsessive taste for taking risks ('Anyone who climbs with me must be prepared to die', von Barth said repeatedly and emphatically) and the tragic death in the mountains of many a solitary climber (from Winkler to Zsigmondy to Preuss) stirred up much fierce debate in the world of European mountaineering about whether the risks of the sport were justifiable. This debate raged until the outbreak of the First World War, and was heightened by the grim German tragedies on Nanga Parbat and the Eiger, in the height of the Nazi period. In this period there

At the end of the nineteenth century the construction of tracks and refuges at high altitude greatly helped the art of mountaineering to emerge from its pioneering days. At the same time, as the sport became more and more popular and widespread, villages which had previously been completely lost in the mountains suddenly became favourite haunts for climbers. Above: the construction of the Margherita cabin on one of the peaks of Monte Rosa (the Gnifetti peak) at 4556 metres (15,200 ft). The refuge was opened in 1893 in the presence of Queen Margherita. The building work and the opening ceremony were put on record by Vittorio Sella, considered to be the best mountain photographer of his day.

also sprang up a certain macabre rhetoric about the 'murderous Alps', and this lived on for many years in minor mountaineering literature.

In the Dolomites, modern 'acrobatic' (to use Guido Rey's term) mountaineering started in 1881 with the climb by Michel Innerkoffler, the guide from Sesto and head of a famous family of guides, to the Cima Piccola di Lavaredo – slightly late in the day compared with the advances that had been made in the Western Alps. But the particular formations of the Eastern Alps and the calcareous peaks in Austria gave rise to a sensational development in the field of rock-climbing. Up until the thirties, when all the major north faces in the Alps were tackled, the most impressive feats took place on the giddy pinnacles of the Dolomites. In 1887 the star of Georg Winkler suddenly appeared. This 'rock artist' was a specialist at 'free' climbing, and did it with great athleticism. At the age of only seventeen he climbed the Winkler tower on the Vajolet (negotiating a crack bordering on grade V in difficulty), the Totenkirchl and the Zinal Rothorn. In the same year he fell to his death on the Weisshorn. His body was recovered, preserved intact, from the glacier in 1957.

Stabeler, Delago, the Schmitt brothers, Pichl (who scaled the south face of the Dachstein in 1901), and later Fehrmann and Steiner all opened up magnificent routes, nowadays considered as 'classic' routes on the Cinque Dita, the Catinaccio and the Brenta. In 1901 the two guides from Val Cismon, Michele Bettega and Bortolo Zagonal, with Beatrice Thomasson from England, blazed the first trail on the gigantic rock-face on the south wall of the Marmolada. A special mention should be made about two typical peaks which, in those days, were among the last untouched peaks in the Dolomites. In 1899, on the Campanile Basso, the Austrians Ampferer and Berger made a clever, short traverse and solved the problem of the last small rock-face, which had been attempted to no avail two years earlier by Garbari, Tavernaro and Pooli, all from Trento, who had had to call off their climb just a few metres from the summit. In 1902, Wolf von Glanvell and Gunther von Saar, with similarly fortunate intuition, reached the summit of the Campanile di Val Montanaia ahead of Cozzi and Zanutti from Trieste.

25

In the years leading up to the First World War, free climbing came close to its upper limits, on the threshold of grade VI. Tita Piaz, known as the 'devil of the Dolomites' because of his individualistic and cantankerous character, came down in favour of the growing argument for artificial climbing, but achieved his greatest climbs free: the Punta Emma crack, in the Catinaccio, solo in 1900; the west face of the Totenkirchl, in the Kaisergebirge (Kaiser mountains); the Campanile Toro and the lofty spike of the Torre Delago on the Vajolet (in 1901, with Glaser and Jori); the first ascent of the De Amicis pinnacle, using the novel device of throwing a rope from the nearby Torre di Misurina.

Angelo Dibona, from Cortina, was one of the greatest and most complete mountaineers of his day. Together with Rizzi and the Mayer brothers, he opened up routes above grade V. Among his most impressive achievements were the north-east pinnacle of the Grande di Lavaredo (1909), the north face of Cima Una and the south-east face of Croz dell'Altissimo (1910), a grade V plus climb, considered to be the hardest of the day and still a taxing proposition. In 1911, again with Mayer and Rizzi, he climbed the north face of the Laliderer, and a year later he tackled the south face of the Meije, where Zsigmondy had perished twenty-seven years earlier. In 1913, during a successful excursion to the Western Alps, he climbed the north-east ridge of the Dent du Requin near Mont Blanc, and the northern ridge of the Ailefroide, the first major route opened up

Shortly before the First World War, free climbing in the Dolomites saw its heyday with the feats achieved by Paul Preuss, Tita Piaz and Hans Dülfer. And in about 1910 the controversy over the use of pitons and artificial apparatus started to gain momentum. The Austrian Paul Preuss came down firmly against them and took the techniques of free climbing to levels never before reached. Above: the soaring spike of the Delago tower in the Vajolet, first scaled by Tita Piaz – the 'devil of the Dolomites', in 1911. Today this is one of the most frequently climbed routes in the group. Right: a historic photograph: Preuss exploring the virgin east face of the Campanile Basso, before climbing it solo, up and down, in 1911. Opposite page: the style of Emilio Comici, pioneer of the sixth grade in the twenties and thirties, shows clearly that climbing is also an art. Left: on the Dülfer route on the Grande di Lavaredo. Right: this photo shows his extremely modern style at Val Rosandra – his 'training-ground' – near Trieste. Comici died in 1940, when the rope snapped during a climb in Val Gardena.

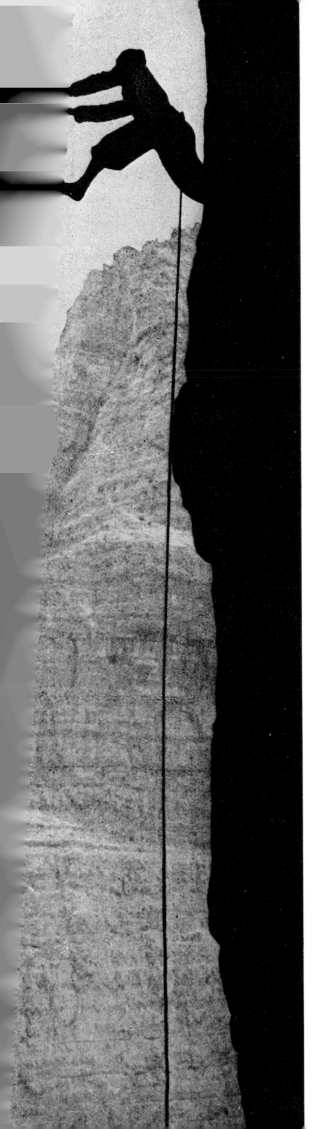

by a climber from the Dolomites in the harsh high-altitude environment.

The Austrian Paul Preuss, another leading figure in those years with many a splendid ascent to his name, often made completely alone, was the most committed champion of pure free climbing. His mountain ethic saw the use of pitons and other artificial equipment as a brutal (or even sacrilegious) development. Preuss was a good-looking, lightly built man, with a natural instinct for climbing, and a perfect balance between body and mind ('he seemed to skim over the rock, as if caressing it', someone wrote of him). He never tackled a stretch of rock which he could not climb down again, without the use of a rope. When he attached himself to a fellow-climber (almost always his friend Paul Relly), he used a knot which would undo in the event of a fall, so as not to endanger the life of his companion. Climbers who reject modern 'fanatical' mountaineering should refer, ideally, to the ideas and activities of Preuss, for he was an extremely modern precursor of free climbing, the ethics of which are now being re-evaluated.

The name of Preuss will forever be associated with the sheer east face of the Campanile Basso (which he climbed alone in 1911, both up and down – a feat which was not matched for seventeen years), the north-east face of the Brenta Crozzon, the east chimney of the Piccolissima di Lavaredo, and a host of others (1200 in all, 150 of which were 'firsts', and 300 of which were climbed solo) in staggering times. He decided against the south ridge of the Aiguille Noire, on Mont

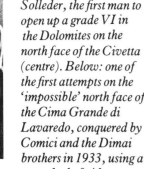

Left: the German Emil Solleder, the first man to open up a grade VI in the Dolomites on the north face of the Civetta (centre). Below: one of the first attempts on the 'impossible' north face of the Cima Grande di Lavaredo, conquered by Comici and the Dimai brothers in 1933, using a great deal of aid.

Below right: the triumphant return of Cassin, Esposito and Tizzoni from the north face of the Grandes Jorasses in 1936. Far right above: climbers tackling the 'Spider' on the fearsome north face of the Eiger. Far right below: Cosimo Zappelli during his winter ascent of the Walker spur in the Grandes Jorasses in January 1963.

Blanc, because he reckoned it required the use of pitons. This 'knight of the mountains' fell to his death in 1913 on the north peak of the Manndlkogel, at the age of twenty-seven, a victim of his own inflexible approach to climbing.

On the eve of the First World War, Hans Dülfer, Otto Herzog and Hans Fiechtl, leader of the Austrian school, were all among the top league of climbers. With them came the birth of modern climbing techniques; the use of pitons for protection was introduced, as was the snaplink or karabiner, and the use of the rope for tension traverses. But Dülfer's routes stand out above all because of their aesthetic sense and the elegance of their free climbing. In 1912 the Austrian maestro managed to scale the smooth rock on the east face of the Fleischbank, and in the same year, with Willy von Bernuth and using just three pegs, he blazed a splendid route on the west face of the Grande di Lavaredo. In 1912, again on his own, he conquered the southern corner of the Catinaccio d'Antermoia, a 250-metre (820-ft) route at grade V plus. Using artificial equipment, which had driven Dülfer to give up mountaineering the year before, Fiechtl and Herzog also managed to climb the south face of the Schusselkarspitze.

The twenties opened up the era of the sixth grade. There was less and less difference between Zurcher and Risch (the north ridge of the Badile in 1923), Langes and Merlet (the Velo peak in the Pale di San Martino), and the Jori-Andreoletti-Zanutti team on the north face of the Agner. The start of the

extreme grade in Alpine climbing is vague and blurred. It is difficult to decide who first succeeded on a grade VI route. In 1923, Fiechtl and Schmid on the north face of the Seekarlspitze, and Herzog and Haber on the Dreizenkenspitze (Ha-He corner: grade VI−, but with a length taken into account, probably VI+) undoubtedly touched the upper limits of difficulty. In 1924, Simon and Rossi opened up an 850-metre (2790-ft) route on the north face of the Pelmo (grade VI-). In 1925, on the north face of the Furchetta, the Germans Solleder and Wiessner opened up the first grade VI route in the Dolomites, pushing their way beyond the high point (the Dülfer pulpit) set by the great Austrian mountaineer and by Louis Trenker ten years before. In the same year, after a first unsuccessful attempt, Emil Solleder and Gustav Lettenbauer attacked the north-west wall of the Civetta, 1200 metres (3940 ft), one of the most awesome walls in the Dolomite range. After fifteen hours of climbing and using just fifteen pitons for protection, they were at the top. The following year saw the turn of the east face of the Sass Maor.

The 'Munich school' also had as a disciple Willi Welzenbach, a specialist (like Hans Pfann) at the various north face ice routes (Dents d'Hérens, Grands Charmoz and so on) who introduced the grading system for the degree of difficulty and revolutionized climbing techniques on ice. In this same period, on Mont Blanc, the Frenchman Armand Charlet, a member of the prestigious *Haute Montagne* group, and the Englishmen Graham Brown and Frank Smythe (Sentinelle Rouge, Route Major, the Pear Route—the Brenva 'trio') made some magnificent climbs on ice, and some excellent mixed rock and ice routes. With little sign of difficulty, the brothers Franz and Toni Schmid, who travelled from Munich to Zermatt by bicycle, scaled the impressive north face of the Matterhorn, in a snowstorm and after a bivouac at 4150 metres (13,620 ft). In 1930 and 1931, accompanied by Brehm and Schmid, Hans Ertl climbed the north face of the Gran Zebrú and the Ortles. And Brendel and Schaller conquered the south ridge of the Noire.

Spurred on by the writings of Domenico Rudatis, who popularized the new hard climbing trends which had been developed by both Germans and Austrians, Italian climbers now started to aim at the most difficult climbs. In 1929 we find Videsott, Rittler and Rudatis himself on the south-west peak of the Cima Busazza, Micheluzzi, Perathoner and Cristomannos on the south face of the Marmolada di Penia, and Comici and Fabian on the north-west face of the Sorella di Mezzo, on the Sorapis, all grade VI routes climbed with the minimum of equipment and extreme courage. On the south face of the Marmolada, Micheluzzi used just six pitons, and was faced with more demanding difficulties than those that occur on the Solleder route of the Civetta.

Emilio Comici, from Trieste, whose mountaineering skills were acquired in the Val Rosandra 'stable', is the mountaineer who best symbolizes this period. With his superb style and gymnast's physique, he climbed for the pure pleasure of climbing, with a sort of narcissistic admiration 'as if seeing himself reflected in the rock'. Comici is part of the great tradition of Preuss and Dülfer, a lover of free climbing and solo ascents, but he was also a keen enthusiast for all technical novelties. His name is inscribed on the north-west face of the Civetta, on the Spigolo Giallo (Yellow Edge) of the Piccola di Lavaredo, and on the Salame of the Sassolungo. But his masterpiece is still the north face of the Cima Grande di Lavaredo (a blackboard-like slab, 600 metres/1970 ft high), previously attempted in vain by Steger and other great mountaineers. It was climbed by Comici in 1933 with Giuseppe and Angelo Dimai, and plenty of artificial aid was used.

What Comici is most respected for is having broken through another psychological barrier and opened up the era of 'mixed' or ice-and-rock routes (using free climbing techniques and artificial equipment) – clinging like a 'drop of water' on the most overhanging of rock-faces. Alvise Andrich on the north-west face of the Civetta, Gilberti-Soravito on the north face of the Agner, Carlesso-Sandri on the south face of the Torre Trieste, Vinatzer-Castiglioni on the south face of the Marmolada, and Soldà-Conforto on the south-west face of the Marmolada all pushed the level of difficulty higher and higher.

The Adolphe Rey routes on the Grand Capucin (1924) and on the Hirondelles ridge (1927) can still not compete with the technical difficulties encountered in the Dolomites. But in the thirties, in the Western Alps, the race was on to conquer the great north faces – cold, fearsome, vertiginous – 'the last great problems of the

After two centuries of climbing, mountaineers eventually overcame most of the physical difficulties encountered in mountains, but went through a period of crisis trying to rediscover the human meaning of climbing, over and above the highly perfected techniques that had been developed. In the Alps, Walter Bonatti closed the chapter on great 'classic' mountain-climbing with a series of stunning climbs. Above: Bonatti in 1965, starting out on his direct, one-man, winter ascent of the north face of the Matterhorn. Right above: Gaston Rébuffat, top-level exponent of French mountaineering in the post-war years. Right below: the outstanding Reinhold Messner, from Upper Adige (one of the first men to argue for a seventh grade). In 1980, for the second time, he climbed Everest without oxygen.

Alps'. This is one of the most thrilling chapters in the whole history of mountaineering.

The epic story of the north face starts on the Croz spur of the Grandes Jorasses. The best mountaineers of the day were gathered: the Frenchmen Charlet, Couttet; Gréloz and Roch of Switzerland; the Austrians Rittler and Brehm (who were to be struck by a fall of rocks at the bottom of the face), Heckmair and Kröner, Welzenbach and Schmid, the Italians Gervasutti, Zanetti, Biner, Cretier, Boccalatte and Chabod, and the Swiss climbers Raymond Lambert and Loulou Boulaz. The face was finally climbed on 20 June 1935 by the German pair, Peters and Maier. The even more difficult Walker spur, which had already been attempted in vain by Allain and Leininger, was climbed on impulse in 1936 by Cassin, Esposito and Tizzoni, a formidable team from Lecco. The lessons handed down by Comici on the Grigna rocks thus bore fruit: Cassin, Ratti, Dell'Oro, and later Bonatti, Mauri and Oggioni were all graduates of the 'Lecco' school.

Riccardo Cassin, Ratti and Vitali (the west face of the Noire, 1939), the 'mighty' Gervasutti and Boccalatte (south face of Picco Gugliermina, 1938), all helped greatly (even though ten years later on) to close the gap that existed in the various technical levels of climbing between Dolomite mountaineers and mountaineers operating in the Western Alps. Teamed up with Ratti, and on another occasion with Esposito and Tizzoni, Cassin conquered two more classic and magnificent north faces: on the west peak of the Lavaredo group (1935) which had resisted some seventeen previous attempts (including one by Comici), and the north-east face of the Piz Badile, a giddy series of smooth slabs of granite, climbed in 1937.

Shortly before the Second World War, other important and impressive routes were opened up by Alfonso Vinci (Cengalo and Agner), Bruno Detassis in the Brenta group, Costantini-Apollonio on the Tofana di Roces, Nino Oppio on the Croz dell'Altissimo and on the Sasso Cavallo. The last of the great north faces to be beaten was the Eiger. This climb claimed its share of human life in the process. The tragedies of Sedlmayer, Mehringer, Hinterstoisser, Kurz, Rainer, Angerer, Sandri and Menti, which were witnessed by onlookers with binoculars from the nearby station of Kleine Scheidegg, heightened the sinister fame of this Oberland monster, and the Nordwand (north face) became the Mordwand (face of death). The Swiss authorities seriously considered banning climbers from it but in 1938, after four exhausting days, the German pair Heckmair and Vorg (who had made an attempt a month before with Rebitsch) and the Austrians Harrer and Kasparek managed to scale the fearsome wall.

After the Second World War, the use of increasingly sophisticated apparatus did away once and for all with the word 'impossible' for the various Alpine faces. The Livanos-Gabriel team that made the Cima Su Alto on the Civetta in 1951 opened the age of highly advanced climbing technology, the age of 'direct' and 'super direct' routes and ascents. In 1958 came the most sensational success of all, made with the use of twenty-odd expansion bolts: this was the direct route on the north face of the Grande di Lavaredo climbed by Brandler, Hasse, Lehne and Löw. It took them four days' hard climbing. The same group of German climbers also opened up a new route on the 'red face' of the Roda di Vael, a feat subsequently repeated by the Frenchmen Couzy and Desmaison and the group known as the *Scoiattoli* ('Squirrels') of Cortina on the north face of the west peak of the Lavaredo group. The Roda di Vael was also climbed by Maestri-Baldessari.

The mountaineering world was now split down the middle, but little by little numbers rallied behind the rejection of mountain acrobatics *per se*, of routes climbed entirely with the use of aid, and of all those phoney so-called 'free' routes, riddled with pitons for protection, where all trace of risk had virtually vanished. The finest climbs were made in the Western Alps, where the great 'mixed' or ice and rock routes, the climate, and the actual formation of the granite made it impossible to cheat. Here the outstanding personalities included the 'lone-wolf' Hermann Buhl, the Frenchmen Terray, Lachenal, Contamine, Rébuffat, Couzy, Desmaison, Mazeaud, and the Italians Walter Bonatti, Carlo Mauri, Andrea Oggioni, not to mention the Austrian Kurt Diemberger, a real enthusiast of the great rock and ice routes, and the German Toni Hiebeler. This was the period of spectacular winter climbs, often involving the use of Himalayan-type equipment (by now all the major routes in the Alps had been climbed in summer in the most hazardous and difficult of conditions); the period also of the sensational one-man

ascents of Cesare Maestri and Hermann Buhl, and the period of record times being set over and over again.

Among all these great names, the Italian Walter Bonatti rightly deserves his high place among the greatest mountaineers of all time. He made his climbing debut in 1949, at the age of nineteen, leading Oggioni, Villa and Bianchi on one of the very first repeat climbs along the Cassin route to the Jorasses. In the winter, with Carlo Mauri, he climbed the north face of the Grande di Lavaredo (already climbed by Kasparek and Brunhuber) and the north face of the west peak in the Lavaredo group. In 1951 he climbed the east face of the Grand Capucin, and in 1954, he succeeded in that extraordinary first solo ascent on the south-west pillar of the Dru. After the tragic attempt in 1961 on the Central Pillar of Frêney, on the flanks of Mont Blanc (with Gallieni, Oggioni and the Frenchmen Mazeaud, Guillaume, Kohlmann and Vieille), came the winter attempt on the north face of the Jorasses (with Zappelli in 1963), and lastly, in 1965, his finest achievement, which wound up that unrepeatable 'golden age' of great and classic mountaineering: the direct, one-man, winter ascent in four days of the north face of the Matterhorn.

In recent years the revolutionary developments introduced by American and Scottish climbers to climbing on both rock and ice, the scientific advances in training, the mastery of all types of psychological conditioning, and the spread of mountaineering and rock climbing as sports, have all brought climbing techniques to previously unthinkably high levels. At a time when mountaineering beyond the shores of Europe is also going through that transitional phase from 'conquering' mountain-tops to the phase of seeking out aesthetically pleasing and difficult lines which can be climbed 'Alpine style', the Alps are still the ideal 'playground' where people can test their capabilities and their courage. Since the mid-sixties, the American approach to free climbing has been making its mark on the red granite of the Aiguilles at Chamonix and on the Dru, in the form of John Harlin, Royal Robbins, and Garry Hemmings. The great English tradition was being carried on superbly by Chris Bonington, Dick Renshaw, Alex MacIntyre, Pete Boardman and Doug Scott. Philipp and Flamm on the Civetta, Messner and Holzer on the Marmolada, and Cozzolino on the Cima Scotoni have all pushed free climbing on rock to its extreme limits. Yvon Chouinard, Walter Cecchinel, Patrick Gabarrou and Jean Marc Boivin, are all extremely impressive ice experts.

In 1978 the seventh grade was officially recognized. The latest sensational exploits (such as retracing the hardest available routes solo, using only free climbing techniques), the absolute mastery of climbing techniques and the consequent demystification of the notion of difficulty, all these perhaps herald, in the Alps, the end of competitive mountaineering in favour of a type of mountaineering which will be experienced above all as an adventure, a discovery, and an inner quest.

Mountaineering comes of age

Yellowing nineteenth-century prints and photographs show us proud mountaineers in their grey double-breasted jackets, clutching their long alpenstocks or with some rudimentary pick hanging on their hip, shod in heavy studded boots, with bulky coils of hemp rope around their necks. Nowadays technology can offer the mountaineer much more reliable clothing and equipment: in fact the very development of mountaineering goes hand in glove with the constant advances being made in the conception and nature of the various materials used.

The use of a rope as a safety device did not become standard until the mid-nineteenth century or thereabouts, when many climbers still regarded their use as unbecoming and even something of which to be ashamed. The primitive techniques and the rather careless systems used by climbers to attach themselves to each other during the hardest stretches of a climb were the prime cause of the catastrophe in 1865 on the Matterhorn: instead of guaranteeing the climbers' safety in the event of a fall, the rope dragged four men into the abyss, and the other members of the team were only saved from death because the rope broke under the weight of the four. But this tragedy caused much reflection upon the dangers that ropes can pose if not used in the correct manner. And seven men tied together on the summit of the Matterhorn is not the right way to make up a climbing team.

Until the early twentieth century, climbing techniques had not undergone any really major changes since the early pioneering days: climbers climbed in nailed boots, with unreliable hemp or Manila ropes which became stiff and unusable when it rained or froze. Ice-axes or picks started to appear between 1860 and 1865, as a halfway tool, a cross between the alpenstock and the short woodsman's hatchet which was used by guides to hack out small steps in the ice. Some of the first applications of 'artificial' equipment for climbing had little follow-up, and were in some cases roundly criticized: this happened with the special pole used by the Maquignaz team on the Dent du Géant in 1882 (and again used in 1924 by Adolphe Rey on the Grand Capucin), the 'hook' described by Whymper, and the metal hook attached to a short length of rope which was used by the very young Winkler on his solo climbs.

The year 1910 marked an important stage in the development of techniques on both rock and ice. In that year the Englishman Eckenstein produced the first ten-point crampons for climbs on hard snow or ice, and a short ice-pick which was much more practical than the heavy ice-axes which had been used hitherto. But the Eckenstein crampons still did not dispense with the slow and tiring business of cutting steps on the steepest slopes. In 1910 the use of the rock piton, hammered hard into cracks, was also introduced. After Dibona and Mayer's ascent of the north-west face of the Dôme de Neige, in 1913, Sir Edward Davidson, of the Alpine Club, summed up the most widespread view of the growing use of artificial climbing equipment as follows:

> We cannot not admire the skill and courage which make feats such as these possible, but at the same time we should like to hope that we shall be forgiven for wishing that the advances made so far, which represent the uppermost limit that it is possible to reach, do not degenerate into mere tightrope-walking and acrobatics.

Claude Wilson uttered some even more drastic words: 'The very term "artificial" equipment sounds like an insult.'

Pitons started to be used even before the invention of the carabiner. The rope was attached to the piton with short lengths of string, or passed directly through the ring, by means of an extremely dangerous manoeuvre by the team leader who found himself forced to untie from the rope in the middle of some exacting stretch of the climb. There is still considerable debate over the origin of the snaplink carabiner. Its invention is attributed to the eminent climber from Munich, Otto Herzog, nicknamed 'Rambo', who was apparently inspired by seeing the numerous pear-shaped spring clips used by the fire brigade to attach firefighters to their ladders. Experiments were carried out by Herzog himself, and by his two

The evolution of mountaineering is closely associated with the progress made in techniques and equipment. Left: the modern technique of ice-climbing, called 'front pointing', as practised here on the Tour Ronde. The climber uses two ice-axes to keep himself in balance and steps up on the front points of his crampons. Above: two demonstrations of late nineteenth-century ice technique. The first crampons had no front points and the climber's foot had to be turned to ensure the crampons dug into the ice. The human pyramid was used to cross short obstacles.

Used for the first time by the Englishman Mummery, and later improved by Dülfer and Piaz, descents by abseil make it possible to negotiate all kinds of obstacles. Above: a swing into space, on the Cinque Torri, near Cortina in Italy. Today's abseil experts, with their modern harnesses, make this spectacular manoeuvre look simple. Opposite page: modern equipment on rock and ice. Nowadays, for pure rock-climbing, mountaineers prefer light, smooth-soled climbing shoes, but these become dangerous on wet surfaces, or on stretches of snow or ice.

contemporaries Fiechtl and Dülfer. Dülfer was the inventor of the rope traverse using tension to negotiate stretches of rock-face without hand- or footholds, and also inventor of the Dülfer ascent technique which is still named after him ('No rock-face is impossible as long as there are cracks in it,' he wrote). These experiments led in no time to the use of pitons and carabiners of modern design. But for many years pitons were considered to be of use primarily on descents, to anchor the ropes, using the rappel system with a double rope. Among the first climbers to use this descent method was the Englishman Albert Mummery on the Grands Charmoz and the Grépon.

On the limestone of the Austrian Alps and the Dolomites, the introduction of light, rope-soled climbing shoes (up until then it was not unusual to find people negotiating the trickier climbs barefoot) was one of the main reasons behind the sensational boom in free climbing in the years immediately before the outbreak of the First World War. The Austrian Paul Preuss was an outstanding exponent of this style during this period and he also featured loudly in the controversy raging over the use of artificial aids. In Preuss's view, anything 'artificial' constituted an insult to the ethics of mountain-climbing, and a step backwards. On 31 January 1913, at a meeting held at the *Alpenverein* (Alpine Club) in Munich, Preuss laid down the six principles which formed the basis of his theory of mountaineering, and which still provide much food for thought, even today:

1 It is important not to be merely a match for the difficulties which may be encountered, but to be clearly superior to them.

2 The degree of the difficulties which a climber may tackle with safety on a descent without the use of ropes and with an untroubled mind should also represent the maximum limit of difficulty which he can master on the ascent.

3 The use of artificial aid is only justified in the event of danger.

4 The rock piton is something to be used only in an emergency; it should not be the basis of a specific climbing technique.

5 The rope should be a means of assistance, not the vital equipment for making an ascent.

6 The principle of safety should prevail over everything else – not of the type that is forcibly obtained by artificial means in conditions of obvious danger, but rather the type of preventive safety measure which, for each individual mountaineer, is based on the proper assessment and knowledge of his own strength and capacity in each particular situation.

Despite initial opposition, the use of pitons spread fast after the First World War, for obvious safety reasons, but also to connect up stretches that could be climbed 'free' on routes and rock-faces that were becoming more and more sheer. Each generation builds on the experiences of the previous generation, and as a result the various accidents and tragedies that occur in mountains serve to provide a better knowledge and understanding of mountains and their hazards. The sport of mountaineering greatly matured and became popular in ever-widening social circles. These developments were spurred on by many famous books, such as Edward Whymper's *Scrambles Among the Alps* (which enthused no less a man than Churchill), Albert Mummery's *My Climbs in the Alps and Caucasus*, Emil Zsigmondy's *I pericoli delle Alpi* (The Dangers of the Alps), all three representing landmarks in a rich Alpine literature culminating in more recent works such as Heinrich Harrer's *Ragno bianco* (White Spider), Lionel Terray's *I conquistatori dell'inutile* (Conquistadors of the Useless), Walter Bonatti's *Le mie montagne* (On the Heights) and Kurt Diemberger's *Tra zero e ottomila* (Summits and Secrets). Acknowledging the constant progress of climbing techniques, Mummery himself writes that 'his' famous Grépon crack, which was considered to be the 'hardest climb in the Alps' in 1881, soon became 'an easy day for a lady'. Ground was also being gained by the idea that 'in the mountains there are not only things that cannot be done; there are also things that should and must not be done' (L. Purtscheller). Before long the first technical handbooks and the first mountaineering guides made their appearance.

The growing emphasis on the use of pitons greatly enlarged the field of action: in the twenties there was already talk of expansion pitons, which were necessary for negotiating stretches of rock-face which could not be scaled with free-climbing methods. In 1925 Rossi and Wiessner used this type of piton to climb an overhang (the *Rossi Uberhang*) on the south-east face of the Fleischbank. In 1933 Comici and

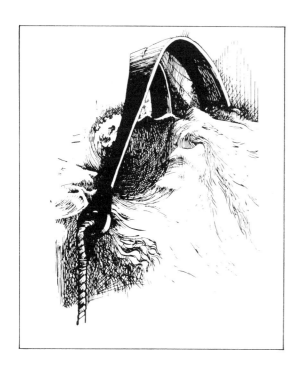

the Dimai brothers managed to climb the first 250 metres (820 ft) of the overhanging north face of the Grande di Lavaredo, using seventy-five such pitons. 'Now I'm convinced that the Cima Grande cannot be climbed,' was the controversial comment of the romantically inclined Julius Kugy. Soon the use of stirrups (or étriers) instead of primitive rope rings and loops, and the great improvements made to the technique in which the climber hoists himself up the pitons by pulley, were pushing the frontiers of rock-climbing ever further. Furthermore, the first and greatest 'mixed' or rock-and-ice climbs (using free climbing and artificial aid) of the classic period were made using a decidedly smaller number of pitons than the number used on repeat climbs, and they were also made in a spirit more akin to that of Preuss or Dülfer than to that of modern experts with artificial equipment. In the words of Comici:

> The climber who singles out and follows the most elegant and logical route to the summit, turning his nose up at the easier alternative routes, well aware of the enormous effort and the constant tension that will be required of him, with his nerves often at breaking-point, challenging the void and those dizzy heights, achieves nothing less than a work of art, a creation of the spirit, a testimony to the artistic sensitivity of man which will remain forever carved in the rock, for as long as mountains continue to exist.

In the Western Alps, up until the thirties, people continued to climb with heavy nailed boots (on occasions replacing them with lighter climbing shoes made of rope or felt for the more exacting stretches), until the Lombardy mountaineer and industrialist Vitale Bramani invented a new rubber sole which was to find huge success: this was the Vibram, which proved itself highly efficient on both rock and snow as a result of its special design. Boots fitted with Vibram soles were worn by mountaineers on all the major rock-faces in the period leading up to the Second World War. In this same period, crampons with points at the front (invented by Grivel in 1932) solved the problem of major ice climbs, the technique for which had already been taken to its uppermost limits with the means available by the German

In about 1910 the mountaineering world was split in two by the controversy over the introduction of pitons and other artificial aids. The problem cropped up again in the sixties, this time over expansion bolts. These are used to scale the smoothest of rock-faces, walls and overhangs, by drilling holes in the rock itself. Today there is fairly widespread rejection of these piton-littered routes and the fanatical technology of ten or twenty years ago, in favour of a return to the lessons to be learnt from Preuss, Dülfer and Comici, the great champions of free climbing.
Left above: artificial climbing with stirrups or étriers.
Above: climbing up a horizontal overhang or roof.
Left below: the 'hook' described by Whymper, one of the earliest pieces of artificial aid in the history of mountaineering.

Welzenbach, and by the Frenchmen Lagarde, Charlet and Contamine. In his account of the first ascent on the north face of the Eiger in 1938, Harrer writes:

> Just before the rocks which separate the second and third ice fields, I looked down, along the endless line of steps we had made, and I saw the New Age arriving at staggering speed. Two men were 'running' across – not climbing – the snow-field towards us. It was amazing to think that, having started that very morning, they had already managed to cover all that distance. They were undoubtedly the best Eiger candidates. It was Heckmair and Vorg, equipped with twelve-point crampons, and I suddenly felt that I was old and eclipsed.

It is worth mentioning that Harrer did not have crampons with him because he had chosen to wear hobnailed boots with a new type of metal stud 'which bit very well on both rock and ice'.

The ever-increasing use of pitons led before long, and inevitably, to the down-grading of many routes. In the account of his ascent of the south wall of the Punta Gugliermina, assessed at grade VI using thirty pitons, Gervasutti notes in 1939:

> To avoid any ambiguity, as happened to me on the south ridge of the Noire, which I had assessed at grade VI− with the use of seven pitons, and which was later the subject of some argument because it had been assessed with the use of more than three times that many pitons, the grading is meant to be valid only with the use of the same number of pitons as used on our ascent.

A larger number of pitons means less risk, and faster repeat climbs, even if, as Messner notes, 'the quality of a mountaineer is in inverse proportion to the weight of the equipment he carries on his back'. In 1937 Comici was able, in four hours and on his own, to retrace his route on the north face of the Grande di Lavaredo which, just a few years before, had involved having a bivouac, and had required numerous exhausting attempts. The excessive use of pitons on so many 'classic' routes that were opened up in the thirties still poses a problem today, and makes it hard to make a comparative assessment of the level of difficulty; it has also given rise to a fair amount of misunderstanding.

In the post-war period, the sports industry gave climbers and mountaineers access to increasingly efficient and sophisticated gear. By the end of the fifties the old hemp ropes were replaced once and for all by synthetic ropes made of nylon, perlon or lilion, with an outer sheath. These are much more flexible, much stronger and remain smooth-running even when wet or frozen. Their standard length is about 40 metres (130 ft), with a diameter of either 9 or 11 mm (about 0.4 in). High-altitude 'duvet' clothing and bivouac sacks which are warm and waterproof make it possible to venture up mountains even in the depths of winter.

In 1956 Bepi de Francesch used the latest 'expansion' bolts to climb an overhang on the Fungo d'Ombretta, in the Marmolada group. These pitons, which are shorter than the normal type made of soft metal, are driven into the rock after a hole has been made with a drill (traditionalists disparagingly call this 'carpenter's work'). This system makes it possible to scale any manner of obstacle. The debate about the legitimacy of these devices and about the 'cult of the most direct route' which they promote is an important chapter in the debate about mountaineering in general. The question is not a new one: every technical revolution has brought with it opposition from the purists of the old school. Things were no different back in 1913. Normal pitons or pegs certainly represent a compromise, an 'artificial' means, but they can only be driven into cracks, and their use, which can be justified on grounds of safety as well, is nevertheless determined by the morphology and structure of the mountain in question. This time around the reactions within the mountaineering fraternity are even harsher, and the new system of 'expansion' bolts is being accused of perverting the moral sense and value of the highest form of mountain-climbing. 'In this way,' writes Walter Bonatti, one of the fiercest opponents of fanatical technology and the piton-cluttered routes of the sixties, 'the sense of the unknown fades away, and with it the very sense of the word "impossible": the very soul of the climb is killed, and it becomes an end in itself,

arid, brutal, and therefore offering no good reason to be made.'

Reinhold Messner also objects to the 'murder of the impossible', of that extreme and ideal limit, constantly evasive, but whose existence is nevertheless vital for the justification of the intense efforts made to get close to it. The extreme example, apart from the numerous super-direct ascents made in the Dolomites, was perhaps the ascent of El Capitan, in the Yosemite Park, by the rock-face known as the Early Morning Light (achieved by Harding and Caldwell in 1970 after twenty-six days of climbing using 330 expansion bolts). This climb was followed from the foot of the mountain by thousands of spectators. 'An ascent is remarkable only if it is made with a healthy respect for certain rules, and with style,' wrote Chris Jones in *Mountain*, although he himself admitted that every climber and mountaineer is nevertheless free to set himself the rules by which he judges his performances.

The trend towards more and more demanding forms of free climbing has, in recent years, found an ideal point of reference in the new technique which has been developed in the training-grounds of Scotland and on the granite walls found in the United States. Hard-steel pitons, which undergo no deformation, are an American invention. But it was soon realized that when these are driven into the rock, they irreparably damage the edges of cracks by splitting the rock itself. Hence the new 'ecological' safety devices making progress in the national parks of the USA, where pitons have been outlawed: chocks, bongs, and then spring and 'cam' chocks, sky-hooks, crack-n-ups and the copper blades which 'hold' for just a few seconds, made with a new flood of ultra-modern alloys, coupled with newer and newer technologies which run the risk of eclipsing the original motivations for climbing.

Nuts or artificial chock stones, which are now used widely, were derived from an unusual technique which was adopted in the forties and fifties by British rock-climbers. They wedged small stones in cracks, and tied a short length rope or tape loop around them. The sixties saw the appearance of the first primitive artificial chocks, small pieces of metal with a hole drilled in them so that a length of rope could be threaded through. In 1961 the 'acorn' model appeared; in 1963 an aluminium model in six different sizes. Then there was also the chock threaded with a steel wire. In 1968 the copper-headed nut appeared and then last of all the 'cam' nut. The Americans Chouinard and Frost produced a whole series of chocks of differing sizes, ranging from the 'micro' chock measuring 6 mm (¼ in) to the eccentric hexagonal chock measuring 8 cm (3 in); plus another complete series of steel pitons or pegs, ranging from the tiny rurps – 'realised ultimate reality pitons' – to the gigantic bongs. Chouinard has this to say about the fast-spreading fashion for nuts in Yosemite:

> I find nuts very useful for artificial climbing, when there are cracks of varying sizes, and when the rock is of poor quality. But I would never replace a piton or peg with a nut in normal situations. I've climbed with one or two nut fanatics, and I can assure you that they took twice as long to set them up as the time normally required when using traditional pegs.

At around the same time, and in the Alps as well, new smooth-soled climbing shoes were introduced, offering better adherence, especially on granite. By now general use was being made of helmets, *baudriers* or cross-belts, descenders for the downward climb, and 'jumars' for climbing fixed ropes. The concept of belaying, now familiar in climbing was based on the concept of the 'dynamic' grip in which the belayer arrests a fall by allowing the rope to run slightly before stopping it so avoiding dangerous jerks. There has also been remarkable progress in the various rescue techniques and in the special and expressly designed equipment for expeditions beyond the frontiers of Europe.

The last ten years have also seen a veritable revolution in ice-climbing. In 1923 Welzenbach had used pitons and specialized rope manoeuvres to climb an overhanging stretch on the Grosses Weisbachhorn, but the technique had remained substantially the 'classic' one, with crampons becoming in the meantime extremely light, and with twelve or fourteen points. Between 1970 and 1972 the British climbers Bill March and John Cunningham, the American Yvon Chouinard, and the Frenchmen Cecchinel and Jager, developed, almost simultaneously, a completely new ice technique, based on the use of a short ice-axe and an ice-hammer on which it is possible to hoist oneself forwards, standing on the

Left: a sequence on an ice-face showing modern front pointing technique. This system of climbing, which was invented in about 1970, requires considerable practice and use of specialized tools, such as a short, curved ice-axe, and an ice-hammer capable of picking into the hardest forms of ice. Front pointing has revolutionized ice-climbing, enabling climbers to move very quickly, and in relative safety. Above: tackling the Rébuffat route with étriers on the south face of the Aiguille du Midi. The rock here is the compact, red granite type common around Mont Blanc.

front points of the crampons. The *piolet-traction* method enables the climber to climb vertical or even overhanging stretches, where he would rely on increasingly specialized and 'aggressive' equipment, with curved or steeply drooped picks, which can be inserted in the steepest of ice. With these new techniques, ascent times on ice are being reduced at a staggering rate, and even the dizziest of faces are being successfully scaled, in summer and winter, not to mention daunting frozen waterfalls, using the very latest and most 'fashionable' techniques which have been introduced by American and Scottish climbers.

ROCK CLIMBING TECHNIQUES

Meteorology

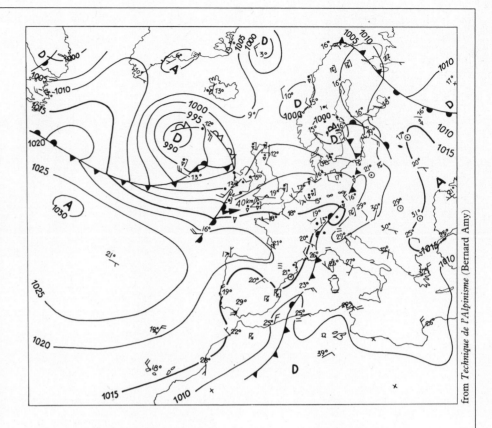

from *Technique de l'Alpinisme* (Bernard Amy)

The most typical phenomenon (even though it may be of only local importance) which affects mountain climates is the alternating pattern of winds. During the day, from 9 or 10 am onwards, the 'valley breeze' blows, carrying moist, warm air upwards towards the mountain-tops. As it rises, the air cools - the temperature drops 6°C 12°F every 1000 metres (3300 ft) - and condenses in the form of clouds. Once the sun has set the 'mountain breeze' gets up, blowing in the opposite direction, carrying the moist air downwards and dispersing the clouds. In summer this pattern of phenomena, caused by the natural instability of the air, can culminate in notorious, and often short-lived, afternoon storms, which are then followed by clear skies during the night. The type of weather which follows on from this is called 'daytime weather' and is typical of a fairly stable general situation.

But bad weather may be the result of much more far-reaching disturbances or fronts, involving the circulation of enormous masses of air of different temperatures and degrees of humidity. These give rise to very complex phenomena in mountainous areas. In summer, Europe is affected by a permanent high-pressure system called the Azores anticyclone. Over central Europe, on the other hand, there is a constant low-pressure zone, associated with the Asian summer depression. Low-pressure areas circulate at higher latitudes and over Iceland. The disturbances or fronts form along the line dividing warm and cold air, and move at varying speeds. Although it is in the main unpredictable, summer weather does follow certain patterns:

1 *Summer weather in ten-day cycles* Following fairly regular cycles, the atmospheric disturbances come from the west and the Alps are affected by successive waves of cold, stormy fronts. Bad weather arrives without much warning, announced by south-westerly winds, but it does not last more than a couple of days. Later on the wind veers to the north-west in mountainous regions and there is a lull, with constantly rising pressures and temperatures, until the next disturbance arrives.

2 *Daytime weather* This is characterized by a zone of relative high pressures in the Alps. There is haze or mistiness in the valleys, stiff breezes, and a development of cumuli during the day and the possibility of storms during the afternoon. This pattern is usually repeated for several days in succession.

3 *The almost stationary front* The depression develops over the Mediterranean and stabilizes along the Alpine chain with long periods of bad weather and rain. Although this type of weather is not very frequent, it can nevertheless ruin a summer.

4 *Ideal summer weather* The Alps are protected by an extension of the Azores anticyclone area. The ridge over France pushes any disturbances northwards. The weather is fine, and there are northerly winds.

5 *The anticyclonic pattern with continental circulation* The high-pressure zone over western Europe ensures fine weather over the whole Alpine region, for very long periods of time, sometimes for as long as three weeks. This situation often occurs in September - October, after the well-known disturbances that happen in late summer. At high altitudes the winds are light and easterly, the sky is clear and conditions are ideal for the mountaineer, especially in the western Alps.

Empirical methods of weather forecasting

Fine weather is indicated by:
Mountain-peaks which 'smoke' with plumes of snow whipped up by north and east winds.
Calm skies, with no morning wind; mist in valleys.
Dew or hoar-frost on fields, regular breeze patterns, with small cumuli.
Cold, still nights, twinkling stars.
Red sunsets, swallows and other birds flying high in the sky.

Signs of imminent bad weather include:
Haloes or hazy rings around the sun or moon.
Skies with 'fleecy' clouds, sudden warmth in the morning, strong winds at night.
Deep red dawns, swallows flying low.
Lens- or fish-shaped clouds on the highest peaks, long vapour trails from aircraft in the sky.

In winter, the meteorological situation is often more stable and weather forecasting is easier. When a high-pressure system sets in over the mountains, there are long periods of fine, calm weather, indicated by the typical presence of mist or fog in low-lying areas, due to the phenomenon of thermal inversion which is common at high altitudes.

Anticyclone - a zone of atmospheric high pressure.
Depression - a low-pressure zone.
Front - part of a disturbance which separates two masses of air.
Isobar - lines connecting points of equal atmospheric pressure (measured in millibars).

The Föhn

As it rises upwards in mountainous regions, air cools as a result of adiabatic expansion and then becomes compressed, being warmed up from the opposite side. This is the phenomenon of *Stau* (cold) winds and *Föhn* (warm) winds, the latter dreaded in the spring because of the avalanches which it can cause.

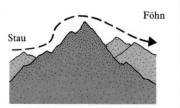

Types of clouds

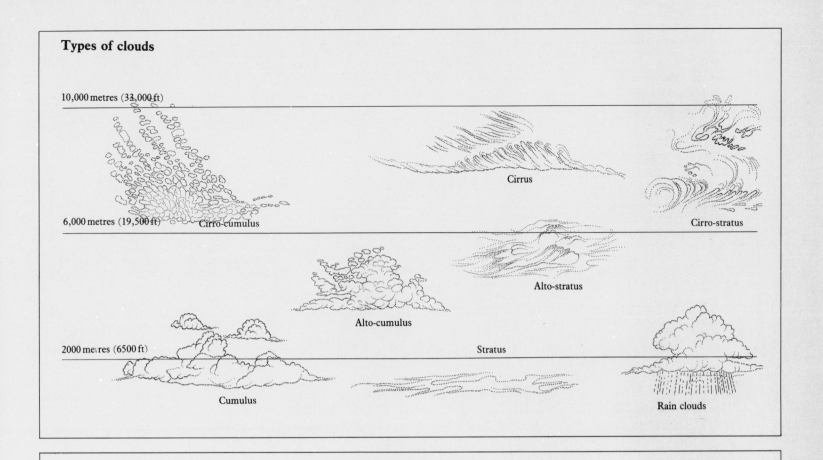

10,000 metres (33,000 ft)

6,000 metres (19,500 ft) Cirro-cumulus

Cirrus

Cirro-stratus

Alto-stratus

Alto-cumulus

2000 metres (6500 ft)

Stratus

Cumulus

Rain clouds

The twelve rules

Altimeter/barometer

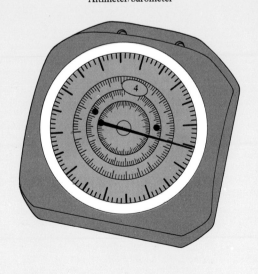

Meteorological forecasts are broadcast daily in all the European countries. They present a very general picture of the situation and are filled in with more detailed information at a local and regional level. In France and Switzerland there are very reliable weather bulletins, addressed particularly at the mountaineering fraternity. But the forecasts never cover more than twenty-four or thirty-six hours ahead. Good knowledge of the overall meteorological situation, whether broadcast over the radio or reported in the press, is very important before embarking on a demanding climb, and can be usefully rounded off by observations using instruments, or by the individual's own experience. The altimeter is an extremely valuable tool for the mountaineer, because it also indicates variations in atmospheric pressure (at a constant altitude) just like an ordinary barometer. The altitude indicated increases as the pressure drops and vice versa. The Swiss Alpine Club has drawn up the following twelve rules for forecasting:

1 The pressure rises sharply (4 - 6 mm) in just a few hours: the following bright interval will be short-lived.

2 The pressure rises markedly during the day: one can expect fine weather for a matching period of time.

3 The rise in pressure is slow, uniform and constant for two or three days: this indicates a period of dry weather.

4 The pressure rises and the wind veers from south to north, passing through the westerly quarter: swift improvement of the weather.

5 Unusually high level with moist air, and windless: mist and fine weather.

6 Irregular pattern of pressure changes: unstable/changeable weather.

7 The pressure drops and the winds veer from north or east to south, south-west: it will definitely rain.

8 Constant and sharp drop in pressure: it will definitely rain, the faster the drop, the harder the rain.

9 Rapid but contained drop in pressure with warm weather and no wind: storms.

10 Drop in pressure persists between 10.30 and 11.30 a.m.: It will definitely rain within twenty-four hours with westerly winds, later if the winds are from the east.

11 The pressure only rises in the afternoon: short bright intervals.

12 Slight drop in pressure during the afternoon: indicates little, especially in summer.

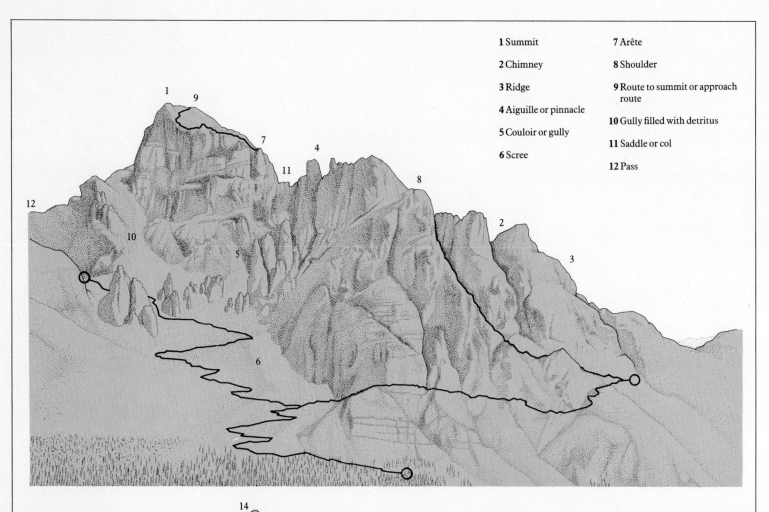

1 Summit	**7** Arête
2 Chimney	**8** Shoulder
3 Ridge	**9** Route to summit or approach route
4 Aiguille or pinnacle	
5 Couloir or gully	**10** Gully filled with detritus
6 Scree	**11** Saddle or col
	12 Pass

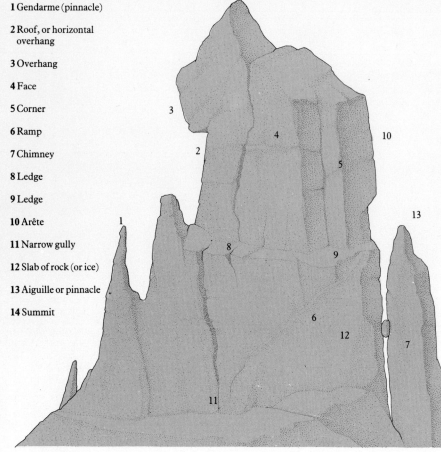

1 Gendarme (pinnacle)

2 Roof, or horizontal overhang

3 Overhang

4 Face

5 Corner

6 Ramp

7 Chimney

8 Ledge

9 Ledge

10 Arête

11 Narrow gully

12 Slab of rock (or ice)

13 Aiguille or pinnacle

14 Summit

The structure of mountains

The type of rock and the physical structures of a mountain are important features when the mountaineer comes to evaluate it for a climb, and he uses a specific terminology to describe them. The diagrams on this page illustrate the meanings of the terms: ridge, spur or shoulder, face, aiguille or pinnacle, together with the more specific terms used to describe a particular ascent route: corner, ridge, chimney, slab etc. At the foot of the mountain there are large deposits of detritus, such as scree, found typically in the Dolomites, or moraine, of glacial origin. The oldest moraine deposits date back to the major glaciations of the Quaternary period, which formed and moulded most of the Alpine chain; the more recent ones date back to the fluctuations of the Lesser Ice Age (AD 1430 - 1850). Rocks of a calcareous (limestone) nature (coral reefs and atolls, sediments of organic matter) have been more deeply eroded by outside atmospheric agents. Granite, on the other hand, has a more compact structure with smooth, sloping stretches.

In the mountains it is vital to know how to keep your bearings and find your way; it is important to work out timetables, and to take the right decisions in relation to the prevailing conditions. If bad weather strikes, for example, the best decision is not always to turn back: sometimes the day can be saved by proceeding to the summit, and then descending by the easier normal route.

Corna del Medale (Lecco) - 0 stances
Length of the climb: 360 metres (1200 ft) - 11 pitches

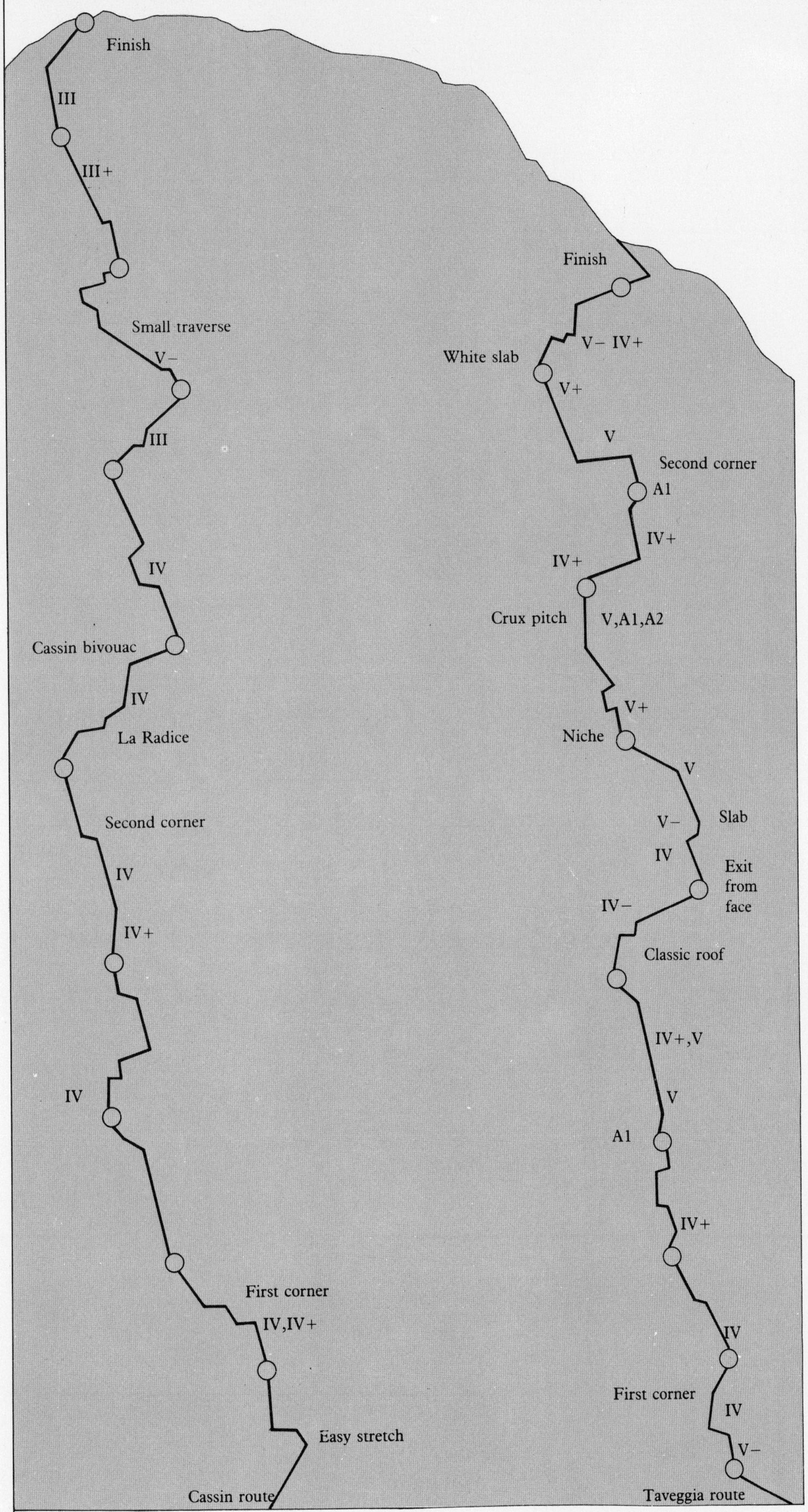

Finish

III

III+

Small traverse

V−

III

IV

Cassin bivouac

IV

La Radice

Second corner

IV

IV+

IV

First corner

IV,IV+

Easy stretch

Cassin route

Finish

V− IV+

White slab

V+

V

Second corner

A1

IV+

IV+

Crux pitch   V,A1,A2

V+

Niche

V

V−   Slab

IV

Exit from face

IV−

Classic roof

IV+,V

V

A1

IV+

First corner

IV

V−

Taveggia route

Following a route

Mountaineering guide books provide very useful hints for working out the overall difficulties of a route, and the individual pitches, and also help climbers follow the route without running the risk of getting lost. Diagrams and maps (see left) make the operation quite a simple one. First and foremost one must identify the starting point, at the foot of the route chosen. Following the various 'signposts', the climb can then begin. The guides also mark the various (or most important) stances and the overall line of the climb, usually in pitches of 30 - 40 metres (100 - 130 feet). The degree of difficulty is indicated by an overall assessment (using the French scale) which takes into account the length and continuity of the various difficult stretches, and by a technical assessment of the most demanding pitch. The term pitch means a convenient stretch of climbing between two stances. The guide book also includes useful hints aimed at finding the normal descent route: this may be the easiest route, but it can also, on occasions, be laborious and hard to follow.

Note
● *On the busiest routes there are usually several pre-fixed belay anchors, but it is a good rule not to trust these too far. It is always dangerous to tackle routes where there are lots of other teams in action.*
● *Achieving guide book times for routes is the best sign of good training.*

Grades of difficulty
(for free rock-climbing)

Welzenbach	French scale	UK
II+/III	PD+	Difficult/Very Difficult
III+/IV	AD+/D	Very Difficult/Severe
IV+/V	D+/TD	Hard Severe/Mild Very Severe
V+/VI	TD	Very Severe/Hard Very Severe
VI	ED	Just Extremely Severe
VI+		Extremely Severe
VII		Hard Extremely Severe

Artificial climbing grades

A1-A2-A3-A4

Rock-falls

Among the 'objective' or external dangers which threaten the mountaineer or rock-climber, rock-fall comes at the top of the list. These falls rumble their way down gullys and cracks, and rock-faces overlaid with ledges covered in loose rocks. Rocks and stones can be displaced by other climbers, or they may be dislodged by movements caused by temperature variations. The first rule is to avoid the most exposed stretches of rock and the most dangerous ascent routes where the rock is loose and crumbling. Snow-filled gullys should only be climbed when you are sure of a constant temperature, i.e. when they are in shadow, or first thing in the morning. The use of helmets is by now fairly standard and always advisable. Warning of a rock-fall should always be announced by shouting 'below'. The first reaction is to flatten yourself against, or run immediately towards, the face, and cover your head with your knapsack. If you have your wits about you you might look up, and thus manage to avoid being hit by dodging the falling rocks at the last moment (you can always hear their characteristic whirring noise as they hurtle downwards). The danger is that you may be hit in the face as you look. The second member of the roped team should always be on the alert for the leader falling after being hit by a rock, and he should be fully prepared to brake any such fall using a dynamic belay.

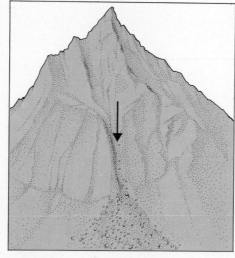

The danger of rock-falls is always greatest in funnel-shaped gullys and cracks. If you have to climb up them it is best to use the small rocks at the side. The safest route is up the ridge.

Lightning

Below: Where to shelter from lightning

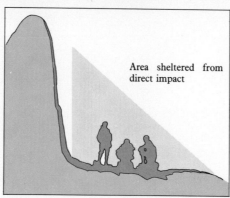

Area sheltered from direct impact

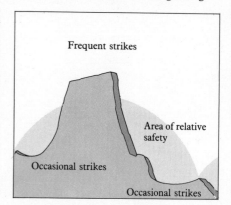

Frequent strikes

Area of relative safety

Occasional strikes

Occasional strikes

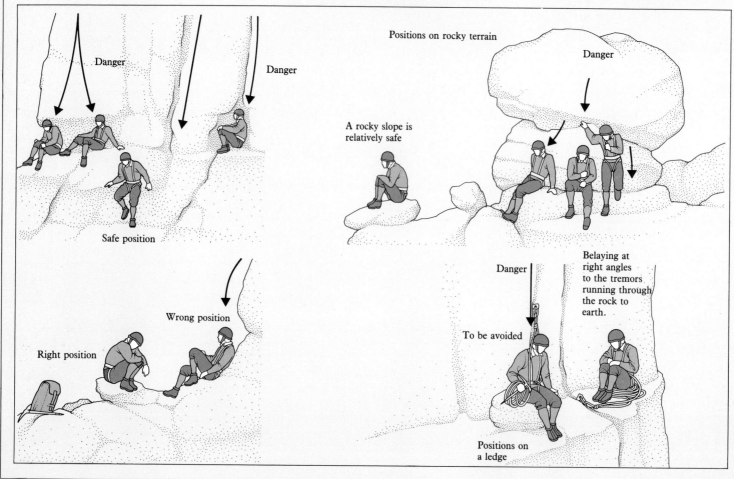

Danger

Danger

Danger

Safe position

Wrong position

Right position

Positions on rocky terrain

A rocky slope is relatively safe

Danger

Danger

To be avoided

Belaying at right angles to the tremors running through the rock to earth.

Positions on a ledge

Types of avalanche

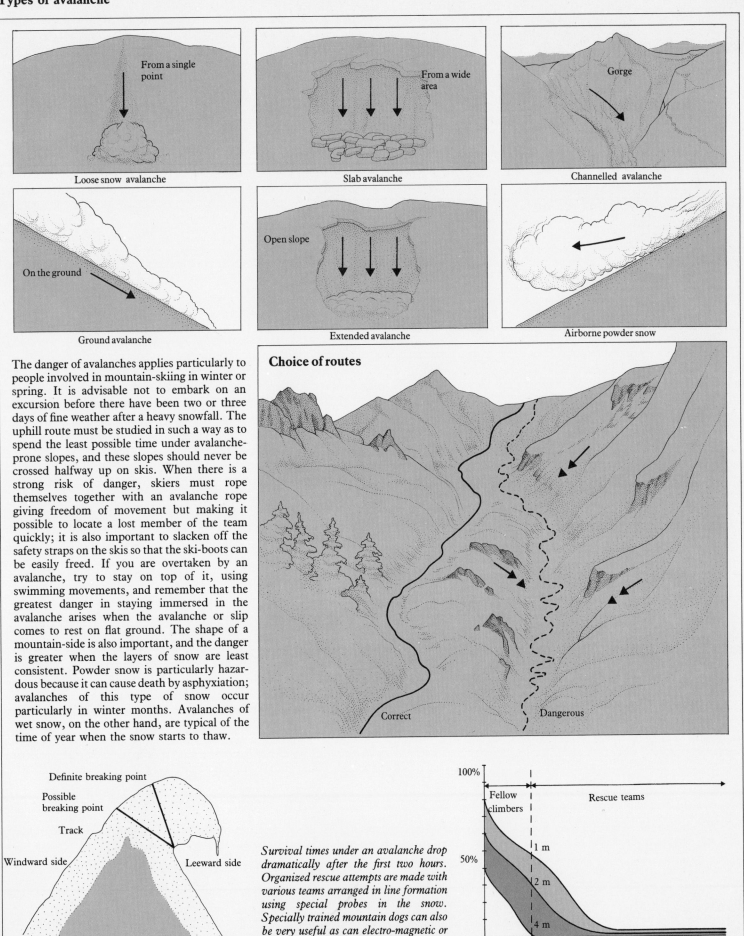

Loose snow avalanche — From a single point

Slab avalanche — From a wide area

Channelled avalanche — Gorge

Ground avalanche — On the ground

Extended avalanche — Open slope

Airborne powder snow

The danger of avalanches applies particularly to people involved in mountain-skiing in winter or spring. It is advisable not to embark on an excursion before there have been two or three days of fine weather after a heavy snowfall. The uphill route must be studied in such a way as to spend the least possible time under avalanche-prone slopes, and these slopes should never be crossed halfway up on skis. When there is a strong risk of danger, skiers must rope themselves together with an avalanche rope giving freedom of movement but making it possible to locate a lost member of the team quickly; it is also important to slacken off the safety straps on the skis so that the ski-boots can be easily freed. If you are overtaken by an avalanche, try to stay on top of it, using swimming movements, and remember that the greatest danger in staying immersed in the avalanche arises when the avalanche or slip comes to rest on flat ground. The shape of a mountain-side is also important, and the danger is greater when the layers of snow are least consistent. Powder snow is particularly hazardous because it can cause death by asphyxiation; avalanches of this type of snow occur particularly in winter months. Avalanches of wet snow, on the other hand, are typical of the time of year when the snow starts to thaw.

Choice of routes

Correct — Dangerous

Cross-section of a cornice

Definite breaking point

Possible breaking point

Track

Windward side — Leeward side

Survival times under an avalanche drop dramatically after the first two hours. Organized rescue attempts are made with various teams arranged in line formation using special probes in the snow. Specially trained mountain dogs can also be very useful as can electro-magnetic or radio devices, if the person buried has the appropriate small transmitter.

100%

Fellow climbers — Rescue teams

1 m

50%

2 m

4 m

1   2   3   4 hours

Equipment

The mountaineer or rock-climber is constantly torn between two conflicting demands: his equipment must be as complete as possible, but he must also keep the bulk and weight of it to an absolute minimum during the actual ascent. It is not always possible to achieve the best balance. Once again, experience can help you to make the right decisions. The true mountaineer can be recognized by the way he prepares his rucksack.

Clothing

Clothing must be warm, light, tough and comfortable. Waterproof nylon clothing keeps the wet out, but does not allow your body to 'breathe'. This means that the inner surface of the material soon becomes damp with condensation. One of the latest innovations, however, is a revolutionary fabric called 'Goretex', which is completely waterproof but also 'breathes' allowing water vapour to pass outwards and so prevents condensation forming on its inner surfaces. Woollen berets or caps and sweaters stay warm even when they are wet. As far as personal clothing is concerned, we recommend a cotton or woollen vest and T-shirt, possibly long woollen underpants or all-in-one woollen or silk combinations, although it is more practical if these are in two parts. Your shirt (made of flannel, cotton or wool) should be sufficiently long not to ride up over your waist while moving, and it should have pockets for keeping sweets and other things. To protect yourself from the cold you can also wear thin silk socks under your long woollen or wool-and-silk stockings. Your sweater should be comfortable, warm, preferably without a roll-neck, or with one that can be opened. Breeches should be of the classic zouave type, stopping below the knee, either woollen or made of elastic material. Jeans are not recommended because they dry out very slowly and weigh too much when wet. Nowadays salopettes are popular because they protect the area around the waist better. As a general rule, several layers of thin clothing offer better protection than a single heavy sweater.

PROTECTIVE CLOTHING

Gloves

These are vital in snow and ice in high altitudes. Woollen gloves are warm, even when wet or covered with snow and ice, but when they are dry they do not keep out the wind. Nylon gloves with a fur lining are preferable. The 'muff' type of glove keeps the fingers together and there is thus less heat dispersion. Fingerless gloves, or mitts, are sometimes used on rock keeping the hands warm while leaving the fingers free to grip the holds.

Sunglasses

Vital in snow and ice to protect your eyes from the glare. In wind and snow you can also use skiing goggles. They must offer good visibility in mist and fog, and they must not mist up.

Headwear

Simple woollen ski hats are best, or the balaclava or hood type when more protection is needed. They must, however, be big enough to cover the ears.

Anorak

A light anorak or jacket is adequate for short climbs. But on rock it is better to wear an anorak made of waterproofed cotton or the newer Goretex fabric. There should be shoulderpads and reinforced sleeves (for protection when belaying and against abrasion on rocks), and these jackets must be simple to put on and take off. There is usually a double system of zips and buttons. It is important for the anorak or jacket to have convenient and safe pockets.

Rucksack

Overgloves

Gaiters

Duvet jacket

Gaiters

These are vital for walking and climbing on snow. They can be ankle-high or knee-high. The best type are of waterproof canvas because these are tougher and therefore especially useful with crampons. Nowadays most have zip fasteners so that they can be put on and taken off even when the boots are laced up.

Waterproof cape

This is useful in heavy rain. The large type with a hood which will also cover the rucksack is highly recommended. One specific type is the bivouac cagoule. It is advisable to wear a beret or cap under the waterproof hood.

Duvet clothing

Duvet jackets and trousers (quilted and filled with either down or a synthetic fibre and down) are now part and parcel of the mountaineer's equipment as the best protection against cold. The duvet jacket usually has a hood and must be large enough to be worn over other heavy clothing. A specialised type, which is lighter and has shoulder padding, is particularly recommended for mountain-skiing. For mountaineering in winter and outside Europe there are also special double duvets. Synthetic fillings are capable of staying warm even when wet while down becomes water-logged. In the event of bad weather, rain or snow, it is therefore necessary to wear, on top of a down duvet, a Goretex cagoule. If the duvet breaks or tears it can be repaired temporarily with adhesive tape or sticking plaster.

Rucksack

There is a huge range of models. Mountaineering types should have the following features: narrow with no side pockets; no internal rigid framework; a strap to fasten it around the waist; a reinforced base and waterproof or water resistant fabric; an easily accessible pocket in the upper section. The rucksack should contain: water-bottle, knife, matches, spare batteries, spare food, first-aid kit and spare clothing.

TECHNICAL EQUIPMENT

This includes ice-axe, crampons, pitons, carabiners, ropes, harnesses, tapes and helmets, many of which are referred to in the relevant chapters. Here we will give just a few general rules regarding choice and maintenance.

Harness

Only choose safe, well-tested models. The harness must be adjustable; it must also support the body in a balanced way from the point where the rope is attached, and it must distribute the jerk or impact evenly in the event of a fall.

Ropes

In terms of single ropes, choose only the makes approved by the UIAA (Union of International Alpine Associations), in an 11-mm (0.4-in) thickness, made of synthetic fibre (nylon or perlon) with a sheath and a central core (breaking strain of more than 2000 kg (4500 lb). The standard length is 40 metres (130 ft). When rappelling or roping down two 9-mm (0.35-in) ropes are useful.

When used intensively, ropes tend to lose their initial characteristics. This can occur in a single season or after about 250 rope lengths of climbing. Humidity (even if modern ropes are water-repellent) and cold reduce their resistance. Heat and light cause deterioration in the polyamide material used. Ropes should not be dried out near a stove, and must be washed out with detergents designed for delicate materials in lukewarm water. Ropes are no longer safe when they have been involved in falls with a fall factor of 1 or worse (see page 65), or if there are visible signs of fraying. The elasticity of ropes is considerable as time passes.

Ice-axe

If the handle is wooden it should be protected with special oils.

Note

On easy terrain, the ice-axe can be conveniently carried with the head uppermost between the rucksack strap and the climber's shoulders.

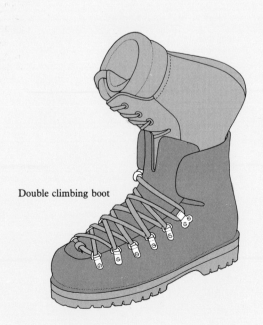

Double climbing boot

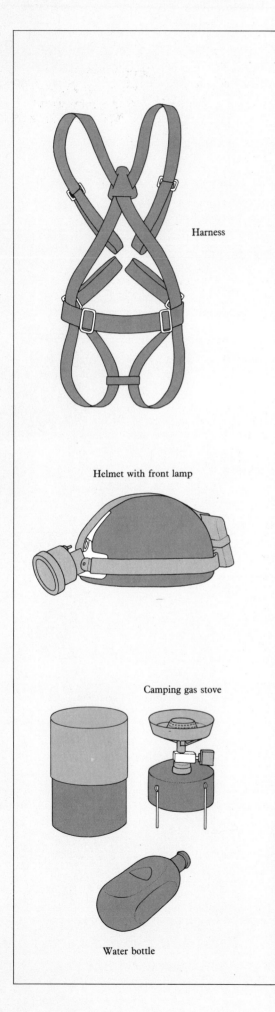

Harness

Helmet with front lamp

Camping gas stove

Water bottle

Crampons

The straps must be made of nylon and they should be checked frequently. Tighten them up well and keep the straps on the outside of the foot. Keep an eye on the adjustment screws. The front points and the front pair of points (at 45° and 90° approximately to give the best support to the climber's weight) must be periodically sharpened. The crampons must fit tightly to the boot.

Note

When crampons and ice-axes are not being used they should be covered with rubber caps to avoid accidents. Camping equipment (tents, sleeping-bags, camping-stoves) is very much the same as that of the ordinary camper.

SKI MOUNTAINEERING

This is becoming more and more popular. The problems are the same as for conventional mountaineering, but they are complicated by the difficulties connected with the best season for skiing (spring or winter) - namely the high risk of avalanches and bad weather. Ski mountaineers generally choose summits which can be easily reached on skis. The major hazard is crevasses in snow-covered glaciers; other hazards are avalanches and snow-slides. Special 'avalanche bulletins' issued by the various Alpine Clubs can be useful for taking stock of the general situation as far as snow is concerned. At high altitudes, in the region of 3000-4000 metres (10,000-13,000 ft), very late spring and May and June are the best and safest times for this activity, when the snow conditions are relatively safe.

Note

The special equipment for ski mountaineering (vital among which are ropes, slings, ice-axes and crampons) includes the short type of ski (which can be turned into emergency stretchers or litters by means of the hole at the tip), seal-skins (best are the adhesive type), fastenings with a rear pivot for climbing, Vibram-soled climbing boots, and rampants for hard snow - these are fixed beneath the soles of the boots and are used like crampons, but make it possible to continue using the skis.

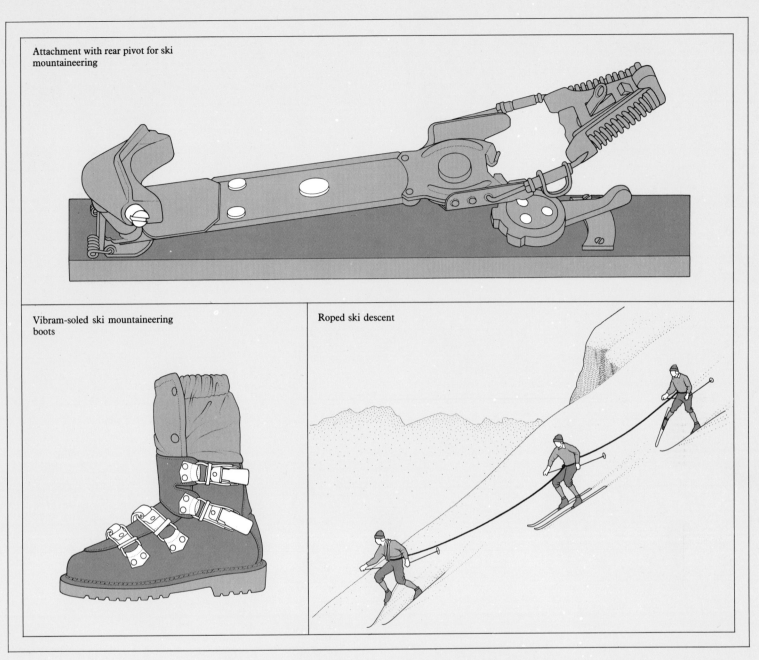

Attachment with rear pivot for ski mountaineering

Vibram-soled ski mountaineering boots

Roped ski descent

The Bivouac

In order to bivouac in difficult conditions, you need to have a lot of experience and familiarity with mountains, but it can be an extraordinary experience. Special hammocks slung from pitons mean that you can sleep on a sheer rock-face. A reasonable bivouac requires a down sleeping-bag, a duvet, a camping-stove (using a propane-butane mixture, best for use in cold conditions), a head lamp and freeze-dried food.

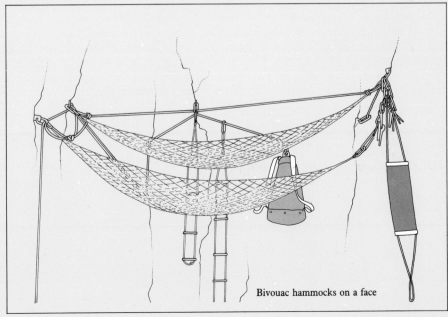

Bivouac hammocks on a face

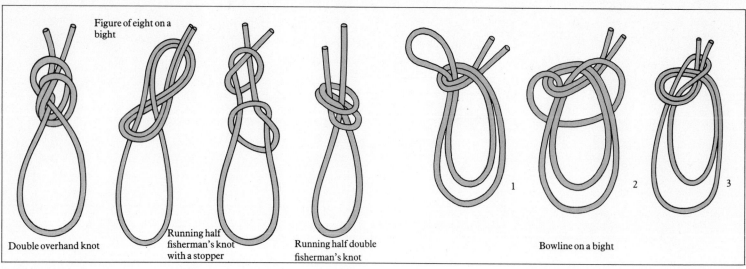

Figure of eight on a bight

Double overhand knot

Running half fisherman's knot with a stopper

Running half double fisherman's knot

Bowline on a bight

1   2   3

There was a time when people attached themselves together with a simple figure-of-eight knot, but the jerk that can occur is very dangerous for the spine and there is also a risk of turning upside-down and slipping loose of the loop in the rope. The simplest knot, and the safest, is the Bowline knot with a stopper. The Bowline is also used to attach yourself to the rope with modern harnesses consisting of combined belts and leg-supports. These are particularly effective at distributing the impact of the rope suddenly tightening in the event of a fall and keeping the body stable even when hanging free.

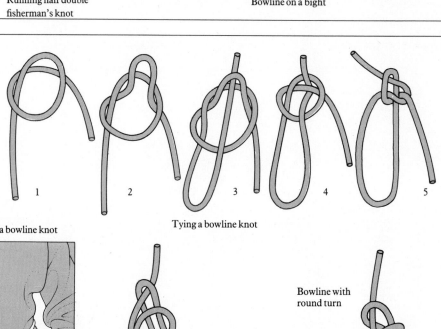

Tying a bowline knot

1   2   3   4   5

Application of a double overhand knot

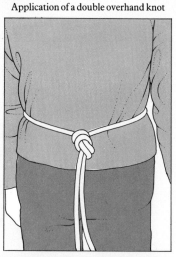

Application of a bowline knot

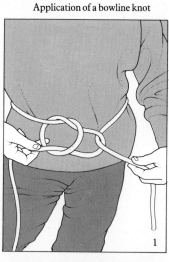

1

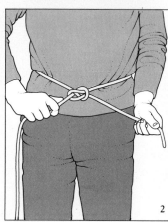

2

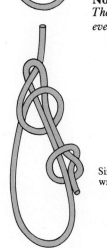

3

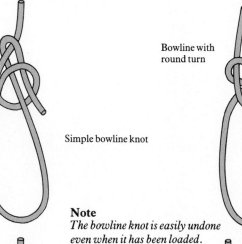

Simple bowline knot

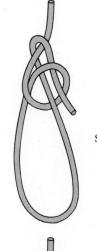

Bowline with round turn

Note
The bowline knot is easily undone even when it has been loaded.

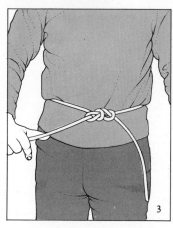

Simple bowline knot with stopper

Bowline knot with round turn and stopper

Bowline knot with
shoulder brace

Note
*In all these knots it is
advisable to leave
enough slack and to
make a stopper*

Note
*On easy terrain, or when descend-
ing, it is necessary to reduce the
length of the rope by making a
series of loops around the body.
But on the last loop you must tie a
stopper loop and attach it with a
carabiner to the harness or to the
loop around the waist.*

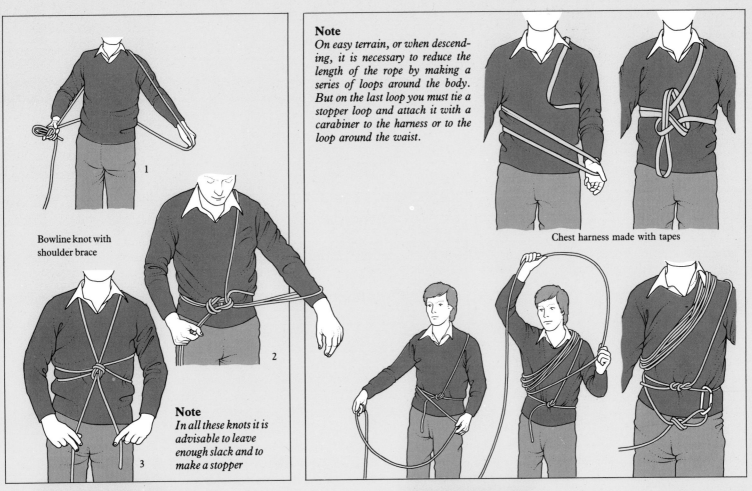

Chest harness made with tapes

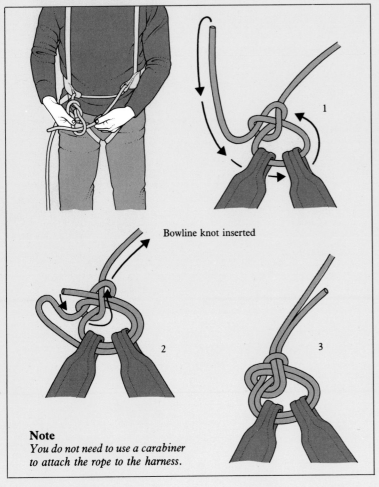

Bowline knot inserted

Note
*You do not need to use a carabiner
to attach the rope to the harness.*

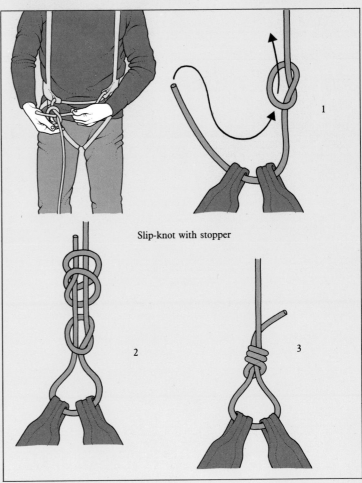

Slip-knot with stopper

Securing equipment

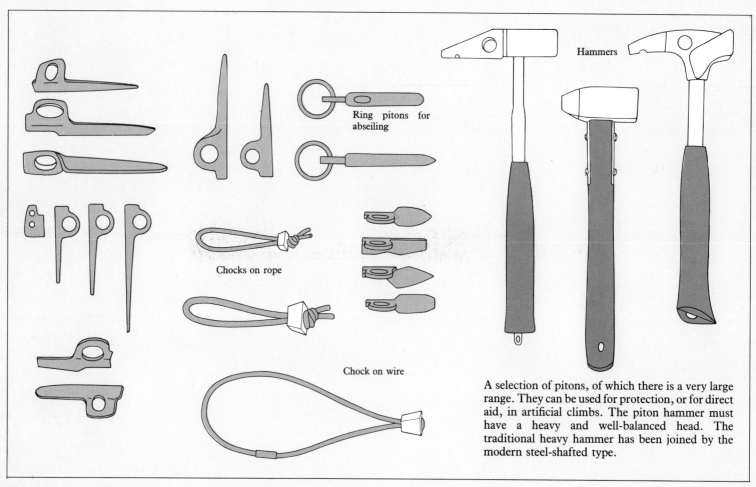

Ring pitons for abseiling

Chocks on rope

Chock on wire

Hammers

A selection of pitons, of which there is a very large range. They can be used for protection, or for direct aid, in artificial climbs. The piton hammer must have a heavy and well-balanced head. The traditional heavy hammer has been joined by the modern steel-shafted type.

The carabiner or snaplink (like the piton) undergoes very considerable stress in the event of a fall, at least as much, in fact, as the stress on the rope. Its breaking strain must therefore not be less than 2400 kg (5300 lb).

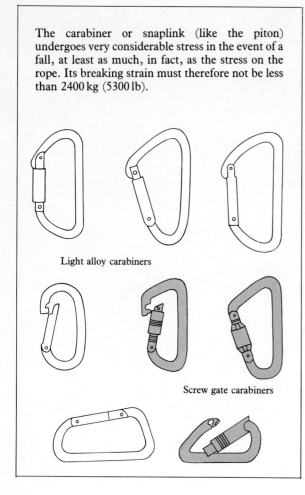

Light alloy carabiners

Screw gate carabiners

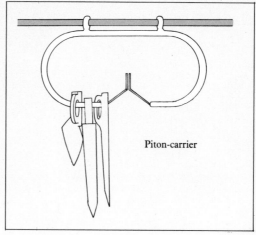

Piton-carrier

Inserting a carabiner through a piton eye

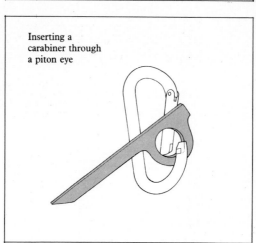

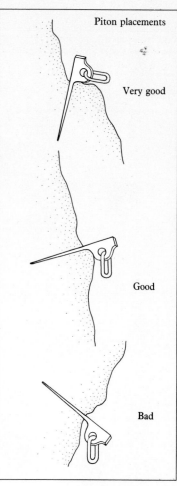

Piton placements

Very good

Good

Bad

The complete series of hard-steel American pitons. The traditional wooden wedge (shown below) has been replaced by larger bongs.

Bongs

Bugaboos

Knife-blades

Angles

Wedge

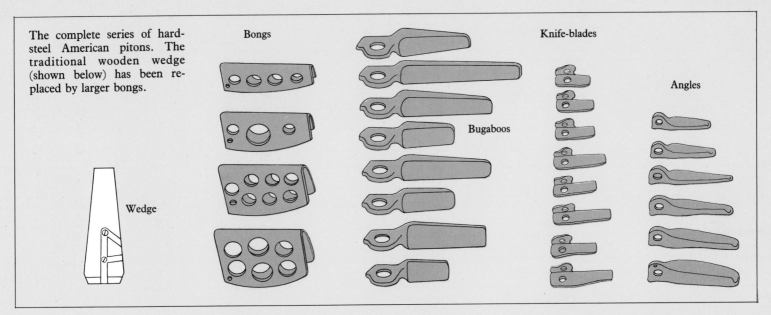

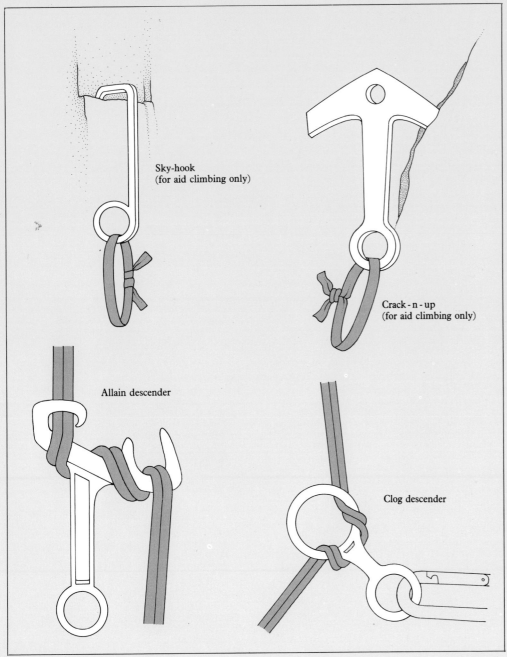

Sky-hook
(for aid climbing only)

Crack - n - up
(for aid climbing only)

Allain descender

Clog descender

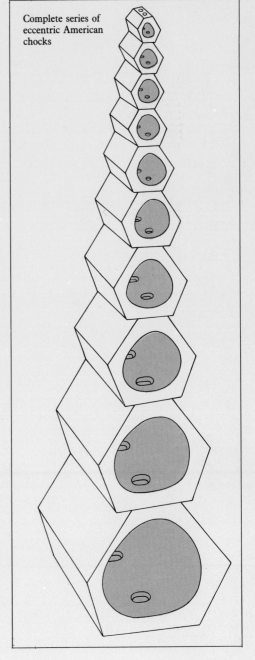

Complete series of eccentric American chocks

Self-locking knots

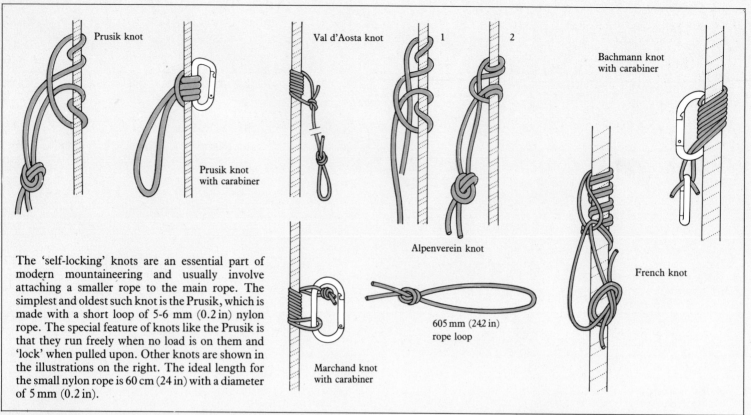

Prusik knot

Val d'Aosta knot   1   2

Bachmann knot
with carabiner

Prusik knot
with carabiner

Alpenverein knot

605 mm (24.2 in)
rope loop

French knot

Marchand knot
with carabiner

The 'self-locking' knots are an essential part of modern mountaineering and usually involve attaching a smaller rope to the main rope. The simplest and oldest such knot is the Prusik, which is made with a short loop of 5-6 mm (0.2 in) nylon rope. The special feature of knots like the Prusik is that they run freely when no load is on them and 'lock' when pulled upon. Other knots are shown in the illustrations on the right. The ideal length for the small nylon rope is 60 cm (24 in) with a diameter of 5 mm (0.2 in).

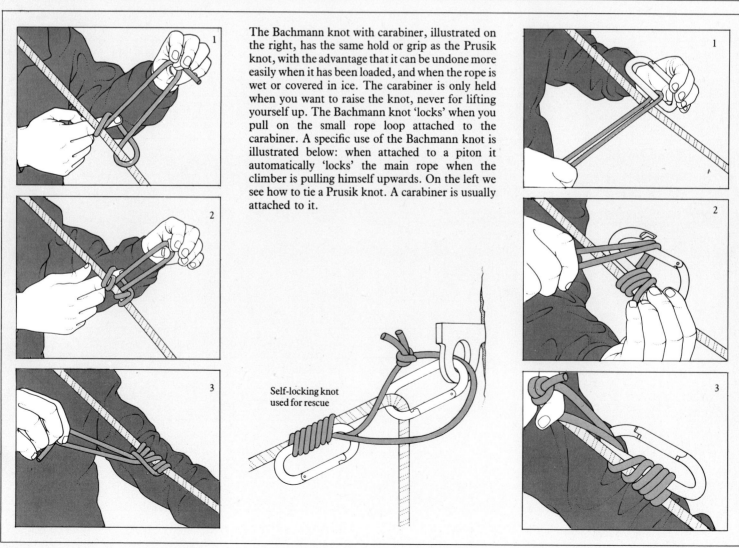

The Bachmann knot with carabiner, illustrated on the right, has the same hold or grip as the Prusik knot, with the advantage that it can be undone more easily when it has been loaded, and when the rope is wet or covered in ice. The carabiner is only held when you want to raise the knot, never for lifting yourself up. The Bachmann knot 'locks' when you pull on the small rope loop attached to the carabiner. A specific use of the Bachmann knot is illustrated below: when attached to a piton it automatically 'locks' the main rope when the climber is pulling himself upwards. On the left we see how to tie a Prusik knot. A carabiner is usually attached to it.

Self-locking knot
used for rescue

The 'locking' loop

In order to stop the rope running in the carabiner (for example when a fall has been stopped), tie a locking loop (as shown below), and possibly even add a counter-loop. The loop is easily undone by pulling on the other end of the rope. It is even safer if you tie a half-hitch onto the carabiner. This knot, invented in Italy, is frequently used as a means of belaying between the first and second members of the team, and vice versa. It works best when a loading of 350-400 kg (800-900 lbs) is placed on it. This kind of belay is dynamic and when holding a fall the optimum run of the rope ranges from 50 cm (20 in) to 1 metre (40 in). There is no point in trying to arrest the fall too quickly: the braking potential of the knot is not improved and you may well burn your hands. Beware, however, that in dynamic belaying, overheating of the rope running through the carabiner may cause deformations and so weaken the rope.

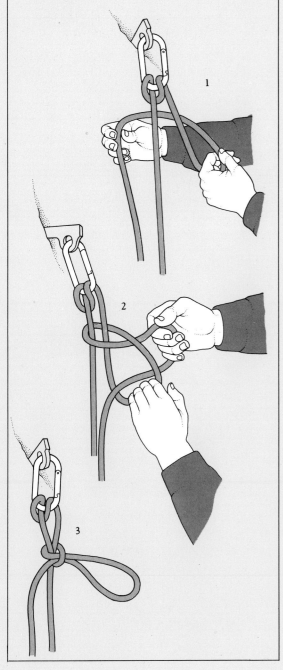

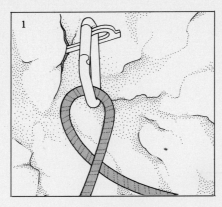

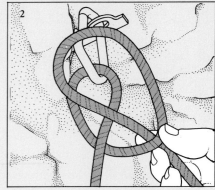

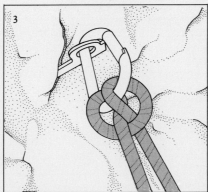

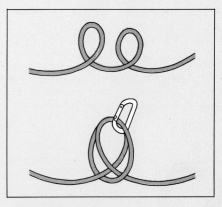

The hitch knot

A typically nautical knot, this is used to block the rope in both directions around a carabiner. It is easy to tie and untie, and is a good knot to use when securing yourself to a single loop with an overhand knot, not least because you can adjust the length of the free rope without undoing it. The illustrations above show how to tie the double hitch, by superimposing two rope loops.

The half-hitch

The use of this knot is particularly recommended in belaying. It can be tied quickly through a carabiner, but be sure to have the gate outermost (see illustration below). The half-hitch can be tied in two different positions depending on the direction of the strain. In the drawings below, the strain is downwards, and the knot acts as a brake.

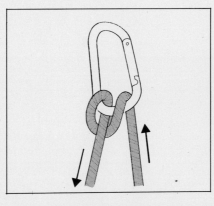

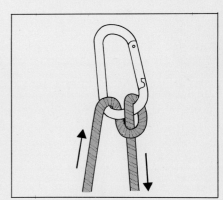

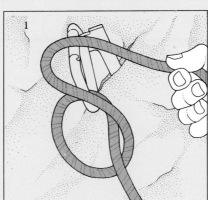

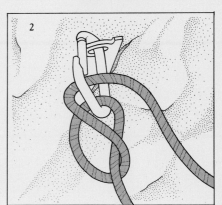

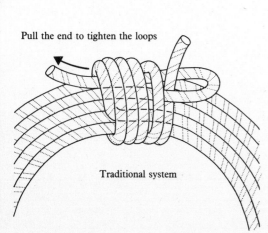

Pull the end to tighten the loops

Traditional system

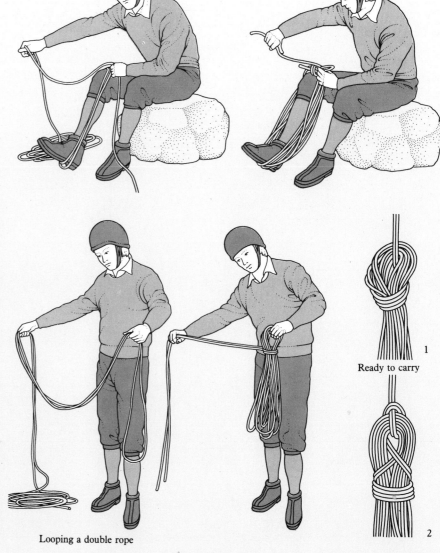

Ready to carry

Looping a double rope

At the end of a climb it is very important to coil the rope carefully, to avoid it becoming twisted, so that it can be re-used without becoming tangled. The traditional system is to loop the rope in the form of a hank, using the knee and foot to do so, and then secure the whole rope by looping one end around the hank (as shown above). The hank can then be slung over a shoulder. To carry the rope over difficult terrain, or when you are about to embark on an abseil, the most sensible system is to loop the rope, starting from the halfway point (and it is helpful to mark it with adhesive tape, for example), and then secure it at one end like a nautical rope. The ends of the rope can then be used to attach the rope to the back, by crossing them over the rope and tying them around the waist at the front.

Note

On the so-called Vie Ferrate *(high level walking routes in the Dolomites), instead of a climbing rope it is advisable to use a small rope sling secured around your waist with a carabiner clipped into it. The carabiner can then be clipped either directly or via another sling and carabiner on to the handrails and ladders on these Dolomite routes. In this way the climber is protected in the event of a slip.*

Note
To unloop the rope it is laid flat and slackened off.

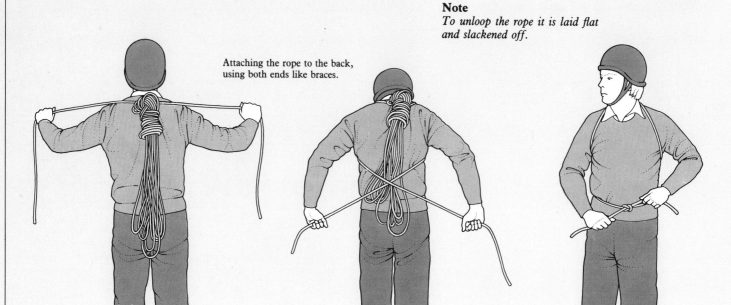

Attaching the rope to the back, using both ends like braces.

Self-locking devices

These are extremely useful for rescue purposes, and make it possible to leave a rope pulled taut; the rope 'locks' itself. The 'Garda' self-locking system was shown for the first time at the 1974 Italian Mountain Rescue Course. It has now taken the place of the Bachmann system in manoeuvres involving hoists and pulleys (see page 106). The carabiners must be of the same type and size; the best shape is the trapezoid one. Another system involves passing the rope behind a carabiner, crossing it in front, and then inserting both ends of the rope through the carabiner. The rope to be 'locked' is the one above the cross-over. A second carabiner is then hooked into the first, and the free-running rope is passed through this (see illustrations on the right below).

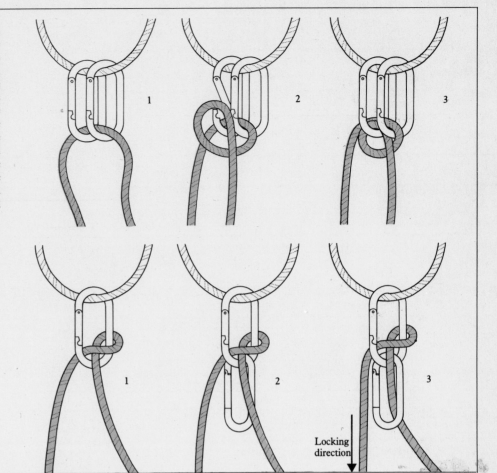

Running free   Locking direction   1   2   3   Locking direction

The carabiner used as brake

This is another system used to lower rescuers or injured climbers during rescue operations, but it can also be used as a descender for abseils. The system is illustrated below. It is essential that the gate of the first carabiner points upwards, and that of the second carabiner (which acts as a brake) is on the side opposite the braking action. Single or double ropes can be used in this system (see right).

The Sticht plate

This recently invented belay plate uses friction to absorb sudden loads on the rope, and is therefore an excellent 'dynamic' belay device. It can be fitted to the harness, or, with a length of rope and a (French) self-locking system, to a safety piton.

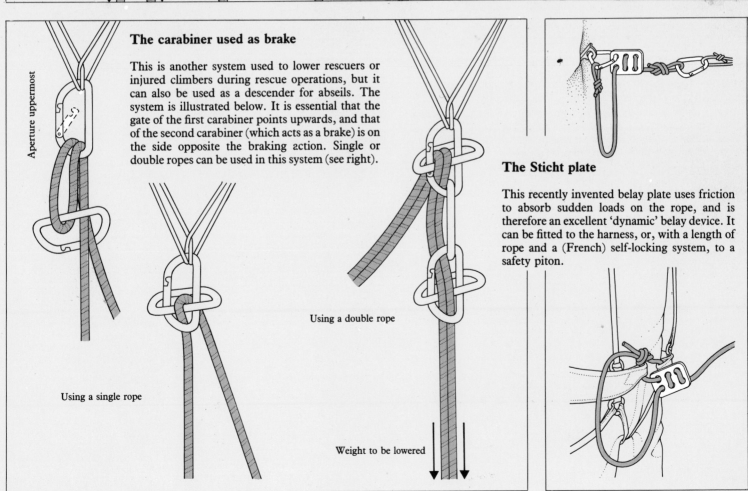

Aperture uppermost

Using a single rope

Using a double rope

Weight to be lowered

Pitons for protection

While climbing a difficult pitch which has no natural protection, the leader of the rope may fix a piton in a crack. He then attaches a carabiner, turns it 180° so the gate is away from the rock, and passes the rope through it, making sure that it runs freely and does not do a half-turn when the piton is passed. If the rope forms too sharp an angle with the rock, use a second carabiner or create an extension with a small loop passed directly through the eye of the piton and the carabiner clipped through the loop.

Turn the carabiner and clip the rope into it

Direction of hammer blows

Rope loop

Hammer blows

Steel carabiner designed for this precise purpose

Carabiner chain

Right

Wrong

No

No

Right

The use of nuts

The modern approach to rock climbing is to use metal nuts (or chocks). Often rope loops 7 - 9 mm in diameter (0.3 in approx) are threaded through the nuts, to give greater dynamic flexibility to the anchor point. The second member of the team has the task of recovering all the equipment left in the rock-face. The use of chocks or American nuts requires a certain amount of practice, but when properly placed they are as safe as pitons. Always bear in mind the direction of pull in the event of a fall.

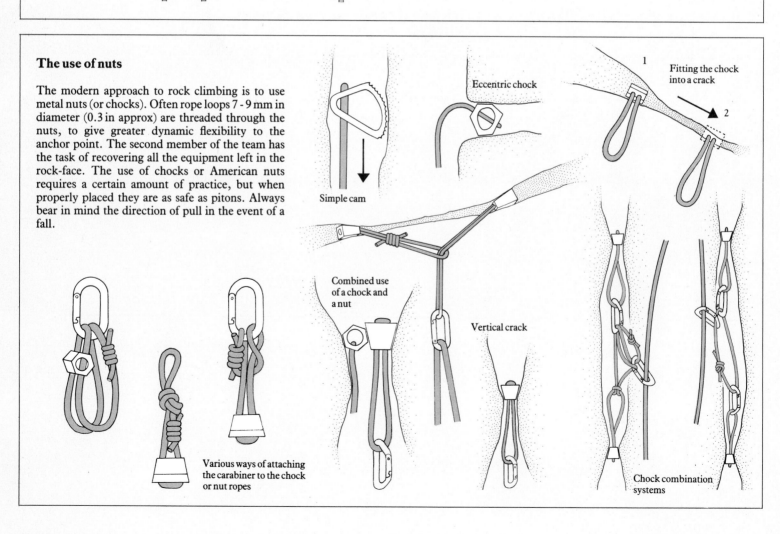

Eccentric chock

Simple cam

Fitting the chock into a crack

1

2

Combined use of a chock and a nut

Vertical crack

Various ways of attaching the carabiner to the chock or nut ropes

Chock combination systems

Ascenders

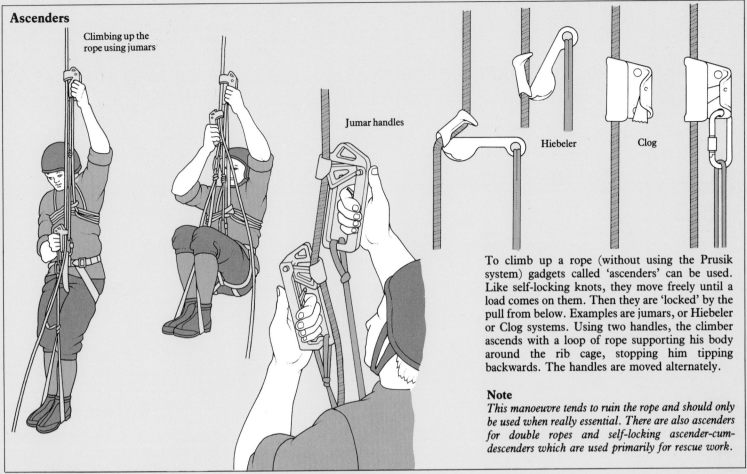

Climbing up the rope using jumars

Jumar handles

Hiebeler

Clog

To climb up a rope (without using the Prusik system) gadgets called 'ascenders' can be used. Like self-locking knots, they move freely until a load comes on them. Then they are 'locked' by the pull from below. Examples are jumars, or Hiebeler or Clog systems. Using two handles, the climber ascends with a loop of rope supporting his body around the rib cage, stopping him tipping backwards. The handles are moved alternately.

Note
This manoeuvre tends to ruin the rope and should only be used when really essential. There are also ascenders for double ropes and self-locking ascender-cum-descenders which are used primarily for rescue work.

Fifi hooks

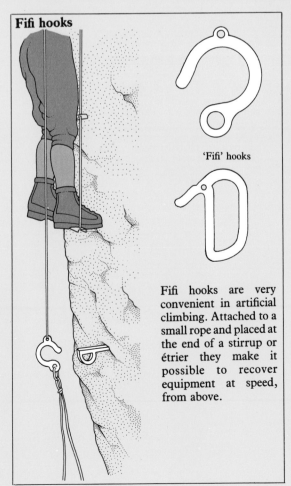

'Fifi' hooks

Fifi hooks are very convenient in artificial climbing. Attached to a small rope and placed at the end of a stirrup or étrier they make it possible to recover equipment at speed, from above.

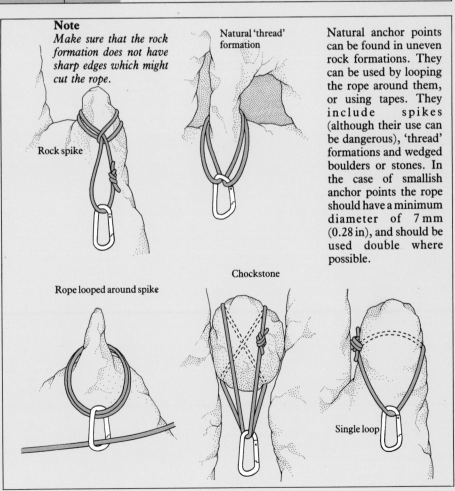

Note
Make sure that the rock formation does not have sharp edges which might cut the rope.

Natural 'thread' formation

Rock spike

Rope looped around spike

Chockstone

Single loop

Natural anchor points can be found in uneven rock formations. They can be used by looping the rope around them, or using tapes. They include spikes (although their use can be dangerous), 'thread' formations and wedged boulders or stones. In the case of smallish anchor points the rope should have a minimum diameter of 7 mm (0.28 in), and should be used double where possible.

Pitons

The effectiveness of a piton depends on the way it has been inserted into a crack, and by the position in which it absorbs the strain or jerk of the rope. As a general rule horizontal pitons are fitted into horizontal cracks, and vertical pitons in vertical cracks, with the eye in the lower position. 'Universal' pitons with an angled blade are of interest. The piton is hammered into place up to the eye; when the eye touches the rock it means that there will be no play. An indication of a piton driven well home is the characteristic high ringing note struck by the hammer blows. European pitons, made of soft metal, adapt to the shape of the crack by becoming 'deformed' inside it; pitons made of hard steel (with a higher breaking point) force their way into the rock until they break or split it, and are harder to use, even if they 'hold' better. It is always a good rule to beware of pitons that you find already in place in a rock-face.

Note

In most cases pitons are the weakest link in the safety chain. In some experimental tests soft-metal pitons have not stood up to loads of more than 1000 kg (2250 lb).

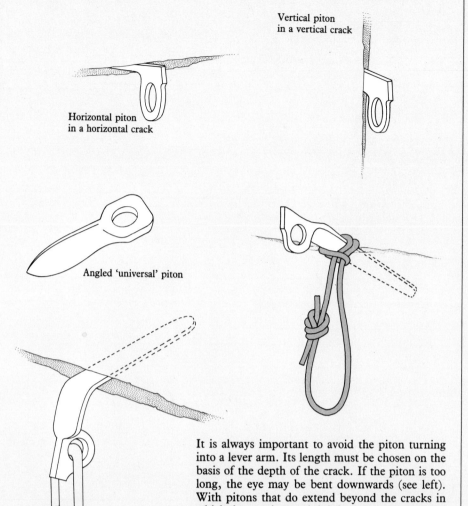

Horizontal piton in a horizontal crack

Vertical piton in a vertical crack

Angled 'universal' piton

1200 kg (2700 lb)

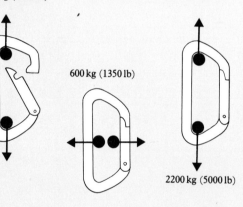

600 kg (1350 lb)

2200 kg (5000 lb)

It is always important to avoid the piton turning into a lever arm. Its length must be chosen on the basis of the depth of the crack. If the piton is too long, the eye may be bent downwards (see left). With pitons that do extend beyond the cracks in which they are inserted, it is best to use a rope loop (see above) or a tape to tie them off. A perfectly inserted hard-steel piton will take a strain of 2000 kg (4500 lb). It must be inserted manually up to two-thirds of its length, and then driven home with just a few hammer blows. A piton can be used up to a hundred times, until cracks start to appear in the metal.

The rurp, introduced by the Americans, is a very short and small piton, shaped like a razor-blade, and made of hard steel; it is used as an aid piton in artificial climbing, in very small cracks in granite.

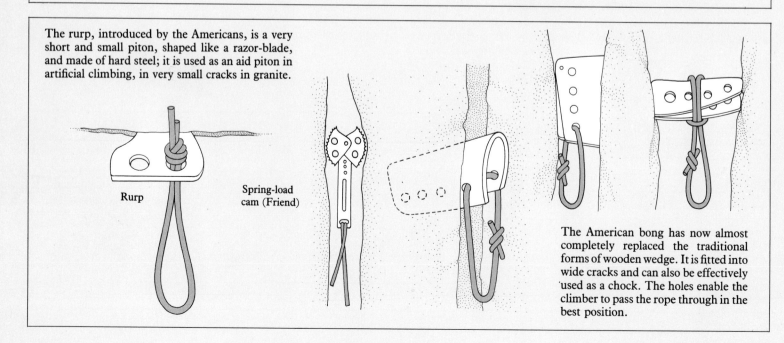

Rurp

Spring-load cam (Friend)

The American bong has now almost completely replaced the traditional forms of wooden wedge. It is fitted into wide cracks and can also be effectively used as a chock. The holes enable the climber to pass the rope through in the best position.

Rope-joining knots

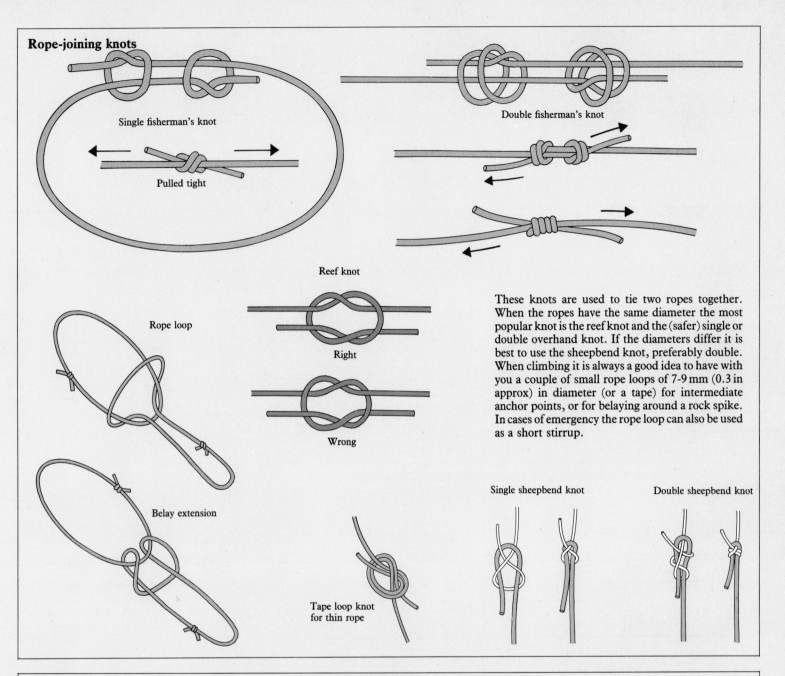

Single fisherman's knot

Pulled tight

Double fisherman's knot

Rope loop

Reef knot

Right

Wrong

Belay extension

Tape loop knot for thin rope

Single sheepbend knot

Double sheepbend knot

These knots are used to tie two ropes together. When the ropes have the same diameter the most popular knot is the reef knot and the (safer) single or double overhand knot. If the diameters differ it is best to use the sheepbend knot, preferably double. When climbing it is always a good idea to have with you a couple of small rope loops of 7-9 mm (0.3 in approx) in diameter (or a tape) for intermediate anchor points, or for belaying around a rock spike. In cases of emergency the rope loop can also be used as a short stirrup.

Tapes

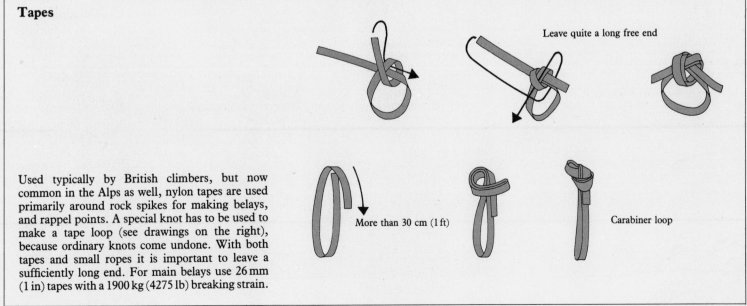

Leave quite a long free end

More than 30 cm (1 ft)

Carabiner loop

Used typically by British climbers, but now common in the Alps as well, nylon tapes are used primarily around rock spikes for making belays, and rappel points. A special knot has to be used to make a tape loop (see drawings on the right), because ordinary knots come undone. With both tapes and small ropes it is important to leave a sufficiently long end. For main belays use 26 mm (1 in) tapes with a 1900 kg (4275 lb) breaking strain.

The search for balance

In free rock-climbing (as opposed to artificial) the basic rule is to keep in balance through a series of successive moves (which occurs automatically when walking up steps, for example), keeping the body-weight on the feet and making intelligent use of hand- and footholds. The climbing boot, with a rigid or semi-rigid sole, is used on toe holds, with the heel kept slightly lowered; small steps are taken, without rushing, moving just one limb at a time. The body must always be kept well clear of the rock so that holds can be easily seen and so that feet can be placed on them accurately.

Climbing in friction boots

Flexible, smooth-soled climbing boots, such as PAs, have greatly influenced climbing technique. They are now used widely on hard rock climbs. Because they rely on friction to give the climber purchase, the sole of the foot has to be pressed against the rock. The more of the rubber sole that can be pressed against the rock, the more friction is created. Rigid boots, by contrast, need positive holds for security and give very little friction.

Action of the legs

Centre of gravity

Action of the arms

Body-weight

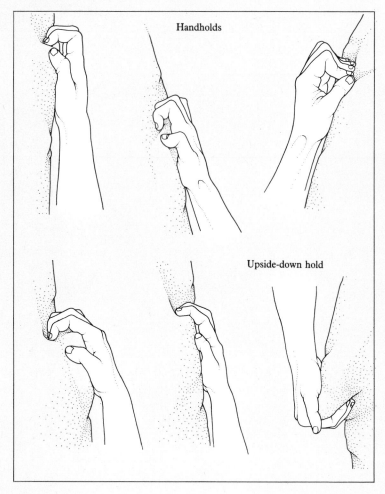

Handholds

Upside-down hold

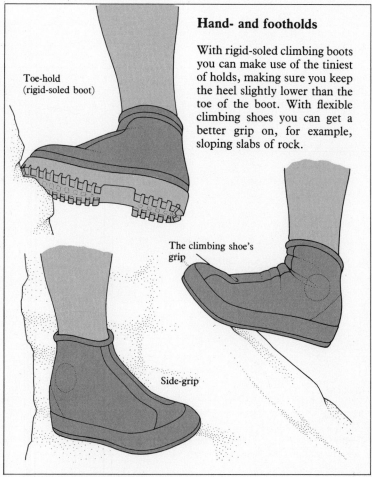

Hand- and footholds

With rigid-soled climbing boots you can make use of the tiniest of holds, making sure you keep the heel slightly lower than the toe of the boot. With flexible climbing shoes you can get a better grip on, for example, sloping slabs of rock.

Toe-hold
(rigid-soled boot)

The climbing shoe's grip

Side-grip

Climbing a rock route

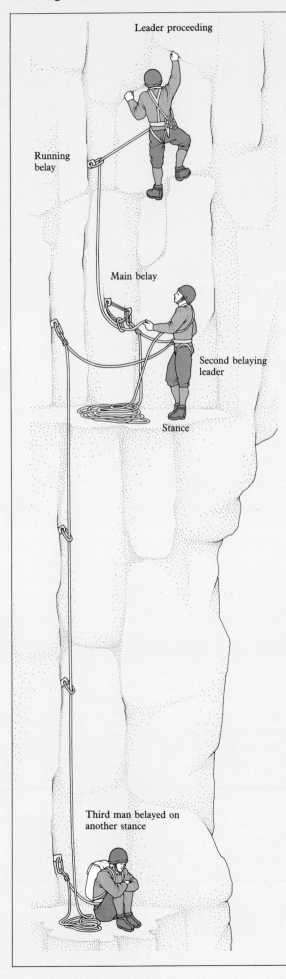

Leader proceeding

Running belay

Main belay

Second belaying leader

Stance

Third man belayed on another stance

The safest and quickest climbing team has two members on the rope. The leader, normally the more experienced of the two, climbs for almost the entire length of the rope (which is now standardized at about 40 metres (130 ft) with an 11-mm (0.4-in) diameter), until he finds a good stance, ideally on a ledge. Here he attaches himself to the rock and then tells his second to join him. During the climb, especially on more difficult pitches, the leader places running belays using pitons or nuts, and then passes the main rope through carabiners attached to them. It is very important to choose solid belay points at the stances. The height of the possible fall is equal to twice the distance of the first climber from the belay point (the position of the last piton or nut). This length, divided by the distance separating the leader and second, gives a coefficient which gives information about the load on the rope and the stress on the anchor point in the event of a fall (F here is called the 'fall factor'):

$$F = \frac{H \text{ (height of fall)}}{D \text{ (distance from team member)}}$$

If the coefficient is equal to 2 (the maximum, if there are no running belays), the fall is an extreme one which would be difficult to hold, even over a short distance, because there would be a massive jerk which would only be slightly absorbed by the elasticity of the rope.

As he makes his way upwards, the leader must keep an alert eye on the quality of the rock, both to avoid a fall caused by a hold breaking off, and to avoid hitting his fellow climber with loose rock displaced from the route. The safety of a hand- or foothold is best tested by hitting it with the palm of the hand, not by pulling on it. As the rope starts to run out, the leader must look for a suitable ledge and secure himself. His call to his second, watching the leader from below, must be short and sharp: 'Climb when you're ready' (when he has secured himself at the ledge and is ready to belay the second up the pitch). When he has taken off his own belay, the second replies: 'Climbing!' In a three-man team the leader climbs, then calls up the second and climbs again. When the leader is belayed above him, the second then brings up the third, and so on. In successive phases, the team moves up the route. The last member has the task of recovering all the equipment that has been used by the leader and second as belays.

Falls

Despite the advances made in the technology of mountaineering equipment, there is still a lot of argument over the basic concepts of belaying in the event of a fall. It is a good idea for every mountaineer to carry out tests and experiments on his own in a training gym. In rock-climbing schools, extreme falls are simulated using weight-drop systems and students are given direct experience of the kind of impact that they can expect. They generally soon realize how unprepared they are when it comes to arresting a serious fall.

In order to be accepted by the UIAA (the Union of International Alpine Associations, the major international mountaineering organization) modern ropes made of synthetic fibres must meet two requirements:
1) They must stand up to two tests with forces of 8 kp (1 kp is the equivalent of about 1 kg/2.25 lb, with a fall coefficient of 1.78).
2) The maximum load does not exceed 1200 kg (2700 lb).

The static breaking strain of modern ropes is about 2600 kg (5850 lb) for 11-mm (0.4-in) diameter ropes, and 1700 kg (3825 lb) for 9-mm (0.35-in) diameter ropes.

The most important factor in absorbing the energy of a fall is the extensibility of the rope. But there are many other factors which help: friction against the rock, the tightening of knots under strain, the climber's body itself, the braking force caused by the rope running through carabiners. Despite these factors, it is essential to minimize the shock loading on each of the elements of this safety chain. Always belay so that the rope is deliberately allowed to run and the fall is arrested gradually rather than with a sudden shock.

Both the half hitch tied around a carabiner and used as a dynamic belay and the Sticht plate offer excellent friction braking and do not need the same skill and judgement as trying to hold a fall dynamically with a shoulder or waist belay. In the diagrams opposite, the shoulder belay is illustrated - a technique used commonly in the Alps by continental climbers. The waist belay is favoured particularly by British and American climbers. Whatever system of belaying is used it is always best to do everything possible when climbing to reduce the potential fall factor. A leader should therefore always try to place a running belay as soon as possible after leaving a stance. Plenty of runners on a pitch dramatically reduce the shock load on the belayer in the event of a fall. The diagrams below show how a main belay can be arranged using a rope sling and two or three pitons. Multiple anchor points at the main belay increase the safety factor and should always be used if time allows. Often in Alpine climbing, speed is essential to make the best of daylight and good weather and less elaborate belays have to be used.

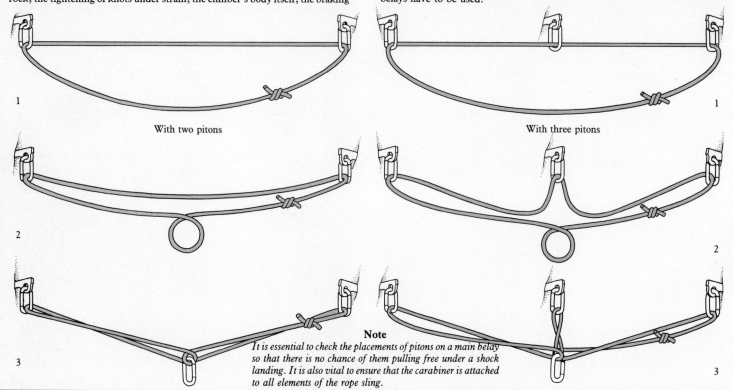

With two pitons

With three pitons

Note
It is essential to check the placements of pitons on a main belay so that there is no chance of them pulling free under a shock landing. It is also vital to ensure that the carabiner is attached to all elements of the rope sling.

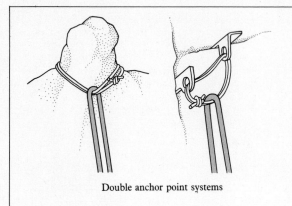

Double anchor point systems

A common belay system involves a double rope loop passed around a rock spike or an anchor point with two connected pitons (see above).

The safety chain

A safe belay: on the piton on the far right a hitch knot is used to protect the climber; on the one to the left the rope running to the second climber is passed through the carabiner with a half-hitch. The thin rope helps to lessen still further the potential impact on the piton, which is usually the least reliable link in the safety chain. A climber must always remember that his safety chain is as strong as its weakest link.

Hitch knot

Half-hitch

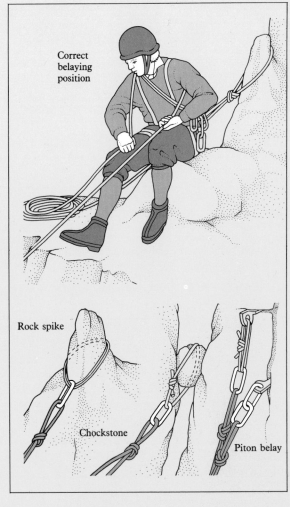

Correct belaying position

Rock spike

Chockstone

Piton belay

Belaying on rock

The shoulder belay illustrated is not recommended when there is the possibility of a serious fall. It is best used only for the leader protecting the second. The rope is passed under the armpit and over the opposite shoulder. To stop a slip, maximum friction around the climber's back is created by drawing both arms in toward the body. The climber must stand in balance ready to brace himself to stop a fall. A useful variant of the conventional shoulder belay is the crossed rope system shown below.

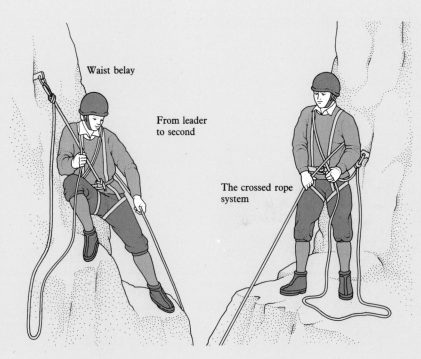

Waist belay

From leader to second

The crossed rope system

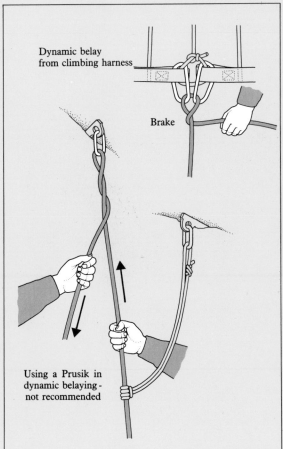

Dynamic belay from climbing harness

Brake

Using a Prusik in dynamic belaying - not recommended

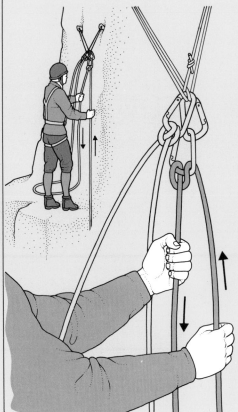

The half-hitch

Belaying a second and a second belaying a leader using a half-hitch system is approved by the UIAA. The rope is pulled through with the hands kept some way from the carabiner, and with a hand on each end of the rope. You can also loop the free end over your back, by leaving about 1 metre (3 ft) of slack. This increases friction in the event of a fall.

Protecting the leader

Belaying the leader, when he has placed three or more running belays on the pitch he is climbing, is relatively easy since the forces on the belay system in the event of a fall are much reduced (assuming, of course, that the runners hold). In this case the shoulder belay can be used, removing the half-hitch which may have been used initially, and passing the rope directly through the carabiner. This change-over must be carried out carefully, and you must warn the leader at the delicate moment when the knot is untied. To reduce the impact of the rope under the armpit (the rope going to the other climber must always be passed first under the armpit, as in the illustration) it can be passed through a carabiner on the harness.

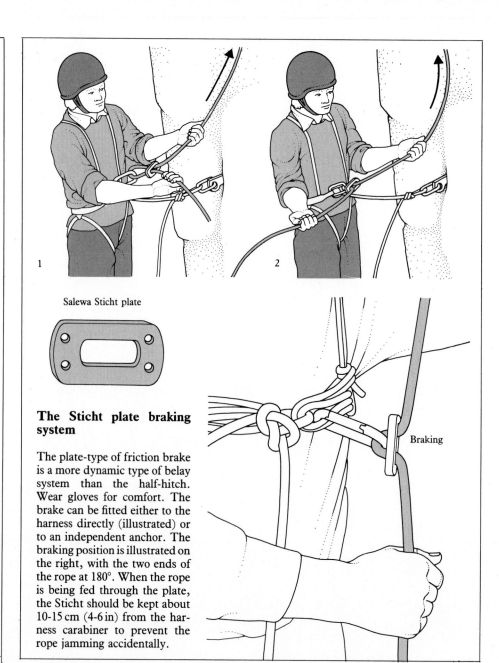

1   2

Salewa Sticht plate

Second belaying the leader, with the rope taken round his back

The Sticht plate braking system

The plate-type of friction brake is a more dynamic type of belay system than the half-hitch. Wear gloves for comfort. The brake can be fitted either to the harness directly (illustrated) or to an independent anchor. The braking position is illustrated on the right, with the two ends of the rope at 180°. When the rope is being fed through the plate, the Sticht should be kept about 10-15 cm (4-6 in) from the harness carabiner to prevent the rope jamming accidentally.

Braking

Note

The most dangerous moments are immediately after the leader has left the stance. It is therefore advisable for a running belay to be placed immediately above the anchor point (see illustration below).

With the ropes crossed and using a carabiner at the waist

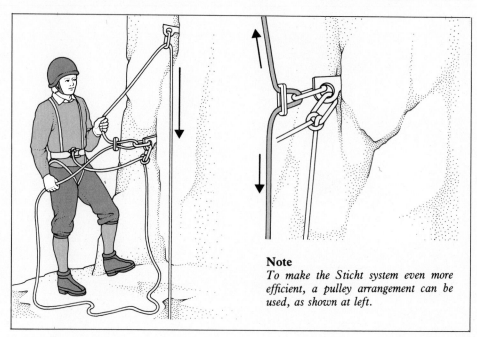

Note

To make the Sticht system even more efficient, a pulley arrangement can be used, as shown at left.

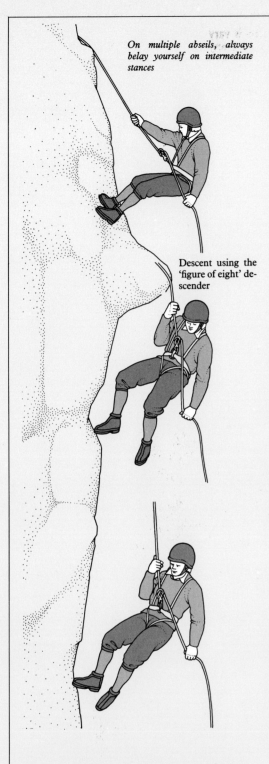

On multiple abseils, always belay yourself on intermediate stances

Descent using the 'figure of eight' descender

- *When the start of an abseil is difficult (low anchor point, overhang) leave the stance from a kneeling position.*
- *Descend smoothly, without jerks. To brake, move the left arm back; to descend, extend it.*
- *During the descent keep your eyes open for footholds to help you maintain your balance.*
- *Use a self-locking knot to link yourself to the main rope as a safety measure.*
- *If the rope jams when you try to pull it down, climb upwards again tied on to both ropes for safety.*
- *Make sure that the rope does not rub against your climbing harness or the heat generated could melt it.*
- *If the rope does jam, do not pull, but try to jerk it free.*
- *If there is a knot joining two ropes at the top, remember which is the end to be pulled to avoid the knot jamming.*
- *In an emergency, you can always make abseil points by cutting off lengths of the main rope.*

Throwing the rope

Abseiling or rappelling

This is the quickest method of descent, and enables the climber to negotiate virtually any obstacle. Nowadays the use of descenders attached to the harness (Clog, Fameau and Allain) is preferred to the traditional Dülfer, Piaz and Comici techniques. It is vital to have a solid anchor point (see page 66).

Note

When you descend in the classic way do not let go of the rope with the hand of the arm which acts as a brake (usually the right). The other hand should not pull on the rope but only steady it.

Piaz descent (the so-called 'classic' abseil)

Using a Bachmann knot to protect one's self on the abseil

Sling harness with carabiner

Locking direction

Fameau descender

With two 11 mm (0.4 in) ropes

With two 9 mm (0.35 in) ropes

One rope Fameau method

Locking off the descender

Climbing down

Many accidents in mountains occur during descents when climbers are usually weary. So the first rule is to have your wits about you. On easy terrain, you can climb down facing outwards, bracing yourself with your hands (without actually sitting down), with the torso leaning forward, and the body well balanced. On rock of average difficulty, keep your hands low to use holds and turn your body sideways and use the edges of your boot on the holds below you. On even more difficult rock, face inwards, with your boots in the normal climbing position. The arms must be kept low and the body held well clear of the rock. Examine the pitch to be climbed down with great care. Once the degree of difficulty goes beyond grade II or III, it is advisable to rope down or rappel. Practising down-climbing is very useful and gives you the chance to turn back at any given moment on a climb without the help of a rope. If you stay roped together, the most experienced climber is, of course, always the last to make the descent, once the other climber or climbers are safely down.

Correct position: hands held low, body well clear of rock to see where holds are

Easy descent, facing out

Difficult descent

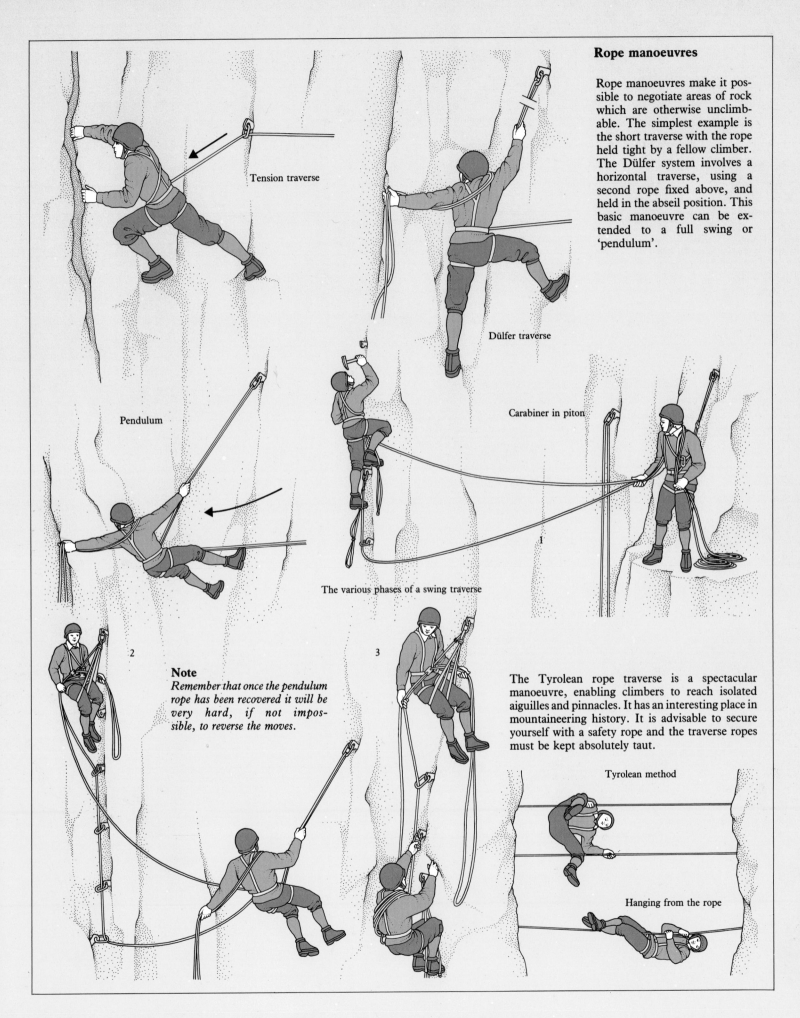

Rope manoeuvres

Rope manoeuvres make it possible to negotiate areas of rock which are otherwise unclimbable. The simplest example is the short traverse with the rope held tight by a fellow climber. The Dülfer system involves a horizontal traverse, using a second rope fixed above, and held in the abseil position. This basic manoeuvre can be extended to a full swing or 'pendulum'.

Tension traverse

Dülfer traverse

Pendulum

Carabiner in piton

The various phases of a swing traverse

Note
Remember that once the pendulum rope has been recovered it will be very hard, if not impossible, to reverse the moves.

The Tyrolean rope traverse is a spectacular manoeuvre, enabling climbers to reach isolated aiguilles and pinnacles. It has an interesting place in mountaineering history. It is advisable to secure yourself with a safety rope and the traverse ropes must be kept absolutely taut.

Tyrolean method

Hanging from the rope

Jamming techniques

These are particularly useful for climbing up narrow, regular cracks in granite; these cracks are often clearly defined with smooth, parallel edges. Jams can be made with the toe and heel of the boot, with the knee and the foot, or with the whole body. Jams can be made with the back of the hand, by closing the fist, or by producing pressure between the hand and the elbow. For the method to be safe it must be carried out resolutely, with swift movements and good technique. In some cracks you might find a hold inside (perhaps a small wedged stone), or you can force against the two sides, as if you were trying to open up the crack. Jamming can be a tiring technique.

Jamming the body in a crack

When the crack is steep and regular, the best position is the one shown on the right, with an arm and a leg jammed on the same side of the body, looking for possible holds with the free limbs on the outer face.

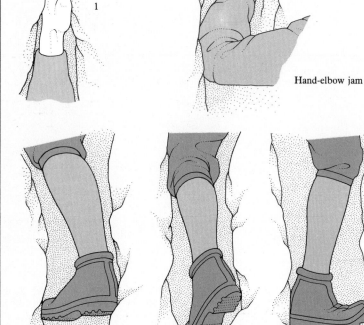

Fist jam

2

1

Pulling in opposition

Using both hands

Hand-elbow jam

The sole of the boot can often be fitted easily in the crack (left). Boots with rigid soles are usually the most comfortable for this type of climbing.

Toe-heel

Knee-foot

Horizontal jam

The layback

This is one of the most thrilling and technically demanding positions, and is very tiring on the hands and arms. It involves arching the body outwards, or to one side of the crack or fissure, gripping one of the sides with both hands. The feet are braced opposite against the face (keeping balance) and grip by pressure, or by finding small protuberances. They must be kept quite high up so that they will not slip downwards. A classic layback is when you can grip the upper edge of a sloping slab of rock with both hands, the slab cutting diagonally across the face. Flexible climbing shoes are the best suited for maximum grip. To avoid tiring yourself out too much keep the arms well extended.

Note
In the position required for the layback, it may be difficult to pause and put a running belay in place. It is therefore advisable to find a runner immediately before tackling the pitch.

In the drawings on the right we see the layback used on a vertical crack. *Above*: a diagonal ascent with arms and legs in opposition. *Below*: a detail of the hand grips.

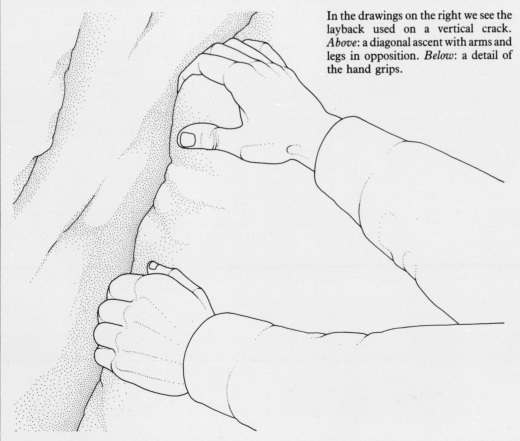

The corner

This is a typical mountain formation, caused by the meeting of two walls or faces at a certain angle. The centre of the corner is usually run through by a crack. It can be claimed by bridging, as in the case of a chimney. It is advisable to stay as near the outside as possible, especially if there are any overhanging stretches. Handholds should not be too high. To raise a leg you press with the hands (or forearms) on the corresponding side of the wall, where possible pulling up on a hold on the other side. There are often good handholds or jams in the central crack, in which nuts can also be fitted for protection.

Note
Bridging technique is also used on a face, especially in very steep or overhanging stretches, where it keeps the body in balance.

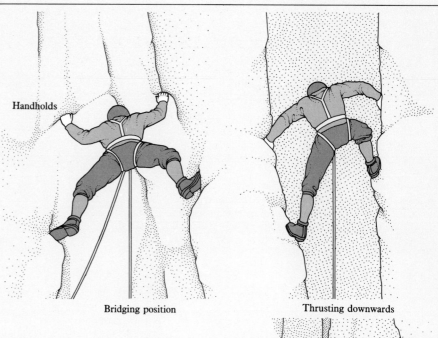

Handholds

Bridging position

Thrusting downwards

Classic corner

The Comici technique consists in using the hands in opposition inside a crack, with the legs in a bridged position. This technique can only occasionally be applied, and it is physically very demanding.

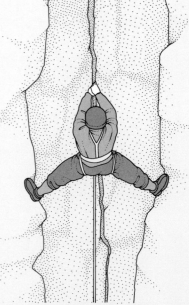

Comici technique

The flexible or P.A. (Pierre Allain) climbing boot has to some extent revolutionized rock-climbing techniques. The sole is smooth, made of a special blend of rubber which ensures maximum friction. The best type of rubber is Airlite. Such boots give a climber a direct 'feel' of the rock and can be used for pure friction climbing on dry rock. In wet conditions they can be dangerously slippery. Take great care on wet rocks or grassy stretches.

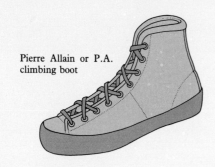

Pierre Allain or P.A. climbing boot

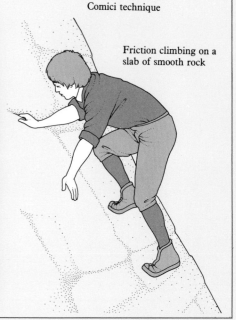

Friction climbing on a slab of smooth rock

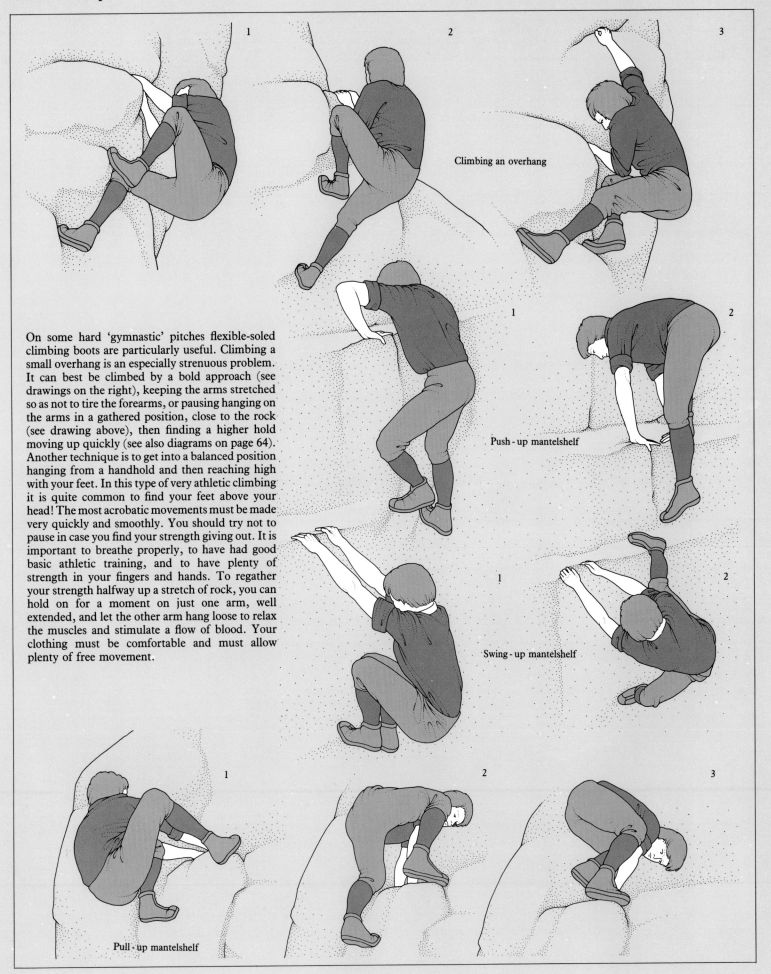

Climbing an overhang

Push - up mantelshelf

Swing - up mantelshelf

Pull - up mantelshelf

On some hard 'gymnastic' pitches flexible-soled climbing boots are particularly useful. Climbing a small overhang is an especially strenuous problem. It can best be climbed by a bold approach (see drawings on the right), keeping the arms stretched so as not to tire the forearms, or pausing hanging on the arms in a gathered position, close to the rock (see drawing above), then finding a higher hold moving up quickly (see also diagrams on page 64). Another technique is to get into a balanced position hanging from a handhold and then reaching high with your feet. In this type of very athletic climbing it is quite common to find your feet above your head! The most acrobatic movements must be made very quickly and smoothly. You should try not to pause in case you find your strength giving out. It is important to breathe properly, to have had good basic athletic training, and to have plenty of strength in your fingers and hands. To regather your strength halfway up a stretch of rock, you can hold on for a moment on just one arm, well extended, and let the other arm hang loose to relax the muscles and stimulate a flow of blood. Your clothing must be comfortable and must allow plenty of free movement.

The wide chimney

A chimney is a vertical split or crevice in the rock which can accommodate the whole body. If the two walls are the right distance apart you can adopt the classic straddle position, pressing each of your boots against an opposing wall. You move upward with your legs spread apart. To get your feet higher, you take your weight by pressing against the chimney walls with your hands. In this way, alternating the movements and with careful coordination, height can rapidly be gained. Chimney climbing is usually not very exposed and relatively safe. Use footholds on the walls wherever possible but if the walls are smooth, it is still possible to keep a good grip by using pressure alone, though it is more tiring. The same straddle technique can often be applied in a corner, if its faces are not too opened out; it can also be used occasionally on stretches of ordinary rock-face.

The narrow chimney

If the walls of the chimney are close together, an opposed position is adopted with the back against one wall and the boots pressed against the other. To gain height, one leg is bent under the body, and pressure is exerted simultaneously on the leg and the arms, with the palms flattened against the wall; the body is then lifted upwards by the seat. The legs are then also raised and the manoeuvre is repeated. If well coordinated, this technique (which is called 'backing up') enables the climber to climb extremely smooth-walled chimneys without undue effort. The pressure created in fact keeps the climber in a very safe position. It is however important to be careful not to raise your body too far above your feet. If you do, your boots may well slip away from the other wall. If the chimney is very narrow, you will have to find footholds. Pressure can be increased if required by pressing against the opposite wall with your arms.

Note
Before setting off study the walls of the chimney so that you start off facing in the right direction: it is not always easy to turn round once in a chimney.

Backing up a chimney

Straddling up a chimney

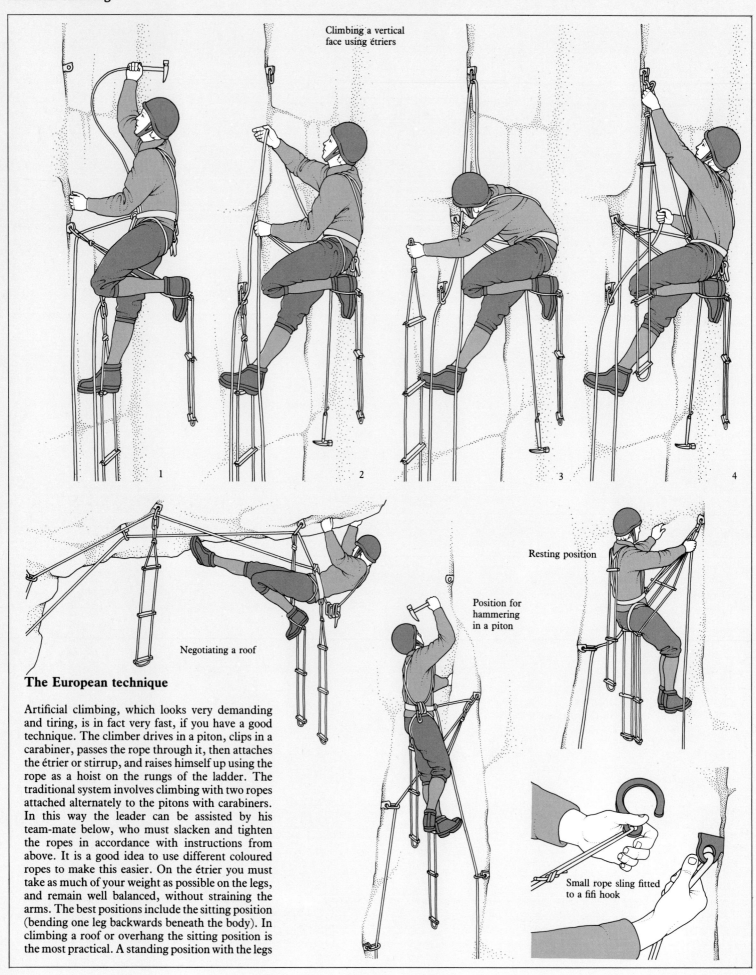

Climbing a vertical
face using étriers

1

2

3

4

Negotiating a roof

Resting position

Position for
hammering
in a piton

Small rope sling fitted
to a fifi hook

The European technique

Artificial climbing, which looks very demanding
and tiring, is in fact very fast, if you have a good
technique. The climber drives in a piton, clips in a
carabiner, passes the rope through it, then attaches
the étrier or stirrup, and raises himself up using the
rope as a hoist on the rungs of the ladder. The
traditional system involves climbing with two ropes
attached alternately to the pitons with carabiners.
In this way the leader can be assisted by his
team-mate below, who must slacken and tighten
the ropes in accordance with instructions from
above. It is a good idea to use different coloured
ropes to make this easier. On the étrier you must
take as much of your weight as possible on the legs,
and remain well balanced, without straining the
arms. The best positions include the sitting position
(bending one leg backwards beneath the body). In
climbing a roof or overhang the sitting position is
the most practical. A standing position with the legs

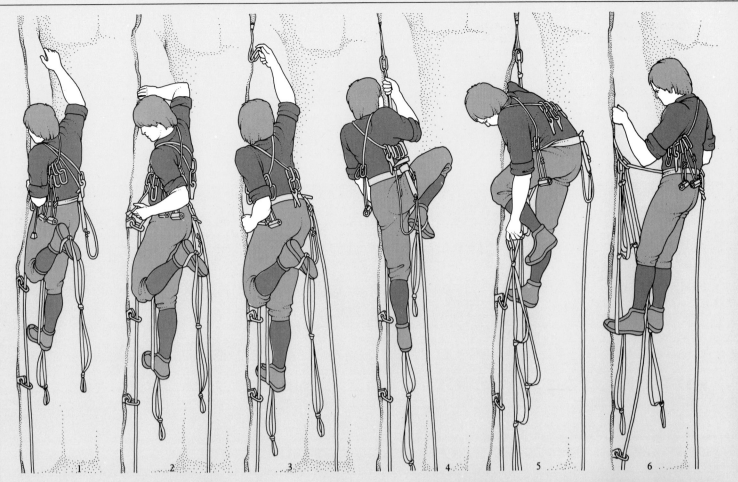

crossed can be used climbing vertical rock. To save time you must try to gain as much height as possible in each movement, driving in pitons about 1.5 metres (5 ft) apart if possible. The fairly new technique of using a small rope sling attached to the harness with a fifi hook (to be passed through the same piton as the étrier) saves a lot of unnecessary effort and exertion by your team-mate.

The American technique

The specific kinds of formation of the granite mountains of California have given birth to a fully fledged American school of climbing. Artificial climbing differs primarily in that just one rope is used, tape ladders instead of étriers, and nuts in preference to pitons wherever possible. The drawings above illustrate this type of climbing. The European type of ladder - the étrier with solid rungs - consists of 6-7 mm (0.25 in) ropes and is on average 1.5 metres (5 ft) in length. There are three or four rungs set at graded distances from top to bottom. The uppermost ones, nearest the piton, are slightly closer together. On very long climbs, and during stops or breathers, a nylon thigh sling can be useful. The second is belayed from above by the leader who keeps the two ropes alternately tight and slack to help the second recover the equipment that has been used. On free climbing pitches, the étriers are folded up, or slung over the head; they are not left dangling from the harness, in case they get snagged on a protruding piece of rock, and cause an accident.

Tape ladder
or stirrups

Étrier

Artificial climbing

The American Yosemite technique involves single-rope artificial climbing. When the climber reaches the end of the rope length he belays himself to pitons or nuts, sometimes also using a thigh sling, and calls up his team-mate. All the belaying methods, in accordance with American and British custom, are dynamic. In some cases the leader merely fixes the rope leading to his team-mate to an anchor point with a blocked loop or hitch knot. The other climber then climbs up the rope using jumar clamps, loosening and recovering the pitons, nuts, ropes and carabiners. The leader recovers the rucksack, however, which probably weighs quite a lot because of all the equipment required for the climb (which may last several days). To bring up the rucksack he sets up a pulley system with a self-locking device such as jumars. To the second jumar, fitted to the rope he takes in, he attaches a stirrup to help himself in the operation of actually hauling the rucksack.

Climbing sequence

1) The leader climbs using the single rope.
2) The leader secures himself at the first stance.
3) He ties off his team-mate's rope and starts to haul up the rucksack.
4) The second climbs the rope using jumar clamps.
5) The second reaches the stance and belays.
6) The leader sets off on the next pitch.

Note
To be able to recover the rucksack easily from above, it must be cylindrical in shape and made of very tough fabric, with no pockets or laces at the sides. A plastic flap over the rop of the rucksack (as shown in the drawings) may also be helpful.

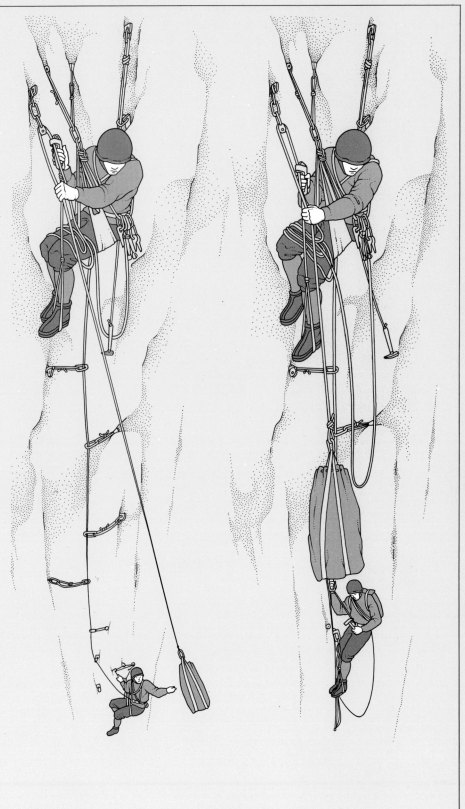

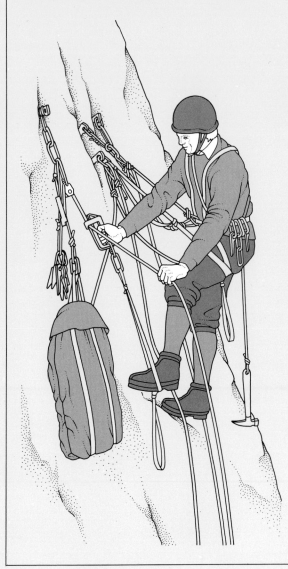

Note
Detail of the recovery system for the rucksack: the climber uses a stirrup (or rope loop) attached to a jumar on the rope he takes in. The rope runs through a carabiner or in a pulley with a self-locking system. The rucksack is attached to a separate anchor point.

Techniques in solo climbing

Solo climbing requires a high degree of safety and perfect self-control: never climb solo simply because you cannot find someone to climb with you. During the climb you can use various self-belaying systems. The one shown in the drawings below is based on the principle of a Bachmann-type self-locking device on the harness. It requires repeated short descents to unclip the rope from the belay point, which, in the event of a fall, is subject to pull from above through the running belays. Other systems involve passing various sizes of rope loops through the carabiner (depending on the height that has to be scaled), and these are then undone from above. It is advisable to pass small rope slings through the pitons to avoid any direct jerk or strain. Anyone who climbs solo must be doubly cautious in all his movements and pay special attention to knots and belay points.

The self-hoist

Two stirrups are used, attached by small slings to the harness. The first is the length of the distance from the waist to the highest rung on the étrier, in the laden position. The second must be able to be passed through a carabiner attached to the next piton. The climb takes place in two phases: first on the longer stirrup, then on the short one which automatically (with the actual weight of the climber) keeps him on the piton at waist level, thus enabling him to make the next movement. This system can also be effectively used by a normal roped party.

Solo aid climbing

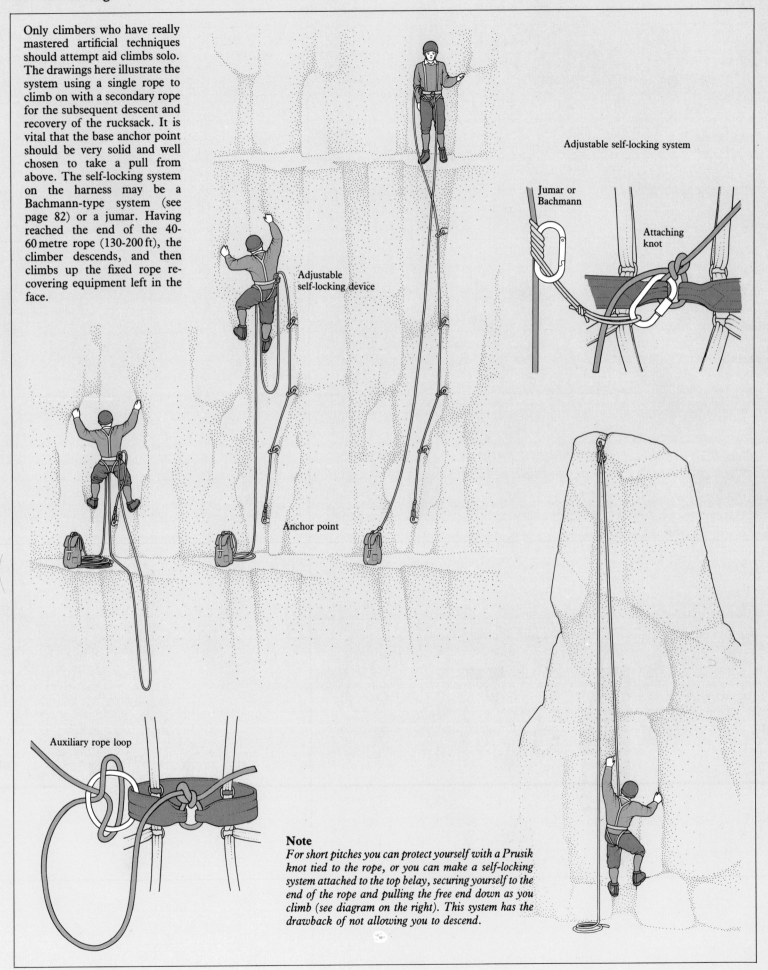

Only climbers who have really mastered artificial techniques should attempt aid climbs solo. The drawings here illustrate the system using a single rope to climb on with a secondary rope for the subsequent descent and recovery of the rucksack. It is vital that the base anchor point should be very solid and well chosen to take a pull from above. The self-locking system on the harness may be a Bachmann-type system (see page 82) or a jumar. Having reached the end of the 40-60 metre rope (130-200 ft), the climber descends, and then climbs up the fixed rope recovering equipment left in the face.

Adjustable self-locking system

Jumar or Bachmann

Attaching knot

Adjustable self-locking device

Anchor point

Auxiliary rope loop

Note
For short pitches you can protect yourself with a Prusik knot tied to the rope, or you can make a self-locking system attached to the top belay, securing yourself to the end of the rope and pulling the free end down as you climb (see diagram on the right). This system has the drawback of not allowing you to descend.

The pendulum using pitons

The drawings illustrate a specific type of solo climbing technique. The climber proceeds by securing himself to the rope which is in turn clipped into pitons. When the piton crack runs out, he makes a pendulum-like movement downwards to reach a parallel crack, and is then able to continue the ascent. When he has reached the end of the rope, and found a good belay, he descends along the auxiliary rope (which is free) attached to the lower belay. As he descends down the upper stretch he recovers the pitons used. He then climbs up the lower stretch, protecting himself with the rope which is tied off at the top belay point. At the last piton he lets himself swing loose and climbs back up the rope with jumars until he reaches the top ledge. He can carry the rucksack on his back or recover it with the auxiliary rope. The type of climbing described here requires a great deal of experience and a very detailed knowledge of the manoeuvres to be carried out. Instead of making a fixed base anchor point, some solo climbers prefer to use the actual weight of the rucksack, thus making for themselves a novel kind of dynamic belaying system.

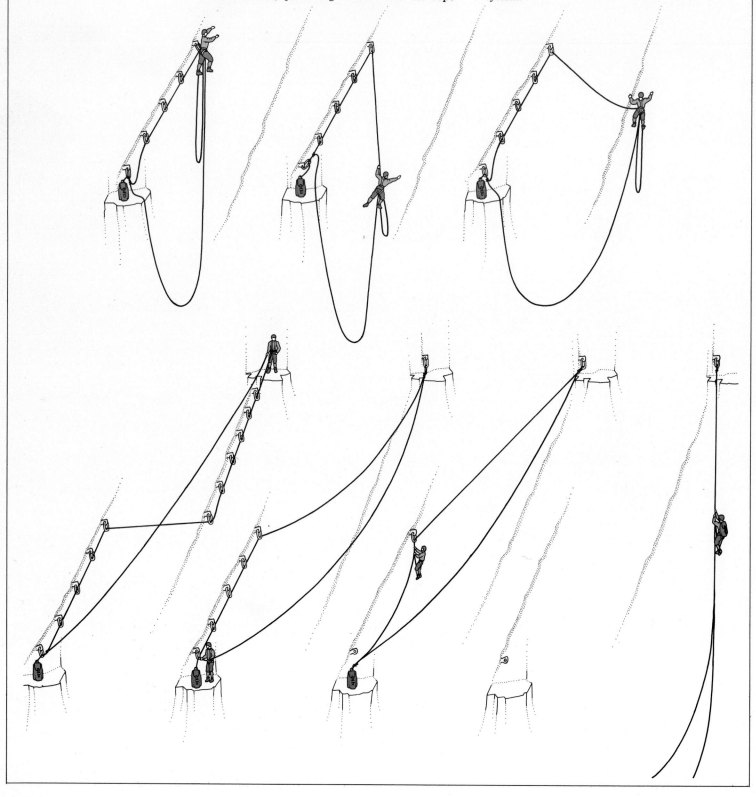

Descending over an overhang

This is where abseiling can run into major problems. The first climber to descend has to set up a self-locking system on both ropes. It is also wise to join the ends together with a figure-of-eight knot (or one of the various slip knots). When he has reached the level of the ledge, the climber adjusts the self-locking system and starts to swing until he can step on to the ledge or platform. He then makes a belay, secures himself to it with a sling and holds the ends of the rope to help his team-mate.

Note
Only pull the rope in if your team-mate is coming down using a descender. The classic abseil where the rope runs over your back is not recommended when an overhang has to be negotiated.

The double étrier system in descent

This can be used to negotiate small overhangs without having to resort to the abseiling. The first étrier is attached to a piton and a rope sling is tied to the end of the second étrier (as shown in the diagram below), adjusting the height as necessary. The climber climbs down to the first rung of the second étrier, recovers the first and then continues downwards. The étrier with the long length of rope (passed directly through the eye of the piton) is recovered very simply by undoing one of the ends.

Note
Adjust the height with a hitch knot (see diagram below).

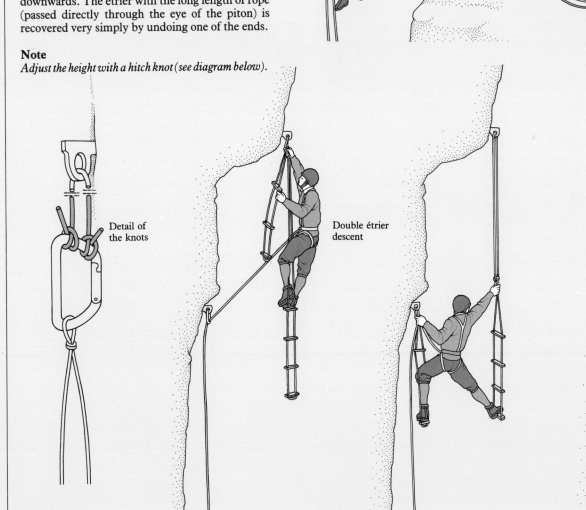

Detail of
the knots

Double étrier
descent

Recovering
one of the
étriers

ICE CLIMBING
TECHNIQUES

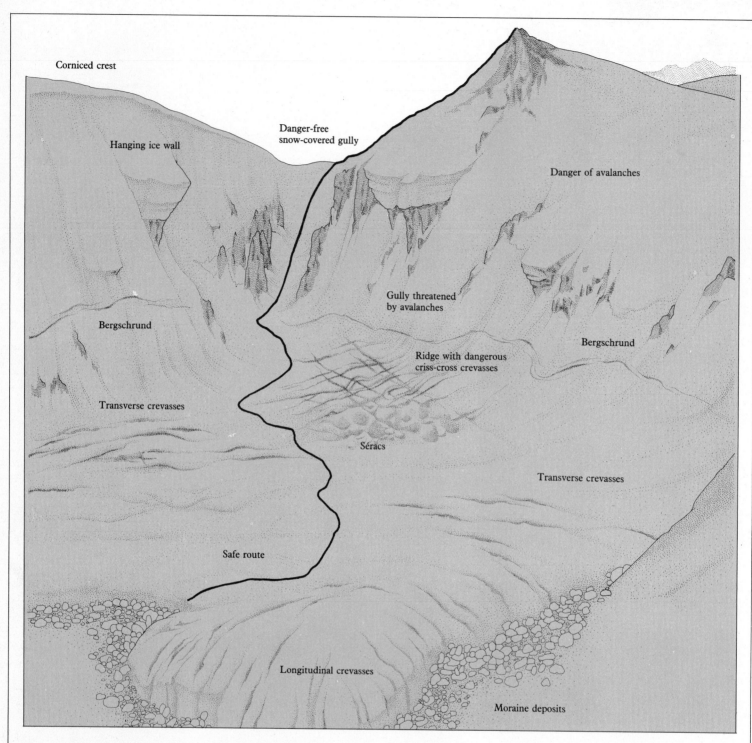

Corniced crest

Hanging ice wall

Danger-free
snow-covered gully

Danger of avalanches

Gully threatened
by avalanches

Bergschrund

Bergschrund

Ridge with dangerous
criss-cross crevasses

Transverse crevasses

Sécracs

Transverse crevasses

Safe route

Longitudinal crevasses

Moraine deposits

The snow-and-ice environment

The illustration above shows a typical glacial environment. The choice of a route is made on the basis of the climber's knowledge and anticipation of the numerous objective dangers posed by the glacier: crevasses (longitudinal, transverse); ice falls involving isolated sécracs, or hanging ice walls; higher up, snow cornices formed by the wind on crests and ridges; and then the risks specific to very high altitudes in mountains, in particular the intense cold, sudden changes in the weather, and the danger of lightning. Glaciers are constantly moving forward, because of the plasticity of the ice which is subject to strong pressures. As you make your way up a glacier you first come across moraine, which is made up of large, often unstable blocks, swept down by the slow passage of the glacier; then

the terminal 'tongue' of the glacier itself, with longitudinal crevasses. Ice forms from the snow which feeds the upper collecting basin, above the permanent snow line, which in the Alps lies at around 3000 metres (10,000 ft). The forward movement of the glacier can often be measured in centimetres per day, but in some cases it may cover over a metre (it moves 107 cm/43 in in the Icefall on Mount Everest). The movement causes crevasses to open and close and sécracs to rise and topple. In the minor 'ice age' which ended in the mid-19th century, Alpine glaciers were much larger and less uneven than they are today. At the present time, after a period of receding, it seems that the glaciers are once more advancing and causing the formation of new obstacles.

Probing for a hidden crevasse with an ice-axe

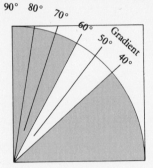

The difficulties of an ice or snow slope depend on its steepness and on the condition of the ice or snow.

90° 80° 70° 60° 50° 40° Gradient

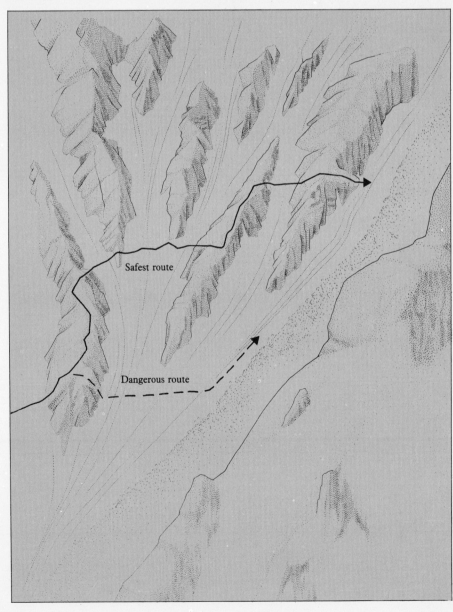

Safest route

Dangerous route

Choosing the route

The first rule in the glacier travel that usually precedes an Alpine climb is that it is best to set out when the temperature is very low, which means very early in the morning. The climb is also planned with an eye on the difficulties and danger which might occur late in the day during the descent. Poor visibility in bad weather, or snow covering up tracks, are two things that can easily cause climbers to go dangerously astray. Crossing a glacier is always a demanding and tiring operation, and must be carried out using the precautions necessary to minimize dangers of accidents (see page 92). Gullies exposed to the danger of avalanches, snow slides or blocks of ice falling from above must never be climbed along the central section (which is the most exposed), but rather along the edges of the formation, using the belays offered by any available rocks (see diagram on the right). North-facing slopes usually stay in good condition until quite late in the day, only receiving direct sunshine in the afternoon, if at all.

Ice can be black or shiny green in colour. Ideal for climbing purposes is hard snow ice, which is white in colour and coarse textured. Difficulties vary with the angle of the slope: more than 50° and up to 60-70° is very steep. Slopes steeper than this can be climbed using specialized ice-climbing techniques but are extremely demanding, physically and technically.

Snow-and-ice climbing equipment

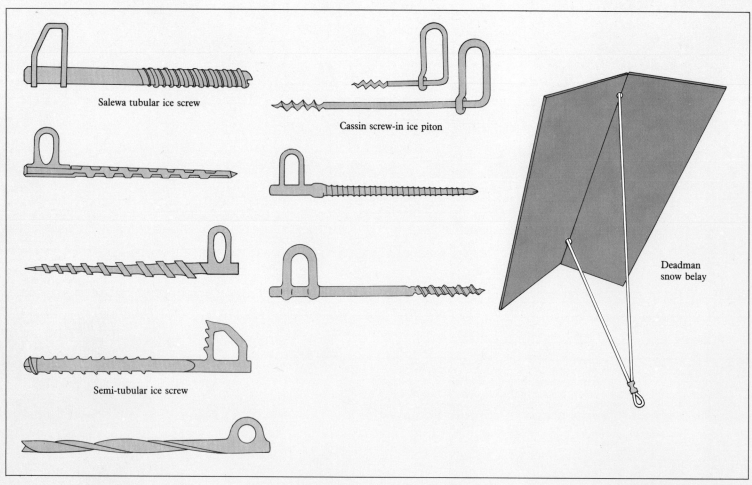

Salewa tubular ice screw

Cassin screw-in ice piton

Semi-tubular ice screw

Deadman snow belay

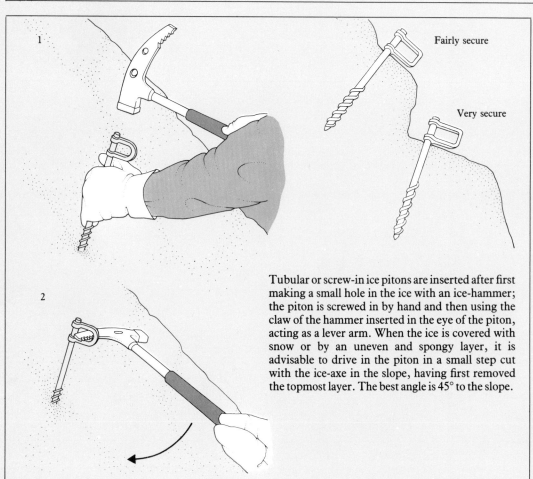

1

2

Fairly secure

Very secure

Tubular or screw-in ice pitons are inserted after first making a small hole in the ice with an ice-hammer; the piton is screwed in by hand and then using the claw of the hammer inserted in the eye of the piton, acting as a lever arm. When the ice is covered with snow or by an uneven and spongy layer, it is advisable to drive in the piton in a small step cut with the ice-axe in the slope, having first removed the topmost layer. The best angle is 45° to the slope.

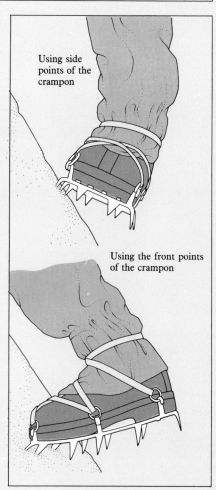

Using side points of the crampon

Using the front points of the crampon

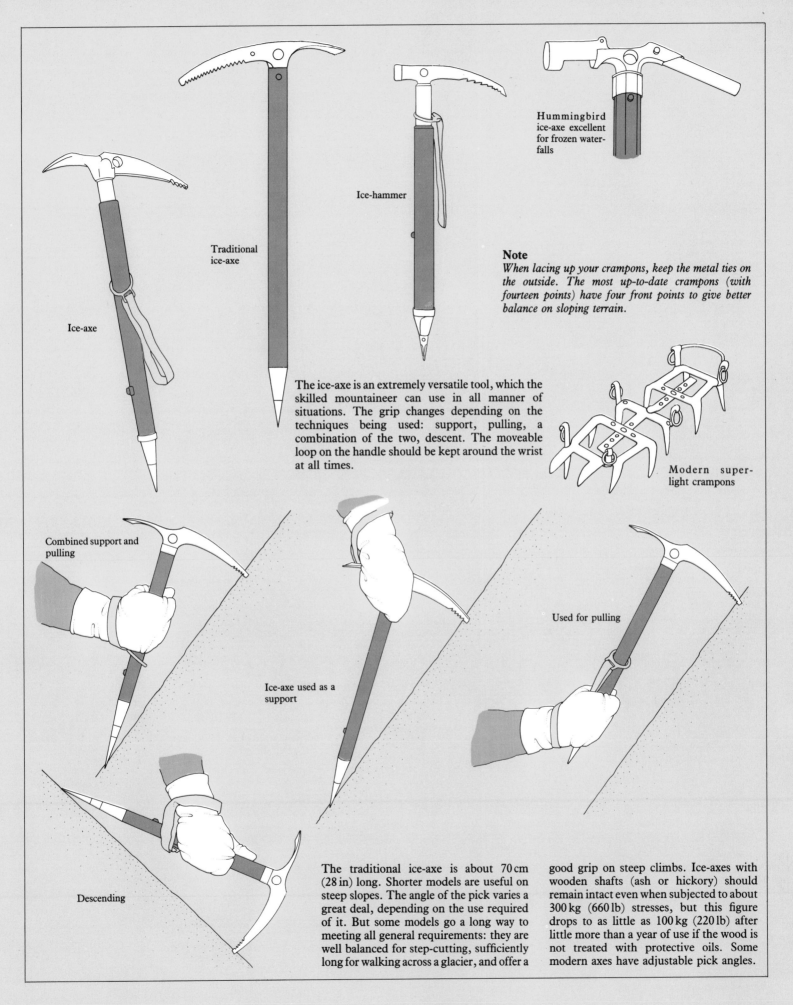

Traditional
ice-axe

Ice-axe

Ice-hammer

Hummingbird
ice-axe excellent
for frozen water-
falls

The ice-axe is an extremely versatile tool, which the
skilled mountaineer can use in all manner of
situations. The grip changes depending on the
techniques being used: support, pulling, a
combination of the two, descent. The moveable
loop on the handle should be kept around the wrist
at all times.

Modern super-
light crampons

Combined support and
pulling

Ice-axe used as a
support

Used for pulling

Descending

The traditional ice-axe is about 70 cm
(28 in) long. Shorter models are useful on
steep slopes. The angle of the pick varies a
great deal, depending on the use required
of it. But some models go a long way to
meeting all general requirements: they are
well balanced for step-cutting, sufficiently
long for walking across a glacier, and offer a
good grip on steep climbs. Ice-axes with
wooden shafts (ash or hickory) should
remain intact even when subjected to about
300 kg (660 lb) stresses, but this figure
drops to as little as 100 kg (220 lb) after
little more than a year of use if the wood is
not treated with protective oils. Some
modern axes have adjustable pick angles.

Movement on a glacier

The first rule, even where there is apparently no problem or danger, is to proceed roped together - never alone. The team should be 5-10 metres (15-35 ft) apart. The last member of the team should carry a few coils of rope, and be ready to take the strain, if the leader happens to slip into a crevasse. You can in fact keep a loop around the ice-axe to be even more prepared - then, in the event of a fall, you just drive the axe into the snow. When the glacier conditions require careful probing of the terrain ahead, the leader should be belayed by his companions (see diagrams). To be able to deal with emergencies, do not attach yourself to the ends of the rope: keep part of the rope in your rucksack. Attachment at the waist can also include a Prusik attached to the harness (this is a good idea because if you are unfortunate enough to fall into a crevasse, it enables you to climb out on your own, using the rope), or with a loop and carabiner. Walking on ice requires a great deal of care and experience, and an instinct for danger zones, especially when there is fresh snow about. Snow bridges over crevasses should first be probed and sounded out with the shaft of the ice-axe.

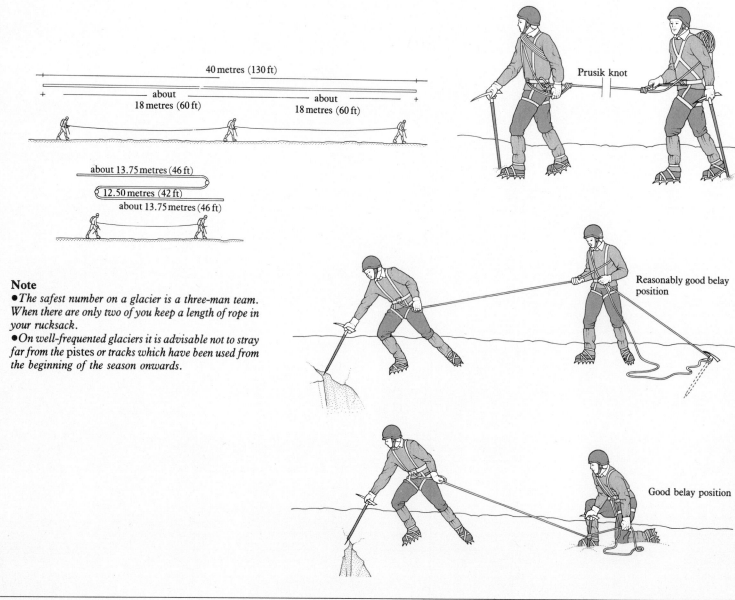

Note
●*The safest number on a glacier is a three-man team. When there are only two of you keep a length of rope in your rucksack.*
●*On well-frequented glaciers it is advisable not to stray far from the pistes or tracks which have been used from the beginning of the season onwards.*

Easy terrain

Climbing in snow and ice conditions always requires a first-hand knowledge of the particular type of terrain in which you will be operating. Snow conditions vary depending on the temperature, time of day, snow structure, and general weather conditions. On easy terrain or terrain of average difficulty you can use the ice-axe rather like a walking stick, driving it into the slope above you. You grip the ice-axe around the head, with the loop around your wrist, and the pick facing forward. As a rule you should not climb along the steepest line up the slope; you should follow a diagonal route, zigzagging your way upwards. In wet or inconsistent snow it is best not to wear crampons, because snow can easily build up beneath them, and clog. In hard snow, without crampons, kick the boots in well at every step: with the tips (if climbing upwards), diagonally, using the edge of the boot (if traversing), and with the heel (if on a descent). The body-weight should always be directed straight downwards towards the feet.

Note
To avoid tripping up with your crampons on easy terrain, walk with your legs slightly wider apart.

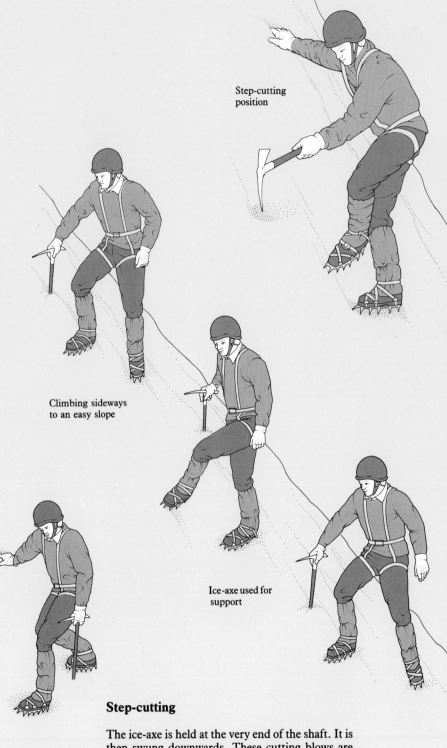

Step-cutting position

Climbing sideways to an easy slope

Ice-axe used for support

Descending

Step-cutting

The ice-axe is held at the very end of the shaft. It is then swung downwards. These cutting blows are alternated with sideways blows. The steps must be sufficiently wide, not too far apart, and cut out diagonally. Sometimes small handholds, cut slightly higher up the slope, can help the climber to keep his balance. When descending, the steps must be closer together. While cutting them, the body is bunched in a forward position.

Note
The most delicate moment on steps is when you move the inside foot forward.

The French technique

On steep ice- or snow-covered slopes, climbing either diagonally upward or traversing, you can adopt the elegant Eckenstein or 'French' cramponing technique, holding the ice-axe in both hands in the braking position, and placing your crampons flat on the slope. When the slope is steep, the ankles must be very bent. On the steepest type of slope the pick of the ice-axe should be used as a means of support. The ice-axe is held in both hands, one over the head of the axe, the other at the end of the handle (the *piolet-ancre* position). The crampons must always be flat against the slope. This system is particularly useful for short and very steep traverses. The ice-axe is only moved when a new and well-balanced position has been reached with the crampons.

Descent position on a steep slope

Ice-axe used for balance

Eckenstein or 'French' climbing technique on a steep slope

Position of the ankles

Crampons placed flat on the slope

Using the ice-axe *'piolet-ancre'*

94

Front pointing

Handholds are cut with light blows of the axe, then finished off with the pick

Pulling up on the shaft, using the pick as an anchor

Ice-axe used for pulling upwards, and support

The pick of the axe used as a support

Climbing up steep snow without crampons

Traversing

On steep and very steep slopes the front points of the crampons help you to climb fast and safely. The foot is dug in with a single movement, and the heel is kept slightly lower than the toe. The ice-axe is held in the anchor position by the pick, either in the anchor position with the adze at face height, or at waist-height, using the head as a support (the *piolet-panne* position). During the climb it may be useful to cut small handholds for the free hand. All movement must be smooth, well-coordinated and perfectly balanced. Always move only one limb at a time. In addition to the techniques described above you can also pull with both hands on the shaft of the ice-axe (if it sticks too far out it is best to hold it at snow level), driven in above the head.

One of the latest techniques in front-pointing uses *piolet-traction*. It consists of climbing using an ice-axe and an ice-hammer, driven into the slope as far above the head as possible. The climber actually pulls on the tools as he moves his feet up. In order to use this technique both effectively and safely, it is worth having carefully selected tools, with a more curved pick than usual. This extra curve, however, makes these tools too specialized for more general use. The best shaft length is about 60 cm (24 in). Such axes are best used on slopes of more than 50°. When the pitch is vertical or overhanging, you may have to resort to artificial climbing methods with ice-pitons, using the same techniques as for ordinary artificial rock climbing. Using a forked or two-ended rope, together with the use of steps, usually avoids having to use stirrups or étriers.

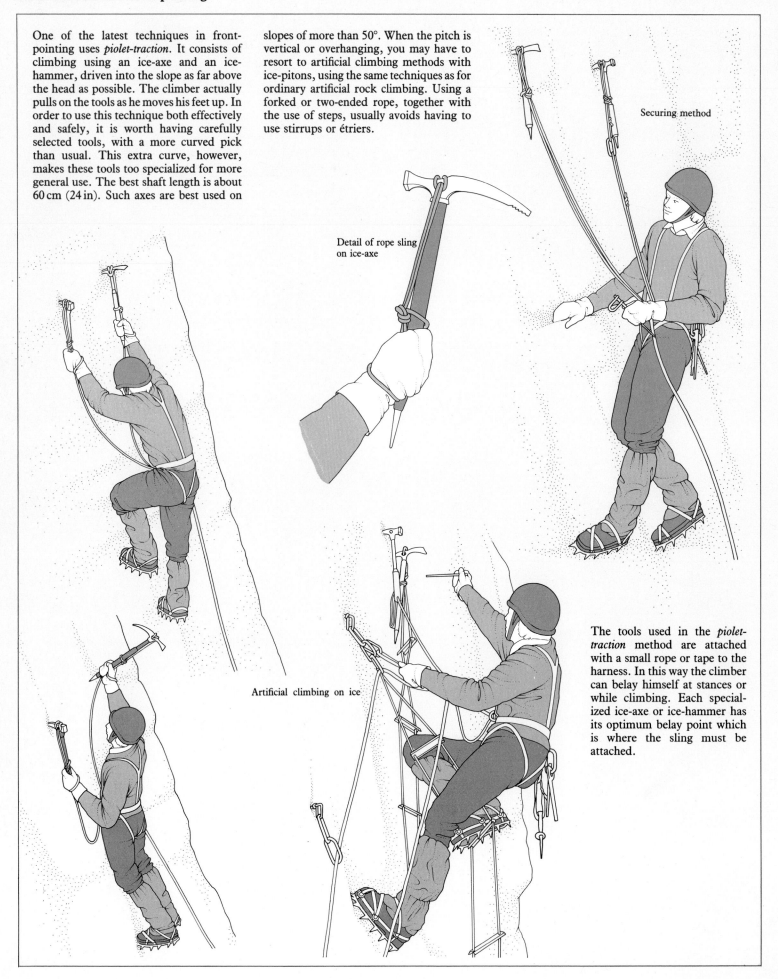

Securing method

Detail of rope sling on ice-axe

Artificial climbing on ice

The tools used in the *piolet-traction* method are attached with a small rope or tape to the harness. In this way the climber can belay himself at stances or while climbing. Each specialized ice-axe or ice-hammer has its optimum belay point which is where the sling must be attached.

Using ice-pitons

Artificial climbing on ice is limited to climbing short overhangs, like those which occur on a bergschrund or on the lip of a crevasse, or beneath a wall of séracs. Tubular or screw-type ice-pitons are driven in up to the eye. It is as well to avoid any direct outward pull. Sometimes it helps to chip an embryo hole first with the ice-axe, to remove any soft layer of snow, and so reach the hard ice beneath. At the end of a pitch, cut out a small ledge that is sufficiently wide to stand on in comfort with crampons, and prepare the belay with at least two ice-pitons. In the diagram below: an anchor point for abseiling using two ice screws and a rope sling.

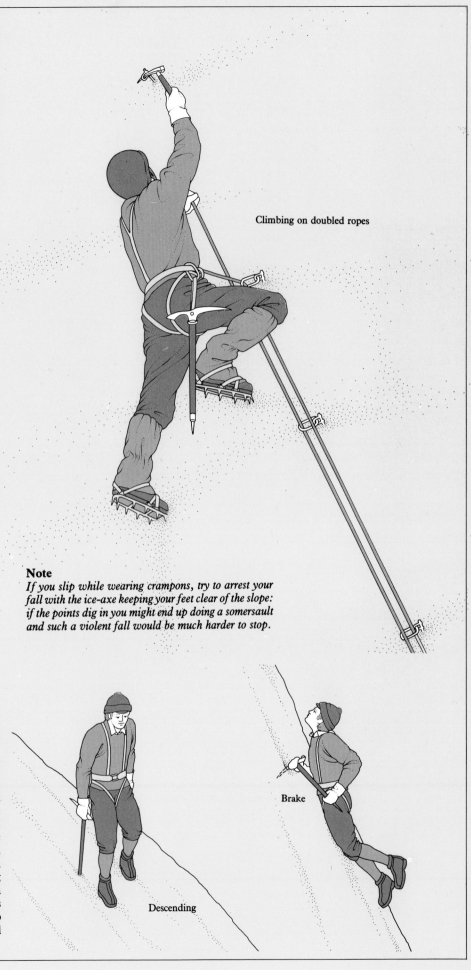

Climbing on doubled ropes

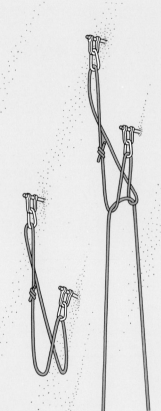

Note
If you slip while wearing crampons, try to arrest your fall with the ice-axe keeping your feet clear of the slope: if the points dig in you might end up doing a somersault and such a violent fall would be much harder to stop.

The descent

Up to a certain angle you can descend facing away from the slope, using short steps, and resting all your weight on your crampons; the body should be slightly hunched forward, and the steeper the slope, the more hunched it should be. On hard snow, without crampons, you can descend still facing outwards from the slope, but digging in the heels hard at each step, with the weight well balanced forward. Hold the ice-axe upside down with the adze turned towards the slope so that you can quickly brake if you should slip. With crampons, in heavy snow, keep an eye out for the snow clogging beneath the crampons: hit them every so often with the ice-axe shaft. When descending, keep the legs slightly apart to avoid tripping up. On very steep slopes face the mountain, and use your ice-axe and front points if necessary.

Brake

Descending

Belaying on snow

On a snow slope the best means of belaying yourself is offered by the ice-axe or by devices such as deadmen. The ice-axe belay involves the use of an ice-axe driven in up to the head, and a 4-metre (13-ft) length of 7-mm (0.3-in) rope. The ice-axe is driven into the slope at an angle of about 30°, and above the stance. The half-hitch can be used to protect the man climbing or any other standard technique such as waist or shoulder belays. If a climber happens to slip, the rope must be allowed to run for 4-7 metres (13-23 ft) to ensure a dynamic arrest so as not to put too much strain on the anchor point.

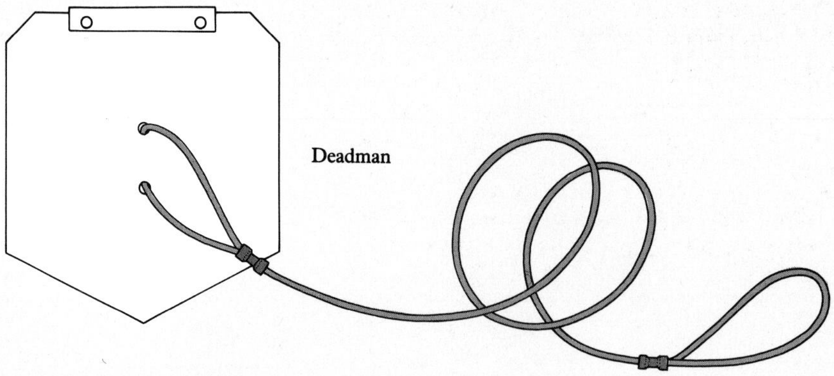

Deadman

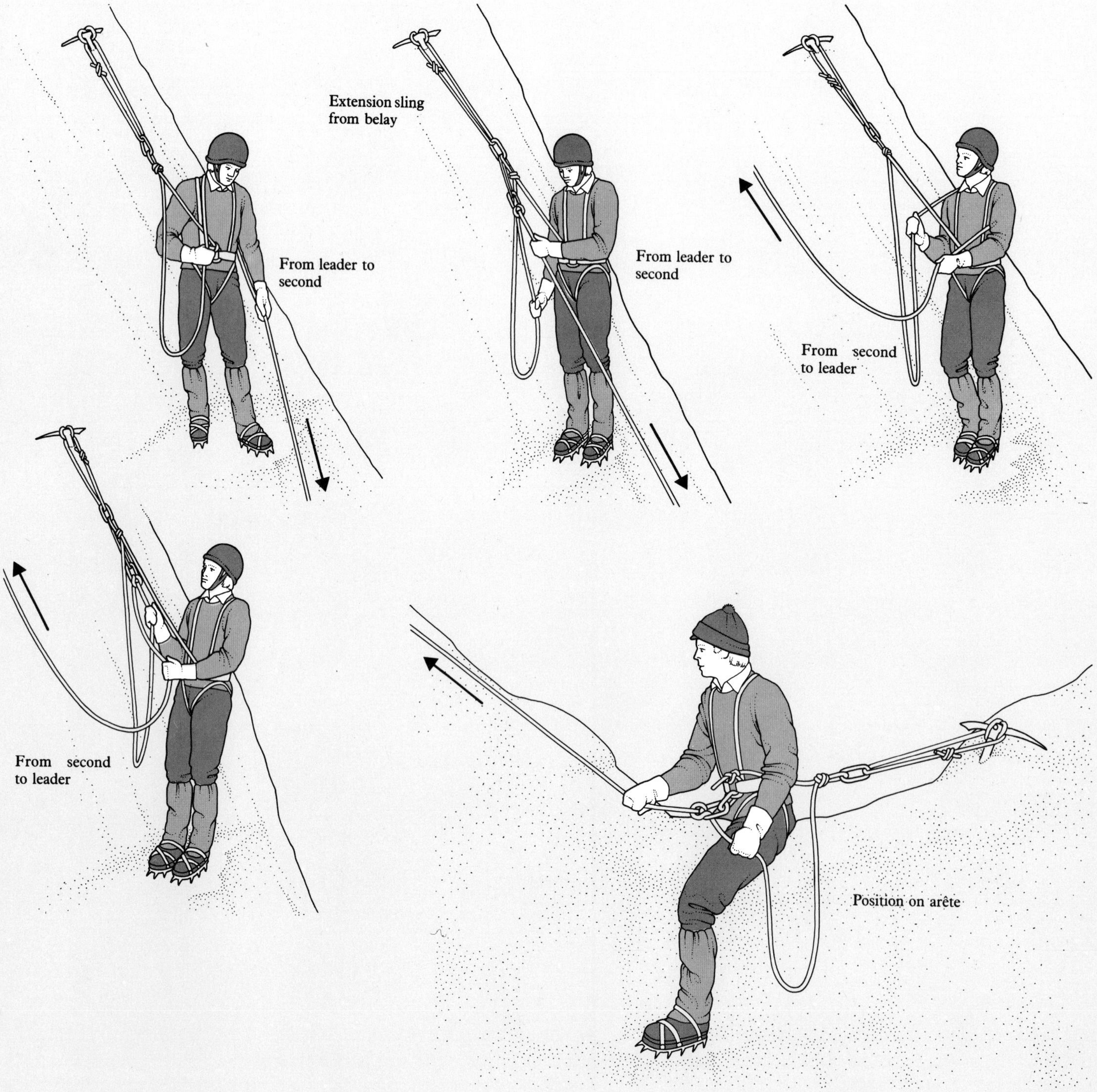

Extension sling from belay

From leader to second

From leader to second

From second to leader

From second to leader

Position on arête

Steep ice slopes

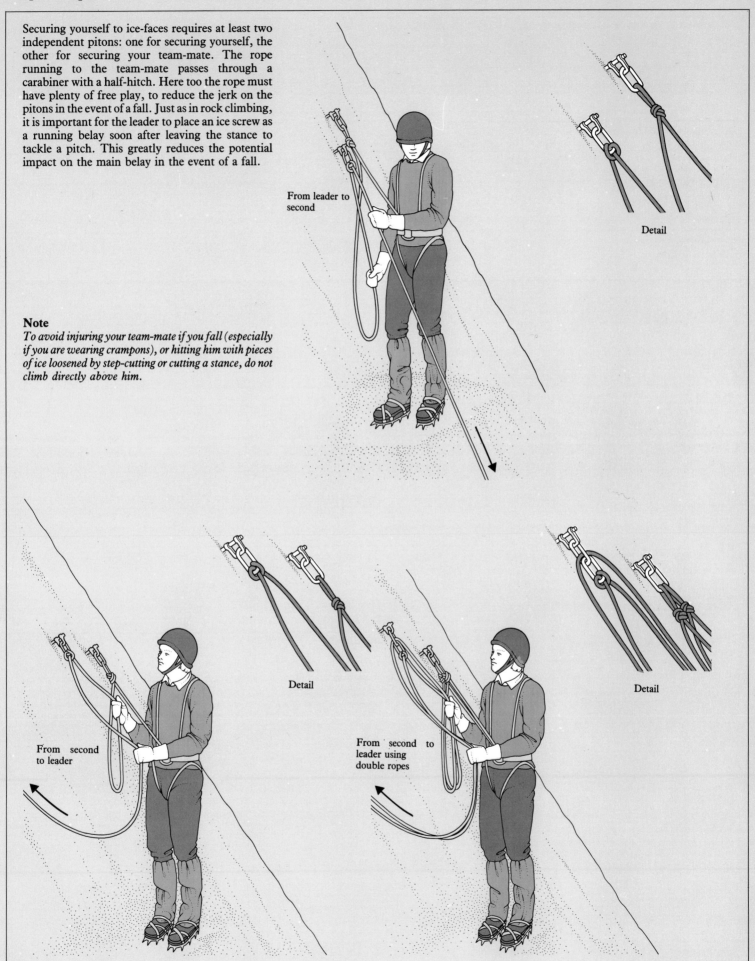

Securing yourself to ice-faces requires at least two independent pitons: one for securing yourself, the other for securing your team-mate. The rope running to the team-mate passes through a carabiner with a half-hitch. Here too the rope must have plenty of free play, to reduce the jerk on the pitons in the event of a fall. Just as in rock climbing, it is important for the leader to place an ice screw as a running belay soon after leaving the stance to tackle a pitch. This greatly reduces the potential impact on the main belay in the event of a fall.

Note

To avoid injuring your team-mate if you fall (especially if you are wearing crampons), or hitting him with pieces of ice loosened by step-cutting or cutting a stance, do not climb directly above him.

From leader to second

Detail

From second to leader

Detail

From second to leader using double ropes

Detail

Belay points in snow

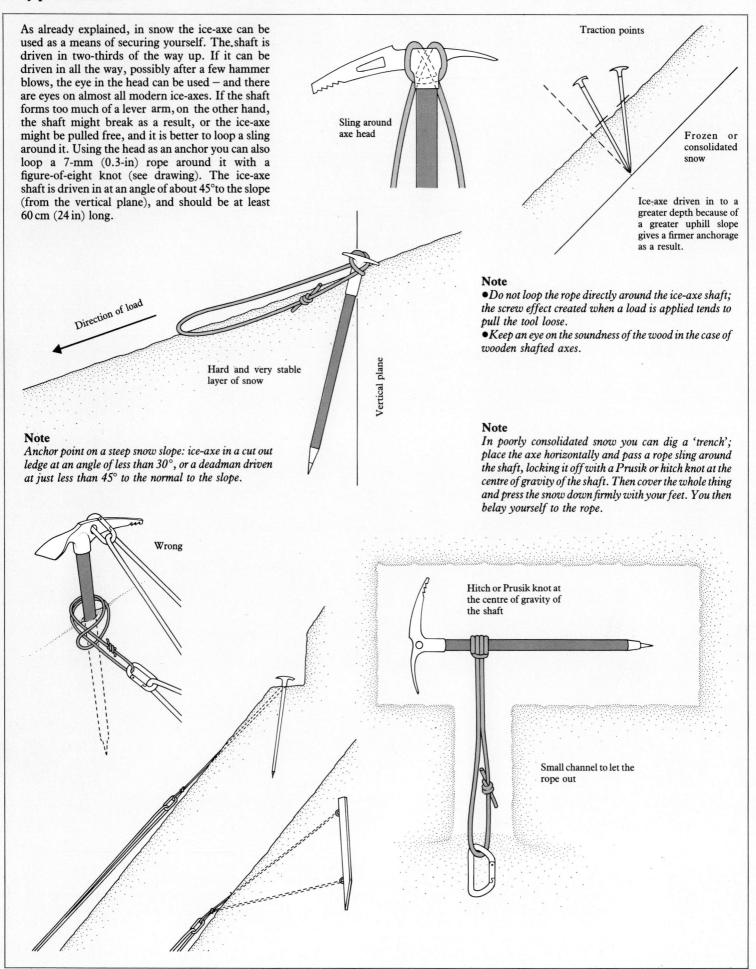

As already explained, in snow the ice-axe can be used as a means of securing yourself. The shaft is driven in two-thirds of the way up. If it can be driven in all the way, possibly after a few hammer blows, the eye in the head can be used – and there are eyes on almost all modern ice-axes. If the shaft forms too much of a lever arm, on the other hand, the shaft might break as a result, or the ice-axe might be pulled free, and it is better to loop a sling around it. Using the head as an anchor you can also loop a 7-mm (0.3-in) rope around it with a figure-of-eight knot (see drawing). The ice-axe shaft is driven in at an angle of about 45°to the slope (from the vertical plane), and should be at least 60 cm (24 in) long.

Traction points

Sling around axe head

Frozen or consolidated snow

Ice-axe driven in to a greater depth because of a greater uphill slope gives a firmer anchorage as a result.

Direction of load

Hard and very stable layer of snow

Vertical plane

Note
•Do not loop the rope directly around the ice-axe shaft; the screw effect created when a load is applied tends to pull the tool loose.
•Keep an eye on the soundness of the wood in the case of wooden shafted axes.

Note
Anchor point on a steep snow slope: ice-axe in a cut out ledge at an angle of less than 30°, or a deadman driven at just less than 45° to the normal to the slope.

Note
In poorly consolidated snow you can dig a 'trench'; place the axe horizontally and pass a rope sling around the shaft, locking it off with a Prusik or hitch knot at the centre of gravity of the shaft. Then cover the whole thing and press the snow down firmly with your feet. You then belay yourself to the rope.

Wrong

Hitch or Prusik knot at the centre of gravity of the shaft

Small channel to let the rope out

Organization of anchor points

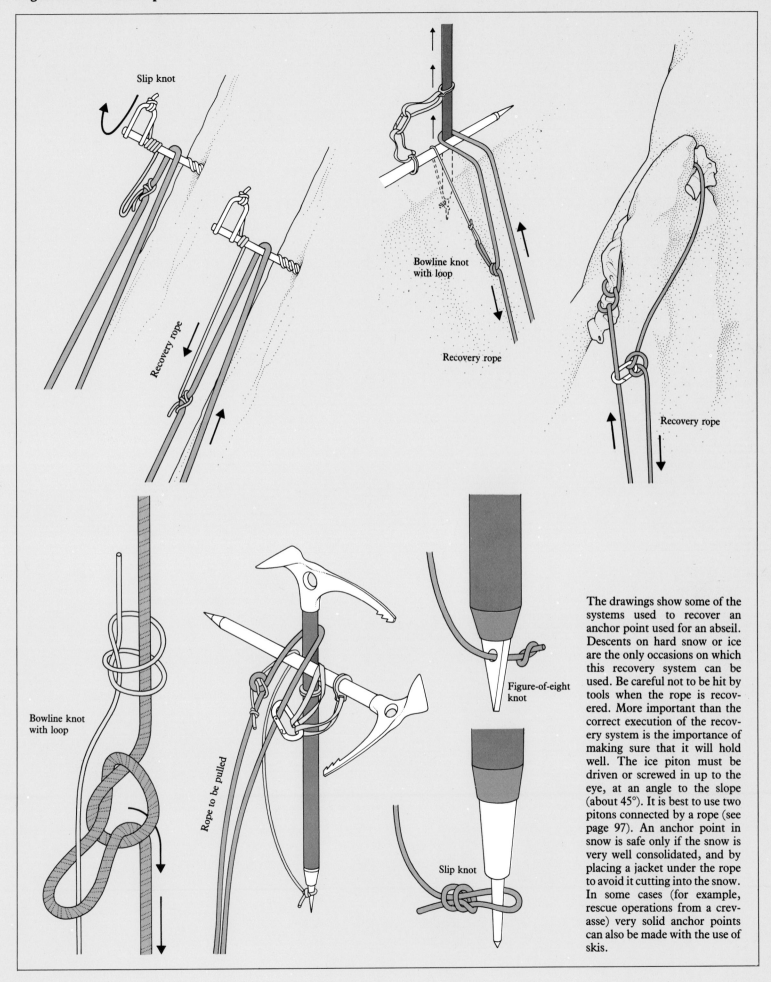

Slip knot

Recovery rope

Bowline knot
with loop

Recovery rope

Recovery rope

Bowline knot
with loop

Rope to be pulled

Figure-of-eight
knot

Slip knot

The drawings show some of the systems used to recover an anchor point used for an abseil. Descents on hard snow or ice are the only occasions on which this recovery system can be used. Be careful not to be hit by tools when the rope is recovered. More important than the correct execution of the recovery system is the importance of making sure that it will hold well. The ice piton must be driven or screwed in up to the eye, at an angle to the slope (about 45°). It is best to use two pitons connected by a rope (see page 97). An anchor point in snow is safe only if the snow is very well consolidated, and by placing a jacket under the rope to avoid it cutting into the snow. In some cases (for example, rescue operations from a crevasse) very solid anchor points can also be made with the use of skis.

MOUNTAIN
RESCUE

Specific knots

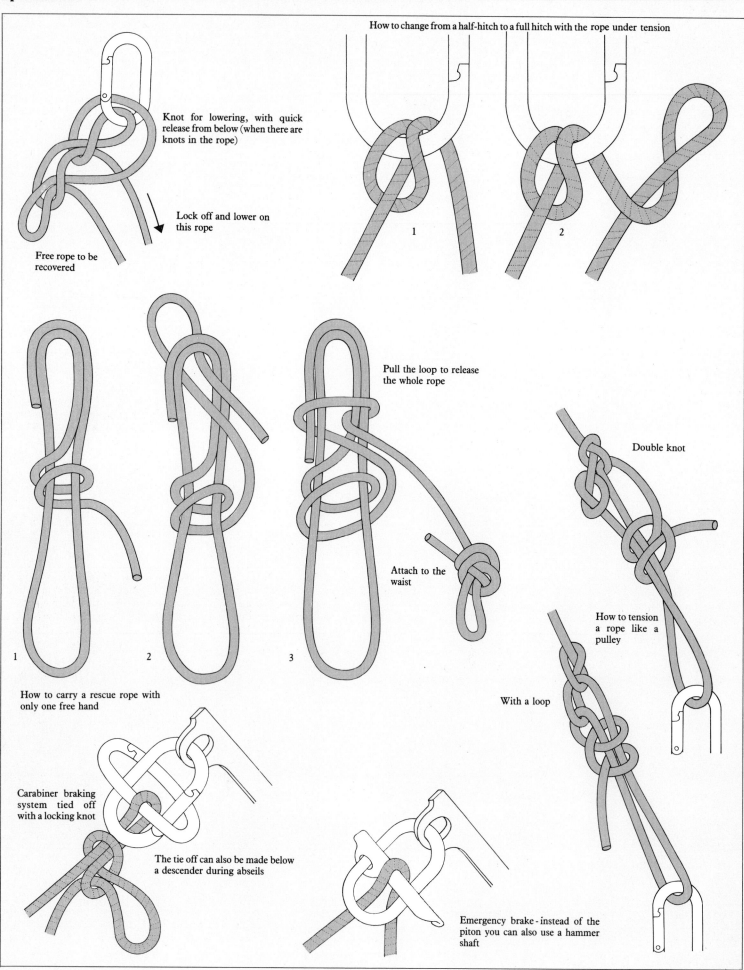

Knot for lowering, with quick release from below (when there are knots in the rope)

Lock off and lower on this rope

Free rope to be recovered

How to change from a half-hitch to a full hitch with the rope under tension

1

2

1

2

3

How to carry a rescue rope with only one free hand

Pull the loop to release the whole rope

Attach to the waist

Double knot

How to tension a rope like a pulley

With a loop

Carabiner braking system tied off with a locking knot

The tie off can also be made below a descender during abseils

Emergency brake - instead of the piton you can also use a hammer shaft

The helicopter

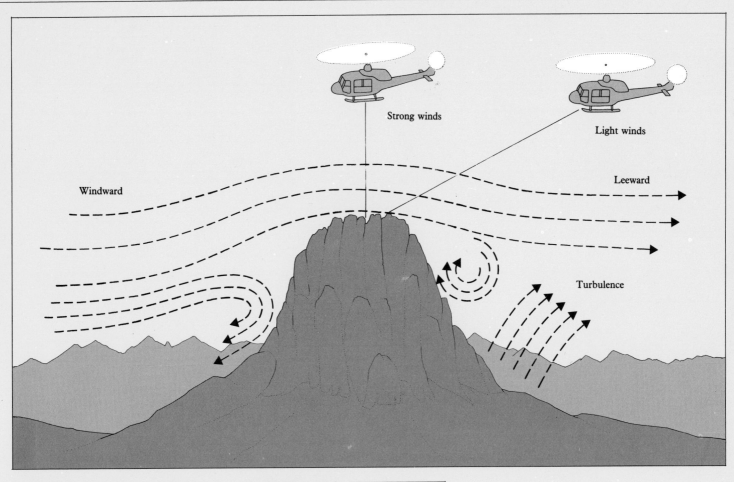

Strong winds

Light winds

Windward

Leeward

Turbulence

SOS

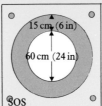

Flare

SOS

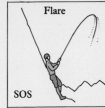

15 cm (6 in)

60 cm (24 in)

SOS

Help not necessary

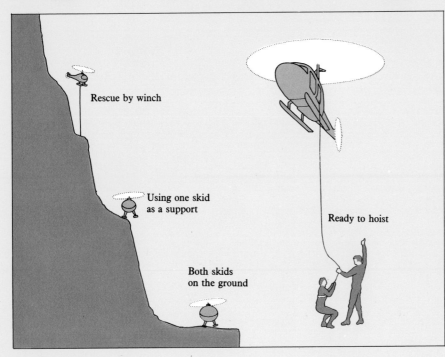

Rescue by winch

Using one skid as a support

Both skids on the ground

Ready to hoist

The use of a helicopter greatly reduces the time involved in rescue operations, and helps to solve otherwise tricky problems, especially at high altitudes. Once the alarm has been raised at any Alpine rescue station, the (usually military) helicopter takes to the air and picks up the rescue team. The rescue can be carried out with the helicopter resting on the ground on both skids, or with just one skid on the mountain-side, lowering the rescuer on a steel cable with the outside winch. The rescuer and injured party are then lifted to safety together by the same winch. In other cases the helicopter can be used to transport men and equipment rapidly to the place where an accident has occurred. Flying in mountains requires special training for pilots because of the danger of turbulence, the reduced efficiency of the aircraft at high altitudes, and the risk of a sudden loss of visibility because of cloud cover. The now standard signals indicating a request for help are firing a red flare or rocket (or SOS night flares), holding the arms raised above the head, and a white circle on a red background. One arm raised means that help is not required. In the event of serious injury rescue is made with a stretcher attached to the helicopter's winch. Alpine climbers usually arrange special insurance to cover the cost of rescue. Most Alpine clubs include such insurance in their membership benefits.

Crevasse rescue

Falling into a crevasse can have very serious consequences, but the fall may be arrested by a fellow-climber. You may however find yourself at the bottom of a crevasse and unable to make your way out on your own. In the latter case rescue can be effected using improvised systems based on the use of the climbing rope, a few slings, and three or four carabiners. The first step to take is to set up a solid anchor point (see page 100). A second ice-axe, or a rucksack, can be laid at the lip of the crevasse to allow the rope to run over the edge more smoothly. If the climber in the crevasse was not tied on to the rope, you must get a rope to him, and secure him, before doing anything else.

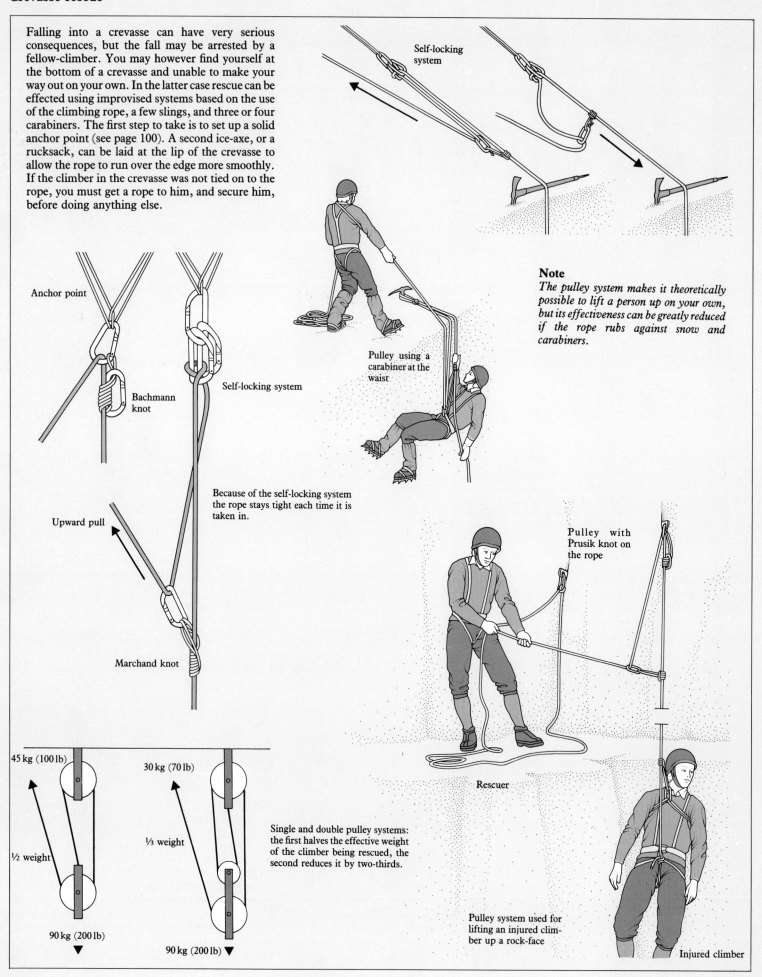

Self-locking system

Anchor point

Bachmann knot

Self-locking system

Upward pull

Because of the self-locking system the rope stays tight each time it is taken in.

Marchand knot

Pulley using a carabiner at the waist

Note

The pulley system makes it theoretically possible to lift a person up on your own, but its effectiveness can be greatly reduced if the rope rubs against snow and carabiners.

Pulley with Prusik knot on the rope

Rescuer

45 kg (100 lb)

30 kg (70 lb)

½ weight

⅓ weight

90 kg (200 lb)

90 kg (200 lb)

Single and double pulley systems: the first halves the effective weight of the climber being rescued, the second reduces it by two-thirds.

Pulley system used for lifting an injured climber up a rock-face

Injured climber

Climbing up the rope using a Prusik knot

Prusik knot

Loop

Pulley

Self-locking system

To climb up a rope it is best to use two slings attached by Prusik knots: the first is passed around the shoulders; the second is used as a stirrup. If you have only the one sling, you can climb up by making a series of frontloops in the climbing rope. You then slide the sling upward, supporting the weight of the body in the footloop.

Note
When crossing a glacier, always have some slings of 5- or 6-mm (0.2-in) rope for this purpose.

A carabiner passed to your fellow climber enables him to set up a pulley system which will (in theory) halve the weight to be raised

A rope lowered in the form of a loop, and lifted back up gradually by one of the rescuers (on the left) can also enable a climber to climb back out of a crevasse. The climber on the right does not pull, but locks off the rope using a shoulder belay after every step upwards.

Prusik

Prusik knot

The self-locking system attached to the anchor point stops the rope from running free

Detail of the self-locking system

Note
Special equipment for crevasse rescue work includes a special 'gripper' (see page 148) and a net, which is passed beneath the body of the climber in the crevasse.

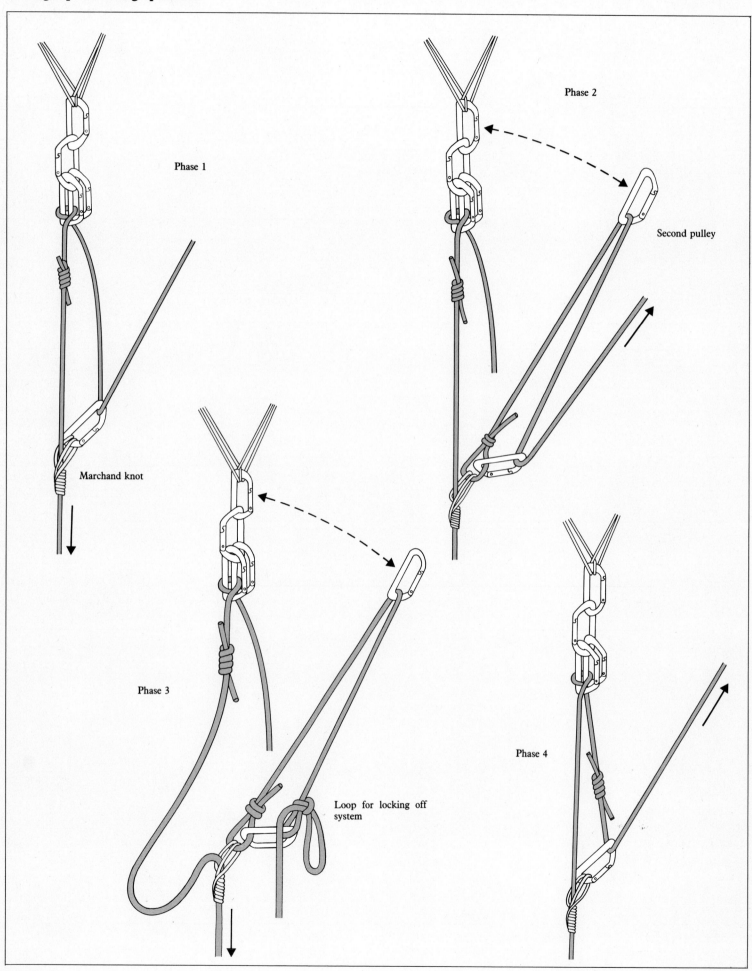

Phase 1

Marchand knot

Phase 2

Second pulley

Phase 3

Loop for locking off
system

Phase 4

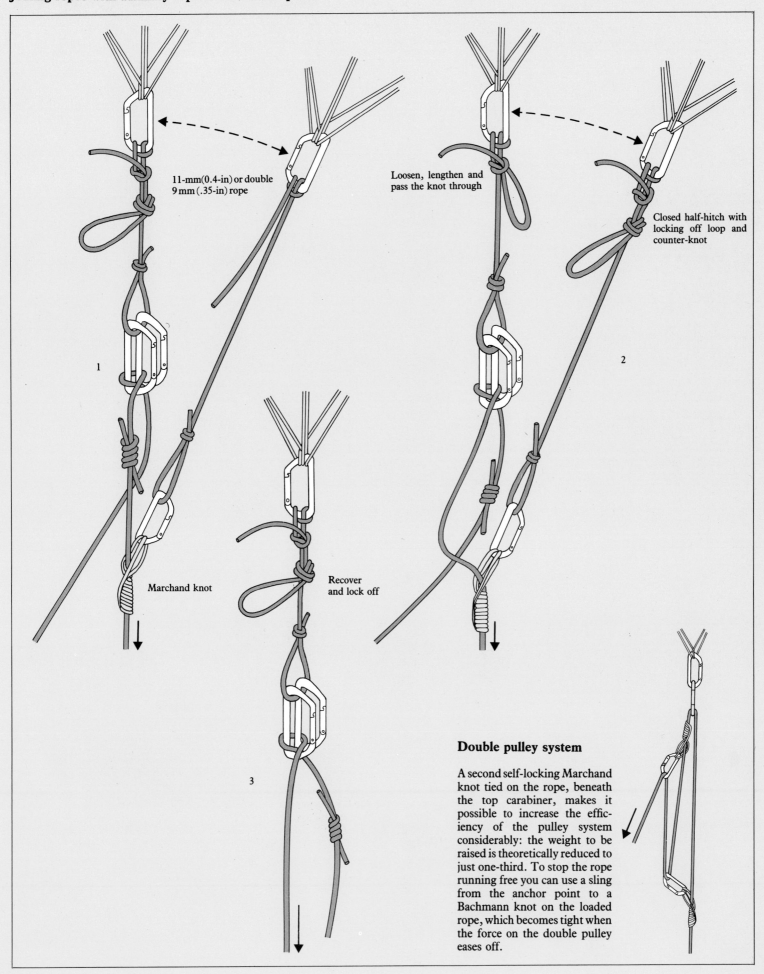

11-mm(0.4-in) or double
9 mm (.35-in) rope

1

Marchand knot

Loosen, lengthen and
pass the knot through

Closed half-hitch with
locking off loop and
counter-knot

2

Recover
and lock off

3

Double pulley system

A second self-locking Marchand knot tied on the rope, beneath the top carabiner, makes it possible to increase the efficiency of the pulley system considerably: the weight to be raised is theoretically reduced to just one-third. To stop the rope running free you can use a sling from the anchor point to a Bachmann knot on the loaded rope, which becomes tight when the force on the double pulley eases off.

Descending with an injured climber

The drawing here illustrates schematically one of the ways a rescuer can descend a rock face with an injured climber. The injured man is held on the rescuer's back and both men use one harness made from the end of the rope with a double overhand knot. A sling, in figure-of-eight form, is passed around the shoulders to hold the injured man in place on the rescuer's back, and the rescuer is then lowered by one of his companions. The belay point from which the lower is made must of course be completely sound, and the rope is prevented from running free by a safety Prusik knot. The rescuer descends kicking off from the rock-face with his feet to keep the two of them well clear of the rock.

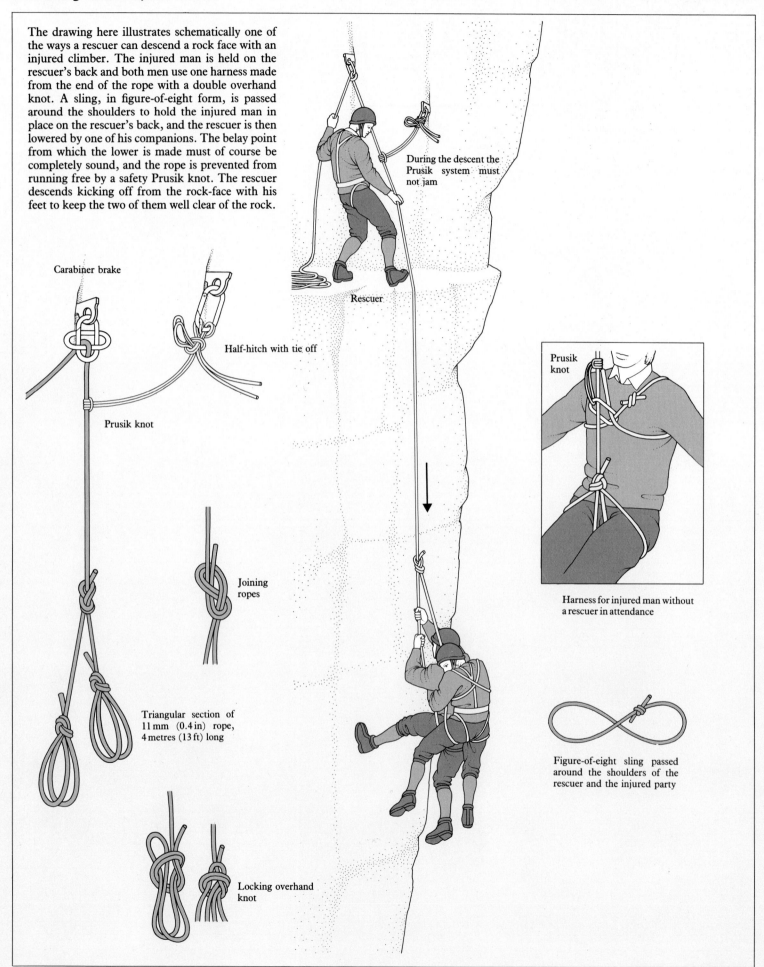

During the descent the Prusik system must not jam

Rescuer

Carabiner brake

Half-hitch with tie off

Prusik knot

Joining ropes

Triangular section of 11 mm (0.4 in) rope, 4 metres (13 ft) long

Locking overhand knot

Prusik knot

Harness for injured man without a rescuer in attendance

Figure-of-eight sling passed around the shoulders of the rescuer and the injured party

Descent using double carabiner brake

This system affords the greatest degree of safety during a descent made with two ropes in the manner of an abseil. The rescuer and the injured climber are attached to the harness with the ends of a triangle made with a length of 11 mm (0.4 in) rope about 4 metres (13 ft) in length. The usual figure-of-eight sling keeps the injured man in place on the rescuer's back. Joining the ropes together and tying the knots are made easier by the use of an auxiliary length of rope, with a small Prusik sling. To join the ropes together easily, the two rope ends should be staggered.

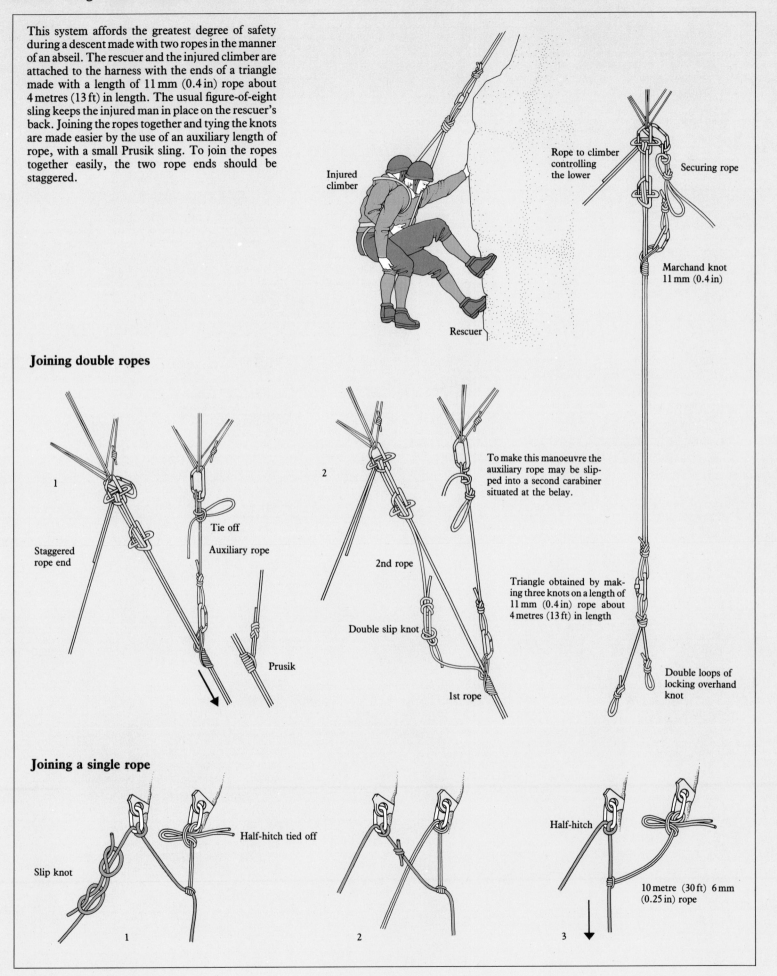

Injured climber

Rescuer

Rope to climber controlling the lower

Securing rope

Marchand knot 11 mm (0.4 in)

Joining double ropes

1

Staggered rope end

Tie off

Auxiliary rope

Prusik

2

To make this manoeuvre the auxiliary rope may be slipped into a second carabiner situated at the belay.

2nd rope

Double slip knot

1st rope

Triangle obtained by making three knots on a length of 11 mm (0.4 in) rope about 4 metres (13 ft) in length

Double loops of locking overhand knot

Joining a single rope

Slip knot

Half-hitch tied off

Half-hitch

10 metre (30 ft) 6 mm (0.25 in) rope

1

2

3

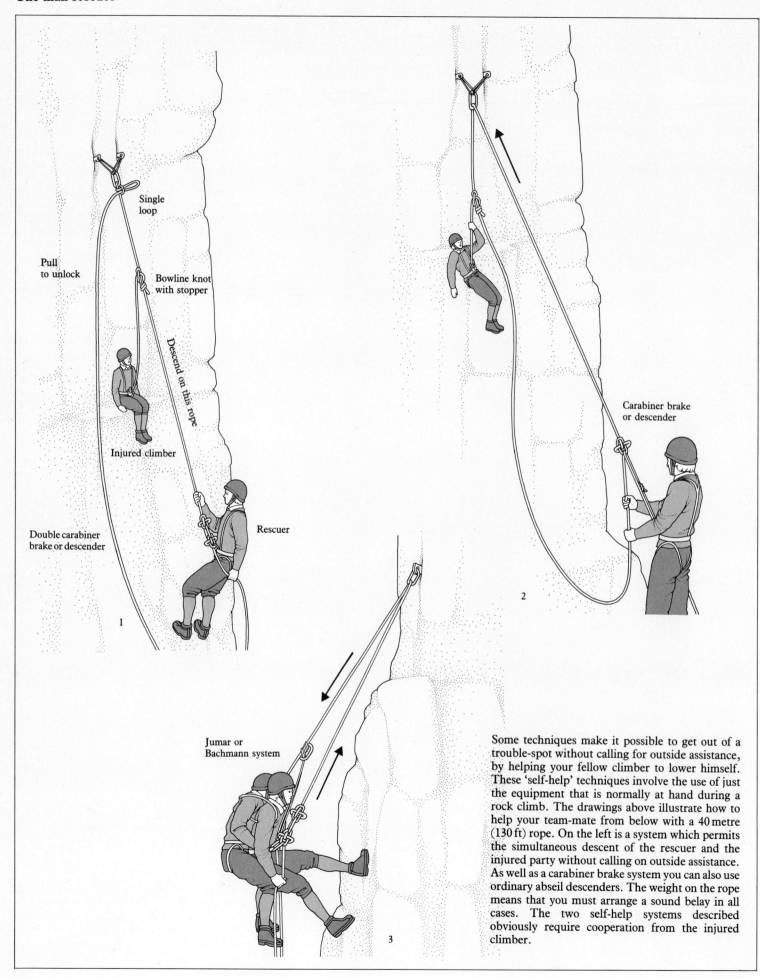

Single
loop

Pull
to unlock

Bowline knot
with stopper

Descend on this rope

Injured climber

Double carabiner
brake or descender

Rescuer

Carabiner brake
or descender

1

2

Jumar or
Bachmann system

3

Some techniques make it possible to get out of a trouble-spot without calling for outside assistance, by helping your fellow climber to lower himself. These 'self-help' techniques involve the use of just the equipment that is normally at hand during a rock climb. The drawings above illustrate how to help your team-mate from below with a 40 metre (130 ft) rope. On the left is a system which permits the simultaneous descent of the rescuer and the injured party without calling on outside assistance. As well as a carabiner brake system you can also use ordinary abseil descenders. The weight on the rope means that you must arrange a sound belay in all cases. The two self-help systems described obviously require cooperation from the injured climber.

Lowering an injured climber

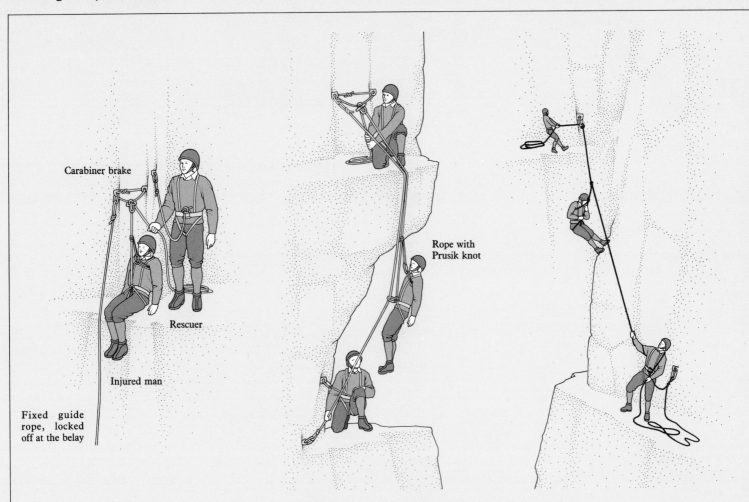

Carabiner brake

Rescuer

Injured man

Fixed guide
rope, locked
off at the belay

Rope with
Prusik knot

Note
*Always belay yourself with a sling when untied from the
main rope to carry out the manoeuvres described.*

If there are two rescuers, the manoeuvres involved are considerably easier. While the first rescuer lowers the injured climber, the second rescuer prepares the next belay on the ledge or platform below, and helps the injured climber to land safely on it. You can also extend half the rope along the face (or a second rope fixed to two pitons above and below) to enable the injured climber (attached to this guide rope with a carabiner) to reach the ledge below. This type of manoeuvre is essential in diagonal traverses or when the ledge has to be reached by swinging inwards from an overhang. The top rescuer lowers the injured climber with a half-hitch or a carabiner brake, and then rappels to the two men below.

*A rescue operation using a Mariner stretcher, below the
Peutérey ridge on Mont Blanc.*

One-man rescue procedures

Leader assisting second on a vertical face

If the second member of the team has an accident, making it impossible to proceed any further, the leader can help in the following ways:

●Undo the half-hitch securing him, and pass the single rope through the carabiner; lock it off with a single loop, making the loop as short as possible so that it can be easily undone from below.

●Fix a descender or carabiner brake on the rope and lower yourself down the rope on which the loop has been made; this will undo automatically as soon as your weight comes on it. In this way the rope will be free to run in the carabiner with the weight balanced between rescuer and injured party: any difference in weight will be compensated for by the way the rope runs in the descender.

●Descend to the injured climber, lock off the descender and with two carabiners attach your own harness to that of the injured climber; if the face is vertical sit him on your lap. If the face is sloping, place him on your back with a figure-of-eight rope passed around his shoulders and back.

●Remove the free from the descender, and, by letting it run, lower yourself to an appropriate ledge or platform. Secure yourself with a sling, recover the main rope and repeat the lowering manoeuvre to the next belay.

Note

This is quite a complicated operation and there can be no improvisation in an emergency. It is advisable to practise the operation in a training gym, and keep a wary eye on the length of the free rope, to make sure it is long enough for the lowering manoeuvre required. If the second climber is too far away to be reached with the end of the free rope, it is best to use a pulley system.

Second assisting leader

If the leader has an accident the rope will have been held by the second climber.

●Check the belay, bearing in mind that the strain is directed upwards. If it is weak, make another one. Secure yourself with an auxiliary rope (Prusik) or a length of ordinary rope (Marchand system).

●Remove the half-hitch, and tie off the climbing rope. Safeguard yourself with a Prusik or Jumar system on the rope leading to the injured climber. Climb up, using the rope, or climbing free, as far as the first piton.

●Above the piton tie a Prusik knot on the rope leading to the injured climber and tie a half-hitch on the running belay point. Pull on the auxiliary rope and lock it off with a suitable knot.

●Pull the rope on which the loop has been made towards the first belay, in order to free it. Undo the rope from your harness and recover the free end. When the loop is undone and the rope is free the weight of the injured man will pull the rope taut; this upper part of the rope is held by the auxiliary rope, with the Prusik knot, attached to the anchor point.

●Make a loop on the rope leading to the injured man, locking it off at the piton and undo the length of auxiliary rope which was holding it.

●Recover all equipment and climb up to the next piton, securing yourself to the injured man's rope with a Prusik knot or a Jumar. Repeat the previous operation.

●Having reached the last piton you will be above the injured man and you can therefore carry on as already described in the section dealing with the leader helping the second, lowering yourself with your companion to a ledge below.

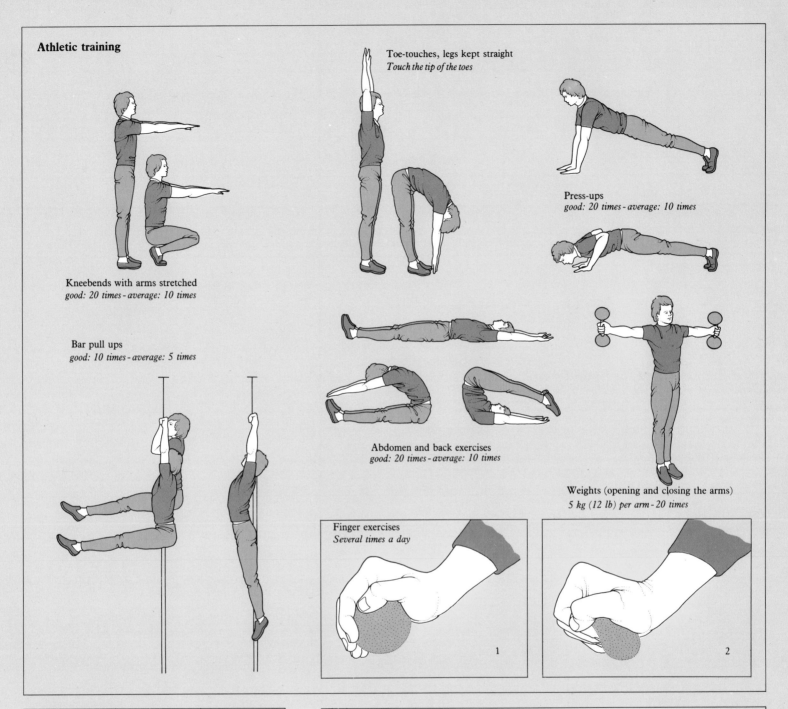

Athletic training

Kneebends with arms stretched
good: 20 times - average: 10 times

Bar pull ups
good: 10 times - average: 5 times

Toe-touches, legs kept straight
Touch the tip of the toes

Press-ups
good: 20 times - average: 10 times

Abdomen and back exercises
good: 20 times - average: 10 times

Weights (opening and closing the arms)
5 kg (12 lb) per arm - 20 times

Finger exercises
Several times a day

1

2

Distance (metres/miles)	Time (minutes)	Times per week
1600/1	8'00"	1
2400/1.5	12'25"	2
3200/2	18'30"	2

Exercises designed to develop muscle strength should be alternated with exercises designed to give a gradual improvement to overall stamina. The above table (compiled by Kenneth Cooper) suggests a good running-training programme. It is important to have continuity of physical activities, to maintain the level of training and preparation reached, and not to over-exert yourself without previously warming-up.

Harvard Step-Test

This is used to measure the stamina of long-distance runners. The test consists in stepping on and off a low bench, alternating the right and left foot, at a rate of thirty steps a minute, for four minutes. When the four minutes are up, sit down and measure your heartbeat after thirty seconds, two minutes and then three minutes, for thirty seconds each time. The recovery capacity of a fit person is assessed by the speed at which the heart beat drops, by applying the following formula:

$$R = \frac{\text{Length of exercise in seconds} \times 100}{\text{sum of three pulse counts multiplied by 2}}$$

The value R increases progressively with training, until it reaches a maximum. You are very fit if it goes beyond 80-90. The height of the step should be 30 cm (12 in) for someone of 1.50 metres (5 ft); 35 cm (14 in) for someone of 1.60 metres (5 ft 4 in); 40 cm (16 in) for someone of 1.70 metres (5 ft 8 in); 45 cm (18 in) for someone of 1.80 metres (6 ft) and 50 cm (20 in) for anyone taller than 1.80 metres (6 ft).

First aid

Every climber and mountaineer has a duty to know the basic principles of first aid, so that he can give instant assistance in an emergency. It is important to keep calm at all times, and only to do what is absolutely necessary. In cases of serious injury, do only the basic things and wait for the rescue team to arrive with a qualified doctor.

Injury from a fall

●Check the victim's pulse and check their breathing, then ease them into a safe, sheltered place. Keep the head, neck and trunk in a straight line during all movement to avoid serious complications if there has been injury to the spine or head.
●Move the injured person by holding them under the arms; do not lift them too far off the ground. Always take great care if there has been any injury to the head or spine.
●If there is more than one rescuer, lift up the injured person supporting the back, and keep him as far as possible in a horizontal position.
●If the injured person is conscious, examine them flat on their back before helping them to a sitting position, or before helping them to stand up and walk.
●If the victim is unconscious, put him in the safety position lying on one side, with one knee and one arm bent forward, and the other arm outstretched. In this way the injured person will not suffocate from vomit or blood.
●Protect the injured person from the ground and cover with anything available against the cold.

Note

Instant checks: *Is the person conscious? Is he breathing? Is his heart beating? Are there any haemorrhages or fractures? Keep an eye on the colour of the skin too. Never administer alcohol or tranquilizers.*

State of shock

Symptoms: Agitation, face and extremities cold and sweating, breathing short and frequent, pulse very weak and fast, drowsiness. Do not give anything to drink, do not try to get the subject to walk; take them immediately to hospital, trying to keep them calm, and tending to the pain caused by possible haemorrhage or fracture. Keep the head low.
●*If the heart is beating but the subject is not breathing*: Quickly clean the mouth and throat, tip the head backwards, pulling the lower jaw forward to stop the tongue blocking the glottis and carry out mouth-to-mouth artificial respiration. You have three to four minutes from when breathing stops to save the victim. Artificial respiration involves holding the head tipped well back, closing the nose and blowing with your mouth half-shut. Let the victim exhale by opening the nostrils. Repeat this operation at regular intervals, and keep calm.
●*If the injured person is not breathing, and there is no heartbeat*: This is very serious. You have three minutes in which to save their life, by giving an immediate heart massage. Lay the subject out on his back on a firm surface. Rest the palm of your left hand flat on the middle of the sternum and two-thirds of the way down (not on the ribs) and with your right hand press down hard and firmly, at the rate of one press per second. If there are two of you, you can carry out this heart massage together, as well as artificial respiration. If you are the only rescuer, alternate these operations, with ten seconds of heart massage and two attempts at artificial respiration. Cardiac arrest is common in cases where a climber has been struck by lightning, and is indicated by dilated pupils. If the massage is successful and the pupils become smaller, continue the process without a break - heart massage and artificial respiration - until you feel the carotid artery pulsing.
Fractures Immobilize the part of the body affected with any means available, without doing anything further.
External haemorrhages If the blood is coming from a vein (it will be darker) block it with a tourniquet applied below the wound (blood travels from extremities to heart). If an artery has been severed, block it with a tourniquet above the wound, or (better still) press the artery at the base of the limb against the bone. Tourniquets must not be too tight, except in the case of very serious haemorrhages, and should not be applied for more than 50-60 minutes continuously, because of the risk of frostbite or gangrene caused by lack of blood circulation.
Frostbite Help is needed at the first signs of loss of sensation, because the effect of cold is painless and very insidious. In the first stage, movement and massaging give rise to a flow of blood and pain in the part of the body that is coming back to life. If the frostbite is already serious - in other words the cold part is white, hard and insensitive - cover it with dry clothing, beware of infections (if there is apparent incipient gangrene or blisters), and do not rub. Do not put the affected area in contact with heat sources, but warm up gradually in water at 40°C (104°F), or at body temperature. Use vasodilation methods. Give the frostbitten climber warm drinks (not alcoholic). Frostbite is aggravated by wind, high altitude, restricted blood circulation, as well as fatigue.

Safest position for an unconscious casualty

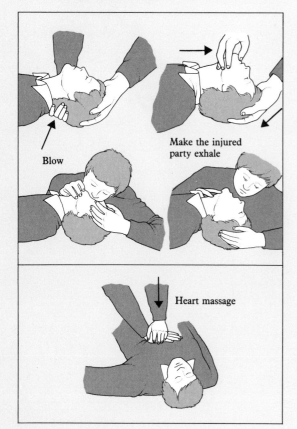

Blow

Make the injured party exhale

Heart massage

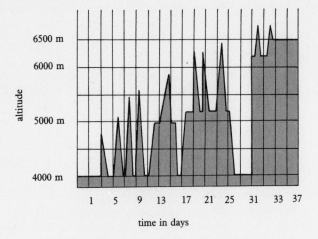

At 8000 metres oxygen falls to one third of its presence at sea level.

Exposure This starts with feelings of exhaustion, drowsiness, sluggishness and indifference. Stop the victim falling asleep, try to get him to react, offer hot drinks - sweet tea or coffee.

If overtaken by an avalanche The first thing to do, to avoid suffocation, is to free the victim's air-passages. If necessary carry out artificial respiration. Shelter the victim from cold.

Exhaustion Symptoms: weak, fast pulse, pallor, shivering and weakness. Offer hot drinks, sugar and glucose; encourage them to keep going after a rest, and proceed slowly.

Mountain sickness Symptoms: tiredness, headaches, nausea, very quick pulse, dizziness, lack of appetite, sensation of seasickness; coma, pulmonary or cerebral oedema in most serious cases. The best solution here is to climb back down the mountain as soon as possible. In serious cases, give oxygen and diuretics.

Snow-blindness Caused by not wearing snow glasses. Sensation of sand in the eyes, blindness. Assist with eye-drops (collirium) or cortisone-based ointment.

Altitude acclimatization

High altitude gives rise to a series of complex physiological reactions in the body, ranging from an initial dizziness to a feeling of having become acclimatized. The mechanism varies from person to person, and the most well-tried system of acclimatization is the so-called 'saw-tooth' one (see above left), which involves successive upward forays alternating with days spent at a lower level. It is not possible to specify exactly to what altitude it is possible to become acclimatized. It is thought that the level lies somewhere between 6000 - 7000 metres (20,000 to 23,500 ft). Beyond 7000 metres (23,500 ft), the process of deterioration is no longer offset by acclimatization, and one crosses the threshold into what has been called the 'death zone'. It is worth noting that a non-acclimatized person who suddenly finds himself above the 7000 metre (23,500 ft) mark will lose consciousness in a matter of minutes.

Schematically the process of acclimatization passes through four phases:

1 Indifference: short exposure at altitude of up to 4000 metres (13,500 ft);

2 Short-term adaptation: pulmonary hyperventilation (with loss of carbon dioxide and water vapour), rise in the rate and flow of blood in the lungs, increase in the number of red corpuscles to offset the lowering of the oxygen level in the blood;

3 Adaptation phase: in which there may still be signs of mountain sickness. Increase in the production of red corpuscles by the bone marrow, periods of imbalance in the neuro-vegetative system;

4 Acclimatization: not always possible. This is demonstrated by a low increase in pulmonary ventilation, normal heart-beat, low arterial pressure, stable polyglobulism: these are similar characteristics to those of people living at high altitudes. One condition that poses a permanent danger at high altitudes is the increase that occurs in the viscosity of the blood and by very marked dehydration. A particular type of adaptation appears to occur at the level of cells (i.e. in the tissues) and enzymes. Despite acclimatization, the same effort at high altitude nevertheless requires a much greater expenditure of energy than at sea level, and fatigue comes on much more quickly.

From *Technique de L'Alpinismo* (Bernard Amy)

PHYSIOPATHOLOGY OF THE MOUNTAINEER			
Causes of symptoms	Symptoms	Defences	
		Natural	*Artificial*
Partial drop in oxygen pressure	Mountain sickness	Acclimat-ization	Directed acclimat-ization
Drop in temperature due to wind	Frostbite General exposure	Heat adjustment	Protection using clothing Food
Drop in atmospheric humidity	Dehydration Laryngo-tracheitis		Food and drink
Radiation	Sunstroke Sunburn Snow-blindness		Sun cream Sunglasses
Physical exertion	Fatigue Exhaustion	Physiological Adaptation	Planned programme

Diet

Stress from fatigue

The energy required to keep the vital processes going (at a temperature of 37°C/98.6°F) comes from a combination of foodstuffs and the oxygen carried by the blood into the tissues, in accordance with the processes of internal metabolism. The glucose required by the tissue cells is stored by the liver in the form of glycogen, extracted by enzymes from carbohydrates, fats and proteins that are ingested as food. With exertion, the consumption of oxygen in the tissues increases. The amount of oxygen necessary arrives from an increase in pulmonary ventilation and heartbeat. But if this is not sufficient, there is a shortage of oxygen. Aerobic metabolism (with oxygen combustion and the release of carbon dioxide and water) is accompanied by another reaction whereby the body draws directly from the glycogen reserves, with the production of lactic acid. There are two consequences: the 'oxygenless' reaction releases a quantity of calories lower by a factor of sixteen than those produced in aerobic metabolism; and the glycogen reserves can only be replaced subsequent to this. In this state the muscles become 'intoxicated' and there is a typical sensation of fatigue. The lactic acid can only be digested when resting, with an inflow of oxygen which turns it into carbon dioxide and water. Training is a complex business, but in essence it reduces the production of lactic acid under stress, favouring the aerobic metabolism and the capacity of the body to increase the inflow of oxygen to the tissues.

A sensible and healthy diet is vital in the mountains. Over and above any normal expenditure of energy under stress, you must also anticipate extra energy requirements caused by certain typical situations: cold (even when you are resting), altitude, and a drop in atmospheric humidity. It has been calculated that at 7000 - 8000 metres (23,500 - 26,500 ft) you have to drink at least 5 litres (slightly more than 1 gallon) of liquid a day to make up for losses. When resting you will be consuming about 1700 calories in twenty-four hours. Under stress, with an oxygen consumption rate that can reach 7 - 8 times the normal rate, consumption can reach as high as 5000 - 6000 calories a day. The optimum food ration, however, is only 50% of the calorie requirement; it is advisable to divide it into small, repeated snacks of 250 - 500 calories each, so as not to overload the digestive system. The calorie deficit indicated is not significant. In choosing the most suitable diet for the mountaineer you must always bear in mind that the exertion required at high altitudes, and at low temperatures, causes hypoglycaemic conditions (combustion of the sugars), gaseous alkalosis (from pulmonary hyperventilation), dehydration, circulation of lactic and pyruvic acids (which cause a sensation of muscular fatigue), with a consequent tendency to acidification of the blood and a reduction of the alkaline reserves. So it is advisable to avoid foods which give rise to acidification, and use those which are alkalogenic. The former include meats, cheese, eggs, cereals and farinaceous products, dried vegetables, and fats. The second include all fresh fruits, vegetables and greens, potatoes, honey, dried figs and skimmed milk. The glucids (sugars) are the best combustible food under stress. When reserves have been exhausted the body summons up its fat resources (lipids). The ideal diet contains 1 gramme of protein for every kilo of weight per day (1 oz per 65 lb), dividing the rest between 70% glucids and 30% lipids. But in normal situations the body tends to regulate itself automatically. A loss of salts (from sweating or urine) can be compensated for by eating sodium chloride tablets; a loss of potassium by drinking fruit juices. Vitamin requirements are usually covered by a normal diet. It is never advisable to drink alcoholic beverages. Sweets, sweet drinks, fruit and jam are specially recommended for overcoming the 'sugar crisis' undergone on ascents.

2100-CALORIE MOUNTAINEER'S DIET
(For two days' hard climbing above 3000 metres/10,000 ft)

Typical daily ration

Powdered skimmed milk	55 g (2 oz)	
Cheese	75 g (3 oz)	
Eggs	1	
Pasta or rice	50 g (2 oz)	
Oat or rice-flakes	25 g (1 oz)	
Wholemeal bread	30 g (1 oz)	
Wholemeal biscuits	40 g (1.5 oz)	
Green vegetables	600 g (21 oz)	Protids 67 g (2.4 oz)
Bananas	100 g (4 oz)	Lipids 63 g (2.25 oz)
Fresh fruit	200 g (8 oz)	Glucids 318 g (11.4 oz)
Dried fruit	30 g (1 oz)	
Fruit juice	600 g (21 oz)	
Honey or jam	40 g (1.5 oz)	
Sugar	15 g (0.5 oz)	
Tea	400 cc (15 fl. oz)	
Mayonnaise (in tubes)	35 g (1 oz)	**2106 calories**

2500-CALORIE MOUNTAINEER'S DIET
(for several days' hard climbing above 3000 metres/10,000 ft).

Typical daily ration

Powdered skimmed milk	40 g (1.5 oz)	Tea (infusion)	400 cc (15 fl. oz)
Cheese	70 g (3 oz)	Tomato concentrate	100 g (4 oz)
Eggs	2	Mayonnaise (in tubes)	50 g (2 oz)
Pasta or rice	70 g (3 oz)		
Oats or rice-flakes	20 g (0.6 oz)		
Wholemeal bread	20 g (0.6 oz)		
Wholemeal biscuits	40 g (1.5 oz)		
Potatoes	150 g (5.5 oz)		
Biscuits	40 g (1.5 oz)		
Greens	450 g (16 oz)	Protids 80 g (3 oz)	
Fresh fruit	350 g (12.5 oz)	Lipids 78 g (2.75 oz)	
Dried fruit	50 g (2 oz)	Glucids 367 g (13 oz)	
Fruit juice	600 g (21 oz)		
Honey or jam	20 g (0.7 oz)		
Sugar	10 g (0.35 oz)	**2586 calories**	

From 100 diete per 100 sport (A. Lodispoto)

Mountain safety code

These are not the 'Ten Commandments', but rather a few basic rules concerned with caution and conduct, tested by experience, which every mountaineer and climber should have constantly at the back of his mind:

1 Be physically prepared (in order to tackle a climb safely and to be able to cope with possible emergency situations. Keep a watchful eye on your fitness, diet and relaxation.)

2 Be morally and mentally prepared (in order to cope with the situation and your own responsibilities; have a clear inner motivation).

3 Be technically prepared (and have the necessary experience to be able to take the right decision at any given moment).

4 Know your own ability and limits (always stay slightly within your limitations so as to have something in reserve).

5 Know your mountain and its dangers.

6 Prepare for your climb carefully (studying the route, times involved, the descent route, the possibility of resting places or escape routes; check all your equipment carefully; find out about the conditions along the route; listen to weather reports and the advice of experts; let friends and the relevant authorities know about your climbing plans).

7 Know when to retreat (when general conditions so require, or when you do not feel on top form, or when you are lacking in confidence; don't let your personal ambition lure you on).

8 Be aware of your own responsibilities (choose your climbing companion(s) well; stay constantly alert, and be cautious; behave with a spirit of solidarity and fraternity towards other climbers; offer assistance to anyone in trouble; know your basic first-aid drill).

9 Respect the mountain (nature, its inhabitants, and the rock itself. Do not leave signs of your climb behind you.)

10 Do not use the mountain for exhibitionist or competitive purposes.

The American school

When a European mountaineer finds himself climbing for the first time in the United States, he will generally feel somewhat disorientated: all the climbing techniques that he has learnt, and all the skills that he has acquired from his European experience, seem to be of little use. He may become giddy studying huge walls of rock, which seem to represent a riddle to be solved with no apparent place to start. Making every effort to stay calm, as he tries to wedge a nut into a crack, he may suddenly hear the light-hearted voice of his American friend wafting up from below with the reminder: 'No protection on this pitch ...'.

In recent years, encouraged more than a little by the awesome photographs published by magazines and by remarkable documentary films, we have seen the development in Europe of an image of all-American climbers and mountaineers as athletic specimens with sun-tanned bodies, their long flowing locks held in place by a colourful headband across the forehead, engaged in breathtaking feats on overhanging rock-faces in California, or making some apparently endless acrobatic swing into the void. Reality, of course, is slightly more varied than this, although it undoubtedly encompasses some of these 'folklore' aspects, which have greatly contributed to the popularity and development of the 'new' style of American mountaineering.

Among the bold pioneers there is one name that must be mentioned, and not so much for the various achievements that he has to his name, as for the spirit behind them: John Muir. This 'apostle of nature', who is regarded as the spiritual father of all those who love and protect the wild beauty of the North American continent, was the first man – in the late nineteenth century – to acquaint people with the splendour of the American mountain ranges, from the Sierra Nevada to the peaks of Yosemite to the Tetons. The interests of the numerous members of the American Alpine Club, which was founded in 1902, were concentrated first and foremost on the highest peaks in Alaska: Mount McKinley (6128 metres/20,300 ft), which was scaled in 1913, and Mounts Logan and Alberta (the former climbed in 1925). After 1920, as mountaineering continued to spread far and wide, so the technical level also improved remarkably, thanks both to American mountaineers who had had experience in the Alps, and to (mainly German) mountaineers who had emigrated permanently to the United States. In 1927, the German-born Stettner brothers tackled the west face of Longs Peak, and opened up the hardest rock route of the day. Another German climber, Jack Durrance, blazed some magnificent trails in the Grand Teton region (rising to 4196 metres/13,766 ft). When it came to training, but also because of his pure love of climbing as an end in itself, Durrance would climb up isolated boulders, seeking out the most elegant and difficult routes to the top. And today many young Americans still prefer to restrict their climbing just to boulders, rising a few metres from the ground, stretching their resources to incredible limits – particularly for those who have not trained specifically for this 'art'. In areas where this 'bouldering' is popular the handholds are white from the gypsum and magnesium used to dry the sweat on the fingers and increase the grip on the rock. The use of hand-and footholds that are slightly removed from the 'route' is strictly forbidden by a set of ethics that grants no concessions whatsoever.

Unhampered by preconceptions and preformulated plans, it was as early as the thirties that American mountaineers discovered the advantages of dynamic belays, and using the waist belay technique, thus absorbing the jerk of a fall with the friction of the rope around their bodies. In 1934, the top climbers were trying to solve a major problem: Mount Waddington. It seemed as if the Californian members of the Sierra Club had the best chance of success; in the Yosemite Valley they had pushed the technical levels of climbing to higher and higher degrees of difficulty. But Mount Waddington demanded all-round mountaineers, experts on both rock and ice. And the man who solved the problem in the end was the German Fritz Wiessner, who had to his credit many a notable climb in the Alps, together with Himalayan experience gained during the ascent of Nanga Parbat, and the first successful climb on the strange 'Devil's Tower' in the United States.

A conspicuous personality in the post-war period was John Salathé. This Swiss-born blacksmith did not discover mountaineering until quite late in life, and

Current reassessment of free climbing has also been stimulated by the sensational performances – athletic to say the least – of American rock gymnasts. Below: a 5.11 pitch on the American grading system (the equivalent of the European grade VII) on the Kloberdanz. Right: the climbing style in Boulder Canyon. Chalk is used on handholds to increase grip.

he took up climbing for health reasons; but it soon became the driving passion in his life. It was he who in Yosemite blazed three splendid routes up the south-east face of the Half Dome, in the Lost Arrow Chimney, and on the north face of Sentinel Rock. His success owed much to his remarkable determination and to his skill, but not least to the special hard-steel pitons which he fashioned, as a craftsman, from the axles of an old Ford. In this way it was discovered that these pitons, which were subsequently improved, could be adapted much more effectively than traditional soft-metal types to the specific structure of the granite faces in the Yosemite region. In 1950, in California, the various categories and classes of climbs were laid down (there are six in all: grade 4 indicates the use of the rope for protecting the climber or climbers; grade 5 is technical free climbing). The scale of difficulty in technical free climbs starts from 5.0, and was designed in such a way as to leave room for grades of increasing difficulty. The most difficult routes are graded around 5.12.

In the fifties, in Yosemite Valley, the 'star' was Powell: this was the 'Powell Era'. His achievements were not mind-boggling, but this man spent very long periods of time in the mountains, climbing completely free. In 1957 the first American sixth grade was chalked up: on the north-west 'concave' face of the Half Dome, Royal Robbins, Gallwas and Sherrick opened up this route in five days, climbing above 5.9 most of the time. And Warren Harding was at the summit to congratulate the climbers: the next move was to be his. The great challenge of Yosemite was El Capitan: a rock wall of more than 1000 metres/3300 ft, smooth and vertical.

The climb up the 'Nose' of El Capitan started on 4 July 1957, using Himalayan techniques, with a series of camps and fixed ropes. The team was made up of Harding and Powell, and later on, Wayne Merry. This formidable undertaking called for a blend of ambition, a taste for major problems, a delight in climbing, especially its technical aspects, and an all-American sense of the spectacular. The climb ended some sixteen months later on 12 November 1958, not least because of

troubles caused by its very spectacular nature – to avoid traffic jams caused by spectators, the Yosemite National Park administration had to tell the climbers to put a stop to their assault on the rock-face for the entire summer tourist season! To reach the top, 800 pitons were used, of which about 90 per cent were for aid. There was much talk of exhibitionism and mountaineering bravado. The riposte to such chatter came from Royal Robbins. He stated that, at that particular historical moment, the only man capable of shattering the mythical taboo of El Capitan was Harding, because he was the only man capable of using the specific technique required. But at the same time he put his own remarks into context: an Alpine-style ascent was still more desirable and Robbins led it up the same route. With Frost, Pratt and Fitschen the climb was completed in seven days. Stimulated by this success, and in order to honour Robbins's dictum that 'what you climb is less important than how you climb it', Frost, Pratt and Robbins himself decided, in 1961, to open up a route that was as much as possible a free climb. This route, which was named after Salathé, was put up in six days of climbing using thirteen expansion bolts; it was regarded as the most logical and beautiful route on the great wall of El Capitan.

The development of American mountaineering in the sixties should not, however, be judged just against these extreme climbs. Powell had turned the Yosemite Valley into a microcosm, with a clearly defined set of 'ethical' principles – the prime source of a new 'mountaineering philosophy' which aligned itself with the values and spirit of the 'Camp 4 community'. Chuck Pratt, Yvon Chouinard, Layton Kor, Ed Cooper and other exponents of the new creed of mountaineering moved from one place to another, travelling like nomads (or real 'hippies'), between them building up knowledge of the different mountaineering environments, exchanging experiences and 'discovering' new mountains: the

Cascades, the Tetons, the Shawangunks, the Eldorado Canyon, and the Tahquitz range.

Royal Robbins, who was the most representative personality in the new stream of American mountaineering in the sixties, soloed the Harding route on the Leaning Tower. This marked the beginning of the era of the great solo climbs, which inevitably soon found its champions and heroes in a country as fond of specialist sports as the United States. In 1964 Robbins hit the headlines with another daring undertaking. Putting aside personal rivalries, he called on the best mountaineers of the time: Chouinard, Frost and Pratt. In nine days a new and extremely demanding route had been opened up on El Capitan. The route was later called the *North American Wall*, because of the shape assumed on the granite face by an intrusion of black diorite (greenstone), resembling a map of North America. Another route was opened up by Chouinard and Herbert on the *Muir Wall*: nine extremely demanding days on the overhanging face, with little equipment available to them, and wondering at a certain stage whether the difficulties anticipated on the descent route might not be more severe than those encountered on the climb up; nine days in a vertical labyrinth where it is hard to keep your sense of direction. A year later Robbins climbed Muir Wall again, this time solo – in 1967, with John Harlin, he had proved to the European fraternity the validity of the techniques used in Yosemite, by opening up a new route on the Dru in the Mont Blanc range.

One of the 'sacred' places for the American school is Eldorado Canyon in Colorado. Left: two photographs which give an idea of the sense of climbing as a game, not concerned with soaring peaks to be conquered, but with individual pitches of extreme difficulty, often only a few metres from the ground. Below: a strangely shaped boulder that has just been scaled – the Wyoming mushroom. Bouldering has now become popular in the Alps as well.

Warren Harding, who was the leading figure involved in the historic ascent of the 'Nose', ushered in the seventies dramatically, and, once again, spectacularly. Together with Dean Caldwell he had been twenty days on the steep face called Dawn Wall, and there was still a long way to go. Rescue teams were prepared, but the two climbers refused any assistance. The climb was all over the newpapers, radio and television, and became a national event. The Dawn Wall saga came to an end after twenty-seven days. Harding and Caldwell emerged at the top to the whirr of cine-cameras and the microphones of interviewers from the media. But the highly artifical nature of the Dawn Wall route was to spur on other forms of mountaineering research. Climbing with Don Lauria, Royal Robbins proposed a plan to 'clean the wall' of the hundreds of expansion bolts and pitons used by Harding and Caldwell. But after a day's climbing, both men were wracked by doubts about the nature of what they were doing, and how they were doing it, and they backed down.

In the Yosemite Valley the piton problem was becoming worse and worse: the steel types were literally breaking up the rock and the edges of cracks. In just a very few years the English-invented nuts completely replaced pitons, and free – or, better still, 'clean' – climbing became the real development and revolution of the sixties. In 1973, Bruce Carson climbed Sentinel Rock solo, and to establish his 'ecological' method of climbing, which 'respected' the mountain, he did not even take a piton hammer with him. In the same year, using the same approach, and climbing with Chouinard, he reclimbed the 'Nose' on El Capitan. With this emphasis on 'clean' climbing, the technical level of free climbing advanced to incredible heights, and there was already talk of an almost magical 5.13 grade: the equivalent of an eighth grade in Alpine terms! These advances naturally required extreme specialization, and there thus developed a split – which was often difficult to bridge – between those pursuing the limits of the purest forms of free climbing, and those who, on the other hand, felt attracted by forms of classical mountaineering. So it is that today American mountaineering sees men like Charlie Porter climbing, solo and without a break, the southern Cassin route up Mount McKinley in thirty-six hours; while there are also scores of nameless young climbers spending whole days studying a few centimetres of rock to find some virtually invisible handhold, pushing the friction of their climbing shoes to the absolute limits. Their form of mountaineering has little or nothing to do with ice, climbing-boots, bivouacs, high altitudes and blizzards. Nowadays many climbers are also refusing to use chalk to sprinkle over their fingers or special protective plasters designed and used to avoid cutting the hands when it comes to hand-jamming: these are regarded as 'artificial' aids which get in the way of the relationship between hand and rock – a form of mechanical climbing which makes the climb easier, on a psychological level as well a physical one – and modifies the characteristics of both the hand 'element' and the rock 'element'.

All this may be rather difficult to understand for those who see mountaineering in a traditional light, as an endeavour in which, on the one hand, the mountaineer figures as a thinking and feeling participant, and on the other, the goal to be reached is static and mineral, symbolized by the summit of the mountain. Under the impetus of the various forms of specialization, the limits are constantly being pushed further and further, and, in America, the sport of climbing is becoming increasingly complex and even philosophical – an opportunity for visionary experiences (there are people who compare these forms of mountaineering with the 'trips' made on drugs) in which the physical climb itself becomes the expression of an inner spiritual climb.

Beyond the sixth grade

Left: a demonstration of bouldering at Courmayeur, using the 'American' approach. The small bag slung around the neck holds chalk for the fingers. Below: soloing a difficult pitch on an isolated boulder near Chamonix. Modern technique using soft-soled climbing shoes means that you have to stay close to the rock. The arms are stretched as fully as possible to avoid tiring them, and the grip is all in the fingers.

At the end of the last century, with the ever-growing number of routes being opened up throughout the Alps, mountaineers and climbers started to feel the need for a scale of difficulty for comparing different climbs. In 1894 the first climbing guide book appeared in Great Britain, written by Haskett-Smith — *Climbing in the British Isles: vol i England*. In the foreword to it, Claude Wilson made reference to the diffidence with which these first attempts to classify and describe ascents was greeted in the elitist and conservative inner circles of the Alpine Club: 'We would hope that this book will not encourage inexperienced climbers and beginners into dangerous situations.' In the same year, Coolidge passed an adverse verdict on the spread of climbing and mountaineering (the German and Austrian Alpine Clubs already numbered 78,500 members between them) and the popularity of mountain 'sports', but he did take some consolation from the fact that 'the decline in the average social status of members has been much more marked in Europe than in Great Britain.'

But warnings and conservative attitudes were of course unable to check the development of mountaineering as a sport, at every level. In 1897 Owen Glynne Jones published another guide (*Rock Climbing in the Lake District*) which proposed a classification with four degrees of difficulty for the sixty-odd existing routes: easy, moderately difficult, difficult, exceptionally difficult. A similar scale was introduced in the Eastern Alps, where, in the meantime, the opening-up of new routes was going on at such a rate that the various mountaineering guides had to be updated annually. Despite the damning words of Sir Martin Conway (1901) directed at rock-climbers 'driven on by the quest for the new and the pleasures of glory', the lines drawn in guide books on diagrams of cliffs, indicating routes became denser and denser.

The four-grade system applied in England and the Eastern Alps became inadequate before very long. The more difficult ascents were all lumped together under grade four, which thus came to embrace routes assessed today as of average difficulty together with the markedly more demanding routes opened up by Dülfer, Piaz, Dibona and others. In 1914 the Austrian Karl Planck stirred up much debate in the mountaineering world with an article in which he stated that the grade four climb had now been superseded, that mountaineers now needed a comparative yardstick with which to assess their own undertakings, and that in a period of time hallmarked by exact descriptions and definitions in every field, these should also be introduced to mountaineering.

In 1926 the German Willo Welzenbach conceived a scale of difficulty with six grades: I (easy, hardly requiring the use of hands); II (barely difficult); III (quite difficult); IV (difficult); V (very difficult); and VI (extremely difficult). The division into six was suggested quite simply by the system of mark assignment in use at the time in German schools. The Welzenbach scale gave order to the classification of routes, but soon showed certain limitations. This system was produced after years of controversy during which it had been argued that such a scale would make mountaineering increasingly athletic and technical, and that it was not possible to define climbs in such a precise and mathematical way. In 1955 the Englishman Irving stated that 'difficulty gradings provoke rivalry among mountaineers and puts an exaggerated stress on the technical aspects of climbing, at the expense of other factors involved in mountaineering'. But the new classification was soon adopted in first French and then Antonio Berti's Dolomite guides and was very successful as far as mountaineers were concerned. With the qualifying terms — superior and inferior grades — the range of grades covered was considered more than adequate.

Domenico Rudatis, who in the thirties wrote a 'manifesto for the acknowledgement and future of the sixth grade' recognised as necessary for any 'sporting' assessment of rock-climbing, gives this interpretation of the 'limits of human possibilities' which are situated at the very top of the scale: 'On the harrowing line that separates limits of daring from limits of existence we find the heroic and sporting feat which really deserves the accolade of sixth grade.' But problems started to crop up when there were attempts to apply the Welzenbach scale to routes in the Western Alps, where the formation of the granite, the mixed

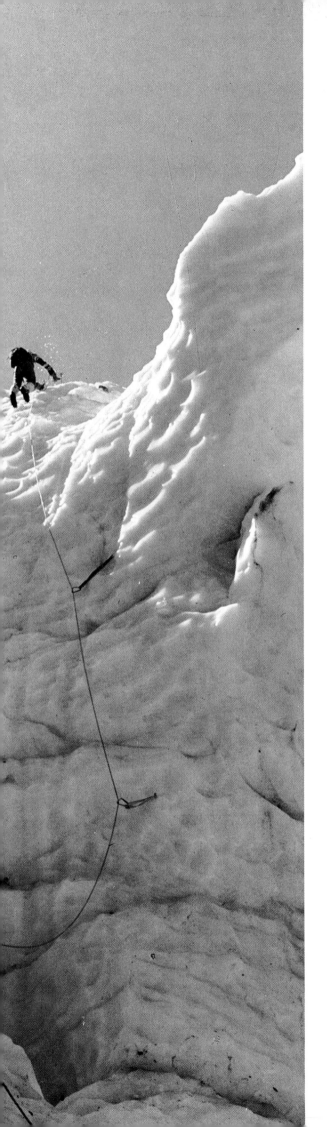

(rock-and-ice) environment, snow-and-ice, high altitudes and the length of the routes required a more overall assessment rather than a purely technical assessment of the individual pitches. Attempts to apply the 'Munich scale' to pure ice routes have had no follow-up. From 1951 onwards the problem has been partly resolved by the adoption of the modified scale adopted in the Vallot guides for Mont Blanc, and devised by members of the French *Haute Montagne* group.

In the Dolomites, the Welzenbach scale (which is taken as an assessment only of free climbing) worked well until it found itself in the area of 'super direct' routes and routes requiring intensive use of pitons. Today, having sorted out this other controversy (Welzenbach had made the distinction very clear cut) the French scale has been accepted for artificial climbs with the grades ranging from A1 to A4. In the overall assessment of a route another French scale is preferred: F (easy – *facile*); PD (slightly difficult – *peu difficile*); AD (quite difficult – *assez difficile*); D (difficult – *difficile*); TD (very difficult – *très difficile*) and ED (extremely difficult – *extrêmement difficile*). In the last ten to fifteen years the traditional Welzenbach scale has nevertheless revealed its limits: it is a scale closed at the top, stopping at the sixth grade, which advances in free climbing are demonstrably exceeding.

1972 saw the publication of a book which was to cause uproar in the mountaineering world: *Il settimo grado* (The Seventh Grade). The author was certainly one of the most qualified men to broach the subject: Reinhold Messner. In the early seventies, many other mountaineers were in agreement that grade VI no longer corresponded entirely with the maximum difficulty encountered on current hard climbs. By strict and specific methods of training, by pushing one's own climbing technique to the limit on boulders just a few metres above the ground, by combining mountaineering with other sporting disciplines, and by preparing both body and mind for a better approach to the mountain to be tackled, people were in fact managing to re-climb classic grade VI routes with a nonchalance and degree of safety which had nothing whatsoever to do with the concept of 'extreme difficulty', or 'limits of human possibilities' implicit in the grade itself. The traditionalists were sceptical, denouncing the excessive use of pitons on the classic routes which, in their opinion (and justly so) often falsified the ideas of gradings. The problem of how many pitons could be used, and of the abilities of the original ascenders–were they superior or inferior to those of present-day climbers? – gave rise to interminable and sterile argument. The main point, however, also comprehensively dealt with by Messner in his book, was somewhat different: grade VI has always been regarded as a psychological measurement, an assessment of risk, courage and challenge, rather than a mere technical fact. But the question involved was the recognition of, above all, technical progress. In bouldering in California and Colorado, or at Fontainebleau, or in the Verdon gorges, and in many other 'training-grounds' where the risk-factor is undoubtedly lower, as is the stamina involved (bouldering is a short, sharp process), the technical superiority of the individual climbs successfully made is undeniable. In an attempt to make a parallel with other continually developing and advancing sporting disciplines, grade VI has been likened to an 11-second 100 metres, grade VII to 10.2 seconds. And no one would now dream of saying that 10 seconds flat or even 9.9 seconds was an impossible target.

While discussion in Europe is still focused on the timeliness or otherwise of admitting grade VII to the scale of difficulty, the problem in other countries is past history by now. Top European mountaineers who have tried Yosemite granite do not conceal their admiration and amazement for the feats achieved by the 'mad men' of the American school, using the purest free-climbing style. Unlike the rigidly classified model of European grading, the Americans, in the fifties, conceived an alternative system called the *Decimal System*. This came into being at Tahquitz Rock in southern California. This system is open-ended at the top: 5.10 is the classic sixth grade; 5.11 the higher sixth; 5.12 the lower seventh, and so on. In the United States assessments for bouldering and mountain-climbing are now separate. People have managed to climb stretches assessed at 5.13 (grade VII +) on the mountain scale, and the basic requirement for negotiating grades B1, B2 and B3 pitches on the bouldering scale (possibly corresponding to grades VIII, IX and X!) is an ability to hang on by just one finger. Referring to the 5.13 grade (which is the equivalent of the corresponding grade 24 in Australia) the American climber James

Preceding pages: front pointing, the equivalent of free climbing on ice. Top: climbing a horizontal overhang or roof with artificial means. This photograph shows the Sarre overhang, near Aosta, an overhang of 40 metres (130 ft), fitted in parts with expansion bolts. In the background you can see Monte Emilius and the Becca di Nona. The main highway to Courmayeur passes just a few metres away. Above: negotiating an overhang in the early stages of the De Francesch route on the Torre Grande d'Averau. Right: recovering an étrier. Despite its spectacular nature, artificial climbing is often less difficult and risky than free climbing.

Bridwell writes: 'In just a few years the standards of free climbing have been raised at a rate that is in direct proportion with the climbing-population explosion'. At any given time there are a few people who are responsible for raising these standards and their attitudes and their genius are passed on to the next generation in a process of continuous evolution. For this reason 'the old men' of yesteryear have all contributed to the present level and to the 'state of the art' of rock climbing.

It is significant, forty years on, and in the words of a young American, that we have seen a comeback of this same concept of the 'art of climbing' expressed with reference to Comici and the battle in the thirties and forties for the recognition of grade VI. As Gaston Rébuffat writes: 'The mountaineer is neither an athlete nor an artist, but a little of each.' In this process of constant evolution, trying to fix limits and to classify what represents the maximum in human performance is pointless. The seventh grade is also seen in this light: taboo until November 1978, it was then officially recognized by the UIAA (Union of International Alpine Associations) the senior international mountaineering organization, when it met for its general assembly at Lagonissi in Greece.

To tackle a grade VI climb, constant and serious preparation is vital, with the help of real professionals. Top condition – of both body and mind – can also be achieved by borrowing techniques used in other sports, such as yoga and autogenous training. It is a good idea to seek out small rock-faces near where you

live; large boulders can become a microcosm where you can try the very hardest possible routes, verging almost on the impossible. When you climb hour after hour on your own, a few metres from the ground, you learn an awful lot about yourself – your personality, your equilibrium, and the strength of your own muscles. And you also realize that the more elegant and stylish your movements, the easier it becomes to climb difficult pitches. Your mental attitude also develops until you no longer feel yourself *pitted against* the mountain, but rather a *part* of the mountain, rock or ice; the mountain is no longer an alien, hostile thing. The struggle against the rock thus becomes a search for a delicate and subtle harmony and equilibruim.

Possibly the greatest merit of grade VII and extreme forms of modern mountaineering (including going above 8000 metres/26,000 ft without oxygen) is precisely that it has spurred on this process of mental evolution, and done away with the cliché of 'fighting the mountain'; it has also transformed the manner of approaching the mountain, which can become a moral heritage for all mountaineers and climbers, even those who are happy to stay at more modest levels. The danger is that there can emerge an irremediable split between the super-champions who spend hours training scientifically every day, and the vast majority of mountaineers who cannot afford this luxury.

As things stand at the moment, and because of the athletic performances that certain routes and pitches require, this split seems more or less inevitable. But this obviously does not mean that those who do not achieve the highest levels should feel inferior in any way. A deliberate non-competitive choice is perfectly legitimate for any mountaineer; in the mountains there is room for everybody. The rational basis of training is aptly summed up by the young German Klaus Gehrke who, in 1979, made the first solo climb up the famous *Pumprisse* on the Fleischbank, assessed at grade VII: when he first climbed it he had found it exhausting; on the second ascent he even managed to enjoy it.

A phenomenon that has exploded in recent years, which is indirectly linked to the search for ever greater technical difficulties and grade VII, is bouldering. The British are past masters here: in Scotland bouldering has a long tradition, with its

own ethics, codes of conduct and champions. A convincing proof of this was given at Val d'Orco, near Turin, by the Briton Mike Kosterlitz; using the hand-jam technique in an overhanging crack rising 8 metres (26 ft) in an isolated boulder, he achieved something that was not repeated for eight years, despite many vain attempts. In all countries bouldering now has its specialists and fans. In France there are the *bleausards* who have been climbing the boulders in the forest of Fontainebleau, near Paris, for twenty years (the first to use resin dust on the hands, called *popofe* in their jargon); and in Bohemia there are sandstone specialists who work to a scale with nine grades. This type of climbing, with no mountain peaks to be reached or conquered, might also in fact encompass that rather odd sport practised by the rock athletes in the Soviet Union who actually compete with each other in climbing races, protected by top ropes.

In Italy bouldering is most common in Val di Mello, near Sondrio, in Val d'Orco near Turin, and in the Susa Valley. The boulderers have also tried to set up their own unique philosophy which in some cases leads them to reject mountains. Their routes are up isolated boulders and rocks, in river gorges, or on slabs which lead nowhere; climbing like this is an end in itself, not justified by training for 'serious' climbs. Following the Americans many of the routes are christened with highly imaginative names. The Mecca for Italian boulderers is the Remenno Boulder, at the entrance to the Masino Valley; this is the largest 'rogue' boulder in the Alps, and has now been explored down to the last nook and cranny. Some exponents of bouldering have even made grade VII routes on places such as the walls of the Porta Venezia gardens in the heart of Milan.

Left above: free climbing without running belays on an overhanging pitch. Left below: corner being climbed by bridging. Below: a crack usually offers a logical upward route, using both the opposition (Dülfer) and hand-jamming technique (illustrated here).

The grandiose scenery of the Himalaya make them the dream of all mountaineers. Here there are ten of the fourteen 8000-metre (26,000-ft) peaks in the world. The other four are in the Karakorum region. Left: the delicate flutings of the Nuptse ridge, looking like a piece of lace made of ice. Top: in the 'death zone' above the 7500-metre (24,500-ft) mark, heading for the South Col on Everest. Above: a difficult stretch, using light aluminium ladders, on the dangerous Icefall below Everest, where thirty climbers have lost their lives since 1953. The problems of high altitude and the dangers of the ice-and-snow environment are the major difficulties encountered by any Himalayan expedition.

Altitude 8000

On Everest's summit – the earth's highest peak at 8848 metres (29,028 ft), climbed in May 1978 without the use of oxygen – Reinhold Messner left a length of rope and the dead batteries of his cine-camera: there were no 'heroic' poses, no unfurling of flags. 'I don't go up mountains to conquer a geological feature,' he is quoted as saying, 'but to discover and explore myself.' A lot of physiologists doubted it was possible, without oxygen bottles, to survive the rarefied air of the 'death zone' (an altitude at which jets fly), where without sufficient oxygen in it the blood has trouble maintaining the basic vital functions of the body. 'I didn't want to put on a show,' Messner says, 'I just wanted to "experience" Everest, without any technical back-up, without a mask between me and the mountain.' Clearly an extreme situation, a ruthless encounter with yourself, and your own courage; and a test of your training and preparation. In August 1980 Messner achieved another awesome feat: the summit of Everest, once again, but this time alone. He climbed the route up the north face in Tibet, which saw all the early expeditions flounder, and George Mallory and Andrew Irvine go missing altogether in 1924 at an altitude of 8600 metres (28,200 ft). 'A chapter in mountaineering beyond Europe has come to an end: what's left to do now?' the newspapers asked, posing a question which had already been asked so many times in the history of mountaineering (and almost invariably answered soon after).

What distinguishes mountaineering beyond the shores of Europe in comparison to traditional mountaineering is first and foremost the environment, taken not only in the physical but also in the human sense. In Nepal, Bolivia, Pakistan, Greenland or the Sahara mountaineers experience the strangeness of the climate and the local peoples, with their own original and often extremely ancient culture. The grandiose majesty of the great mountain ranges beyond Europe, and the logistical problems they involve, take us back to the dawn of mountaineering, when men travelled on foot or by mule from Aosta to Courmayeur. But one wonders if mountaineering in the big ranges of the world is not gradually going through the same experiences as traditional mountaineering, even with the same identity crisis, or if it can be regarded as a form of mountaineering *per se*, with ingredients and characteristics which justify a quite independent definition. There is no doubt that the experience of climbing outside Europe, above all in the Himalaya, is much more total and complete for a mountaineer than any other.

Mountaineering outside Europe came into being with the first explorers who, out of a taste for adventure, or for scientific reasons, or to spread a religious belief, or for reasons of state or economic interest, pushed outwards into the most remote corners of the earth. In many cases the place-names still used today to indicate a precise geographical area or a mountain were coined by these pioneers. A daring Englishman, William Moorcroft, started out from Leh and visited the Nubra Valley, reaching a point only 50 km (30 miles) from the Siachen glacier. It was this explorer who called the entire mountain chain Karakorum in his report. Others were less lucky: Adolph Schlagintweit, who had travelled with his brothers Hermann and Robert for three years in the Baltoro region, and climbed up the Mustagh pass, was killed in Kashgar in 1857. When the taste for exploration in the pure sense was replaced by a desire to climb, many other names started to lengthen the list of casualties: some under an ice-avalanche, some let down by a snow bridge that turned out to be too fragile, some lost on a treacherous ridge, and some swept off by the waters of a river in spate, before even glimpsing the mountain.

The enthusiasm for climbs outside Europe soon started to take a hold, and won over many a famous name in traditional Alpine circles: these included Whymper, who stood atop the summit of Chimborazo in Ecuador (which had been attempted in vain by Humboldt) in 1880, and Mummery, who vanished on a daring early attempt on Nanga Parbat (8126 metres/26,660 ft). Overcoming huge obstacles, and pretending to be pilgrims or shepherds, there were those who made their way across the Tibetan border into the secret realm of the Dalai Lama, which was closed to foreigners. In 1897, E. Fitzgerald's English expedition reached the top of Aconcagua, the highest mountain in South America at 6959 metres (22,831 ft). Another remarkable man was Luigi Amedeo of Savoy, Duke of the Abruzzi, accompanied by his faithful guides from the Val d'Aosta and the

photographer-cum-mountaineer, Vittorio Sella; this group climbed the peaks of St Elias in Alaska in 1897, and the Margherita and Alexandra summits on Ruwenzori in Africa in 1906. During one of the first exploratory journeys into the K2 region, the record of the day was set at 7200 metres (23,620 ft) during a noble attempt to scale it.

The doors to the Himalaya, giving access from the Tibetan side, started to open in 1904, with the English military expedition commanded by Sir Francis Younghusband, who also managed to wrest from the Tibetans the first concessions for mountaineering expeditions. As early as 1852 a technician working for the *British Trigonometrical Survey* of India had discovered that the peak known as 'Peak 15', on the frontier between Nepal and Tibet, hidden behind apparently higher mountains, was in fact the highest, and this mountain was named after the director-general of the trigonometric survey, Sir George Everest. In 1921 a British expedition made a first attempt, finding an access route from the Tibetan glacier of Rongbuk. The expedition included one of the best mountaineers of the day, George Leigh Mallory, who pushed up to the North Col, at 7000 metres (23,000 ft), from where he was able to see an obvious route leading to the top. In the following year, with a larger expedition, Mallory set a new altitude record at 8230 metres (27,000 ft), but he was forced to turn back. Without conceding defeat, Mallory was again in the leading team that attempted the ascent two years later in 1924. After a series of unsuccessful attempts, 6 June saw the last assault on the final pyramid: Mallory and his friend Irvine left Camp 6, heading for the summit. The last person to see them was a member of the support team, Noel Odell, who got a glimpse of the pair at an altitude of 8600 metres (28,215 ft), proceeding with grim determination and a lot of willpower. Then the two men were lost in cloud and became part of the legend of this great mountain, Chomo Lungma, the 'Mother Goddess of the Earth'. Did they ever reach the top of Everest? No one will ever know. A rusty ice-axe, belonging to Irvine, was found nine years later, at the 8500-metre (27,900-ft) mark, the only remaining trace. A further three attempts were made by the British in the thirties, but Everest seemed to be impregnable and invincible.

After the war, mountaineers were able to make use of the research carried out in

Major Himalayan expeditions approach the mountain-top by setting up a series of advanced camps which must be constantly kept supplied by a shuttle of climbers and porters. Left: Camp 1 on Everest, at 6100 metres (20,000 ft). Left below: physiology experiments carried out at high altitude during the Italian expedition to Karakorum in 1909. Below: inside a tent, at 7200 metres (23,600 ft), on the Lhotse face. Bottom: oxygen bottles at the foot of the Western Cwm on Everest. Weighing 5 kg (11 lb) each they last for five hours and are usually used above 7500 metres (24,600 ft).

high-altitude flights. Oxygen bottles became lighter to carry, and oxygen masks and regulator-valves were improved. Warmer and more efficient clothing simplified the problems of spending long periods of time at high altitudes. In 1950 a strong French expedition set up its base-camp at the foot of Annapurna (8078 metres/26,503 ft), one of the fourteen 8000-metre (26,000-ft) peaks in the Himalaya, which had resisted twenty-two previous attempts to climb it. Overcoming all manner of problems, the climbers set up the upper camps, supplied by a constant and exhausting shuttle service from below. On 2 June, just a day or two before the arrival of the monsoons, Maurice Herzog and Louis Lachenal reached the summit of the first 8000-metre (26,000-ft) mountain in the world. The descent was dramatic. Suffering from serious attacks of frostbite, overtaken by an avalanche, the two men limped down the mountain where they were tended to by the expedition's doctor, Oudot. Herzog in particular suffered terribly from the anti-frostbite injections administered to him. Delirious and near to death, he was carried on a stretcher for four weeks through the valleys of Nepal, and was finally saved, although all his fingers and toes had to be amputated.

After the Second World War Tibet had closed its frontiers, but Nepal had opened hers. In 1951 the Englishman Eric Shipton, who had taken part in the previous expeditions to Everest in the thirties, made a preliminary reconnaissance of the unknown southern flank of the mountain. In the following year attempts from this approach mounted by strong Swiss expeditions ended in failure. In 1953 the most highly prepared expedition which had ever tackled the colossus of the Himalaya set out from Darjeeling, and settled in at their base camp on the Khumbu glacier. The leader of the expedition was Brigadier John Hunt. The mountaineers, helped by thirty-four sherpas used to high altitudes, negotiated the treacherous Icefall barrier, and pushed onwards into the great snow-filled valley known as the Western Cwm. Then they climbed up the Lhotse face as far as the South Col of Everest, at 8000 metres (26,200 ft), surveying the whole of the upland plateau of Tibet. The first summit attempt, made by Bourdillon and Evans, came to a stop only 88 metres (290 ft) from the top. From where they stopped, these two mountaineers, exhausted and wracked with disappointment, were the first men to see the last ridge leading to the summit of Everest. But behind them the team was busily preparing a strong back-up rope, made up of the New Zealander Edmund Hillary and sherpa Tenzing Norgay. After a night spent at Camp 9, at 8500 metres (27,900 ft), the two men set out at dawn on 29 May for the final assault. They found themselves beyond the point reached the year before by Tenzing and the Swiss Raymond Lambert and then tackled the last ridge to the summit. The news of the 'Conquest of Everest' was announced to the world via radio to London, on the eve of the coronation of Queen Elizabeth II.

Next year the second highest mountain in the world, K2 (8611 metres/28,251 ft) in the Karakorum, was also climbed. Its summit was reached by Lino Lacedelli and Achille Compagnoni, members of the expedition led by Ardito Desio. Within ten years the summits of all the fourteen 8000-metre (26,000-ft) mountains in the Himalaya – Karakorum chain had been climbed. Of all these successes, there is one in particular which should be mentioned: in July 1953 (two months after Everest had been climbed) the Austrian and German press announced in its headlines that Nanga Parbat (8126 metres/26,660 ft) in Kashmir had been climbed for the first time. This was the 'cursed mountain' which had already claimed some twenty-nine climbers on previous attempts. The leading figure in this sensational venture was Hermann Buhl, considered to be one of the best all-rounders of the post-war period. He left the last camp beneath the Silver Saddle alone, with no oxygen, and reached the summit, climbing some 1350 metres (4420 ft) in sixteen hours, in a state of semi-hallucination, and surviving a terrible bivouac on the way down at 8000 metres (26,200 ft). 'For as long as men climb mountains, and they will always climb them,' said Kurt Diemburger, who was Buhl's friend and fellow-climber four years later in the victorious ascent of Broad Peak, and also present when Buhl was killed on the Chogolisa by a collapsing cornice, 'people will remember his legendary feat.'

In the fifties and sixties mountaineering outside Europe was still in its pioneering phase. The expeditions were massive: hundreds of porters carried tons of equipment for days on end as far as the base camp, at the foot of the mountain. And the base camp became a completely self-sufficient citadel for one, two or more

months. From the base camp climbers set off on the slow task of setting up the higher camps, with a constant shuttle service delivering supplies. The technically most difficult stretches of the upward route were kitted out with fixed ropes and light aluminium ladders, which were also used as bridges over crevasses. Dozens of mountaineers were kept busy every day transporting food and drink, gas, oxygen, tents and so on, up to the last and highest camp from where the summit bid would be made. Difficulties included the climate (bad weather or wind can stop an expedition for days on end and endanger the final result), objective dangers (avalanches, serac falls, the collapse of snow bridges), and the need to make the most of the most suitable short seasonal periods: all expeditions in the Himalayas are conditioned by the monsoon cycle (winter and summer). In Patagonia the very high winds only abate for a few days each year. Where the climate is usually more favourable (for example, in the Andes or Sahara) there can be considerable logistical difficulties.

All problems become accentuated at high altitudes, when the summit soars to 7000 or 8000 metres (23,000 or 26,000 ft). Individual reactions are often unforeseeable and can take the form of nausea, headaches and migraines, insomnia, loss of appetite and tiredness. The mountaineer keeps going even when exhausted, driven by willpower alone, 'like a sick man sleep-walking', to use Eric Shipton's description. The moral qualities of endurance, balance of mind, and determination become more important even than technical preparation. Altitude sickness generally starts to appear with a seasickness-like sensation, where the individual feels indifferent, lack-lustre, and completely stripped of energy and determination. But it can, in extreme cases, also lead to pulmonary or cerebral oedema. The only solution here is to take the climber to the bottom of the mountain as fast as possible.

The reactions of the body at high altitudes have now been scientifically studied by whole teams of doctors and physiologists who went with the earliest expeditions. These studies have shed light on the specific mechanisms of acclimatization which come into play as low down as 4000 – 5000 metres (13,000 – 16,000 ft), after a fairly long period at that altitude. After two or three weeks, the acclimatized individual manages to put up better with the exertion, and reduce altitude troubles. The increase in the red corpuscles and the constant dehydration (at 8000 metres/26,000 ft the body must take in at least 7 litres/ about 1.5 gal. of liquids a day to make up for the physiological loss of fluids) nevertheless make the blood thicker and stickier, exposing the climber to the risk of oedema and increasing the risk of frostbite. Above 7000 metres (23,000 ft) it seems to be impossible to become acclimatized. Higher still, you are in the 'death zone', where mountaineering calls for short-lived brilliance. In spite of the various studies made, there is still some uncertainty about the best method of acclimatization. The traditional 'saw-tooth' system, which consists of making your way up to increasingly higher points and then climbing back down again, has been somewhat replaced today by a system involving one or more fast upward climbs after a basic period of acclimatization. This system is also the one used by the members of 'lightweight' expeditions which have introduced the most interesting innovations in recent years in the evolution of climbing.

In the first period we described in the history of mountaineering, when the 8000-metre (26,000-ft) peaks still all had to be climbed, the determination to reach the top 'using any means whatsoever', the ignorance about human limits at high altitudes, and the spell cast by the novelty of the whole idea relegated the problems of mountaineering ethics to the wings. In many instances a strong nationalistic emphasis was one of the basic motivations. This justified the use of techniques and organizational approaches more reminiscent of a military operation than a mountaineering expedition. This type of 'heavy' expedition also embraced those made on account of or in the name of an organizing committee, a city, or club, firms manufacturing specialized equipment, or private individuals. In the seventies people started to address themselves to problems of extreme technical difficulty such as the south face of Annapurna, the Rupal face of Nanga Parbat, the West Pillar of Makalu, or the south-west face of Everest, but people were also starting to feel more strongly the need to rediscover a proper relationship between men and mountains. It was seen that adventure can be had just as easily in places other than the Himalaya with its colossi; magnificent and unknown mountains were

Left: climbing at 6500 metres (21,300 ft), using pre-positioned fixed ropes. Left below: the final wall of the Icefall on Everest. The sun comes over the ridge when the climbers are already safely past this hazardous stretch. To reduce risks to the minimum where falling séracs are concerned (glaciers move forward at a speed of about a metre a day), it is best to start off very early, when the potentially unstable ice structures are still in shadow. Below: high above the Western Cwm and the distant peak of Pumori, a climber proceeds wearily to the South Col at 8000 metres (26,000 ft). At this altitude every step forward requires a huge effort from the mountaineer, and all his reactions are slowed down.

The victorious ascent by Hillary and Tenzing up the 8848 metres (29,028 ft) of Mount Everest ended thirty years of dramatic attempts to reach the earth's 'third pole'. Bottom: Tenzing triumphant at the top of the world, on 29 May 1953, in the historic 'snapshot' taken by his fellow-climber. Below: bent double over his ice-axe, at 7800 metres (25,600 ft) a mountaineer tries to catch his breath. Right: turning back from the South Col when the Italian expedition to Everest of 1980 was forced to concede defeat. At more than 100 km/h (65 mph), the wind was whipping up whirlwinds of snow from the ridge of Lhotse.

discovered in Norway, Patagonia, Greenland, Baffin Island and even the Sahara. The solitude, isolation and awareness of relying uniquely on his own strengths bring the mountaineer to a deeper awareness of his innermost experience. An extreme example of this form of mountaineering was the ascent by the English pair, Joe Tasker and Peter Boardman, on the west spur of Changabang (6864 metres/22,520 ft). Having reached the foot of the face unaided by any porters, the two men climbed for almost a month, in extremely difficult conditions, in total isolation. In 1982 both men were killed during a lightweight attempt on Everest.

Bureaucratic problems (climbing at 7000 and 8000 metres/23,000 – 26,000 ft in the Himalaya requires permits from the local government) and financial problems were beginning to make large expeditions more and more complicated to mount. Guido Machetto, who tackled the 7708-metre (25,290-ft) peak of Tirich Mir with Gianni Calcagno in 1975, describes in the following paragraph his theory of the

spirit of a 'lightweight' expedition:

On a traditional expedition, each man has his job to do: you have the leader, the second-in-command, and the administrator or book-keeper (who deals with the financial side of things and pays the porters), the doctor, the chef, the director of photography, and the predetermined leading and back-up teams of climbers. If everything is running smoothly the expedition can proceed. But people never work at 100% all the time: there is always someone who falls ill, someone who turns out to be unsuited to the situation, and someone else who refuses to play second string to other climbers. In too many cases the organization breaks down for such reasons: and the story of mountaineering outside Europe is studded with failures caused by them. The members of a two-man expedition, as I see it, must feel that they are the members of a 'commando' team.

For their particular climb, Machetto and Calcagno had trained very hard indeed, keeping to a special diet, preparing their bodies and minds for the challenge lying ahead. Questions relating to the greater validity of one form of expedition as compared with another have become particularly persistent in recent years, after the demonstration of the adverse effects of the constant movement of expeditions in the Himalayan valleys: pollution (which is already serious at the base-camp on Everest because of the accumulated refuse there), the hewing down of timber, and the repercussions on the local socio-economic system which have led almost everywhere to the corruption of traditional cultural values; lastly the contamination and upheavals caused by the sudden inflow of money.

There is a strange and quasi-magical identity, nowadays, which seems to link Reinhold Messner (who has climbed an 8000-metre/26,000-ft peak seven times without oxygen) and other exponents of extreme forms of mountaineering at high altitudes, with those Japanese monks who, step by step, sought inner 'enlightenment' as they climbed their way up Mount Fuji: a volcano, a triangle, a symbol – two converging lines which, ideally, would seem to join earth to heaven.

*The world's mountains offer more than just the frozen
wastes of the Himalaya, Karakorum or Andes. Far
left: a team climbing the Bastion d'Aioui, in the
Moroccan Atlas mountains. Left: climbing on the
warm volcanic basalt of the Hoggar in the Sahara.
Right: In Greenland, on Apostolen's Tommelfingen.
In terms of mountaineering, many mountain ranges
are still waiting to be discovered, and offer excellent
opportunities for lightweight expeditions.*

Preparing yourself to climb

By its very nature, mountaineering is a dangerous sport. And unfortunately its history includes a long list of tragedies and accidents, often caused by banal things: a rope breaking, losing grip on a hold, a rock-fall or a snow cornice collapsing. The widespread use of cable cars, plus the opening of refuges at high altitude, make it possible nowadays for anyone, in just a few hours, and without having to make any particular physical and mental preparations, to find himself suddenly transported from his drawing-room or office to a spot 3000 metres (10,000 ft) or more up a mountain, facing thrills and dangers which he did not even suspect existed: sudden changes in the weather, fog or mist, rock-falls, and treacherous snow bridges. Every summer hordes of ill-equipped people head off from the cable-car stations, and venture up tracks and glaciers wearing no more than tennis-shoes and T-shirts. The sense of false security caused by modern technical equipment for climbing pushes other people, who have neither sufficient training nor experience, into situations where the problems confronting them are beyond their limits. So, every year, there is a long list of victims in the Alps: 253 deaths, 474 injuries, 41 missing persons, and 393 people saved after highly risky rescue operations – and these figures are for the Italian Alps alone, in 1980.

Most of these accidents are not an act of fate, but caused by lack of experience, lack of caution, and lack of a sense of responsibility. The real mountaineer – the climber who really knows his mountains – both fears and respects them. Twenty per cent of fatal accidents in fact occur on terrain considered to be 'easy' – people simply slipping off a track or piste. Sixty per cent occur during descents, when alertness wavers and tiredness dulls the reflexes. The Alpine Rescue Organizations have drawn up a statistical list of the causes of the accidents that have occurred. Only 32 per cent can be referred to real mountaineering activities. Sixty per cent come under the heading 'tourism', 6.3 per cent under the heading mountain-skiing, and 2 per cent under the heading caving.

Causes of such accidents are listed below in order of the greatest frequency:
1 Slipping on grass or tracks (16.17 per cent)
2 Losing the way (15.42 per cent)
3 Bad weather (10.92 per cent)
4 Slipping on snow or ice (9.42 per cent)
5 Collapse or loss of grip on a hold (8.5 per cent)
6 Not feeling well (7.67 per cent)
7 Being incapacitated (6.41 per cent)
8 Rock-falls (3.67 per cent)
9 Falling on skis (3.42 per cent)
10 Avalanches (2.58 per cent)
11 Being too slow (1.75 per cent)
12 Falling into a crevasse (1 per cent)
13 Other causes (13.07 per cent)

It is also shown that 82 per cent of people who get into trouble are men, 23 per cent were roped together, 8.9 per cent were alone, and only 2 per cent were with a professional guide.

There are standards of caution which have now been classified, and these represent a kind of 'Seven Commandments' for anyone venturing into the mountains.
1 Study closely the upward and descent routes
2 Always stay well within your own limits
3 Leave word of where you are going
4 Heed the advice of more experienced people
5 Look after your equipment
6 Tackle problems methodically
7 Respond at once to any call for help, and if necessary fetch further help

The best way of starting mountaineering in a serious manner is to attend one of the many courses organized every spring by the various sections of your Alpine Club. In Italy, for example, the Italian Alpine Club also coordinates the rescue service, handles the construction and repair-work to refuges, and organizes mountaineering activities at every level. The Alpine Club also embraces the

Left and above: practising the recovery of a climber from a crevasse on the Brouillard glacier in the Mont Blanc range. The photographs on this and the following pages were all taken on the advanced Alpine climbing course held every year at the Monzino refuge in Val Véni. The Alpine Rescue Organization was founded in 1954, and nowadays rescuers are equipped with the latest techniques and equipment.

organization of professional guides and aspirant guides, who guarantee maximum safety to their clients.

The first person to classify the various types of dangers inherent to mountaineering was the German Emil Zsigmondy, who divided them into two major categories – 'subjective' and 'objective' dangers. The former are associated with the personal capacities of the individual; the latter occur independently of the mountaineer's own preparation and determination or volition, and are linked to the nature of the environment in which the climber is operating. The objective dangers are also independent of the technical difficulties of an ascent: some easy climbs are very dangerous, and there are some extremely tricky climbs which involve virtually no objective dangers. The first duty of a mountaineer is to acknowledge and know his own capacities and limits, his resistance to fatigue, the degree of training he has achieved, and his reactions in situations of emergency or danger. This understanding can be reached by degrees, on gradually longer and harder climbs. Good physical condition is the first, but not the only, requisite for anyone

Below: rescuing an injured climber on a rock-face. The rescuer lowers himself on a winch with a Mariner stretcher, designed specifically for this type of rescue. Right above: men in the Alpine rescue service lower themselves in pairs from a helicopter of the Military Alpine Service in Aosta. The helicopter is essential in modern rescue operations. Right below: when the alarm has been received, rescuers head for the place of the accident, carrying all the necessary equipment.

undertaking mountaineering activities. Training can help you to improve your muscular strength by 100 per cent and your endurance under fatigue by 50 per cent. But some ascents do require specific training. So, on major ice and mixed routes you will need special technique as well as endurance; on rock routes you will find yourself needing more technique still, muscular strength and an innate sense of climbing sharpened by experience, often called 'style'.

Training should preferably be started at the beginning of the season or in spring. A good starting point is to go to one of the 'training-grounds' which can be reached easily from the city: short rock-faces or lone boulders on which you can develop strength in your arms and fingers, a sense of balance, and pure technique. But experience gained on a training-ground nevertheless has certain major limitations, both technical and psychological. It is a wise idea to approach longer climbs gradually. It is also a good idea to alternate exercises aimed at developing muscular strength (knee-bends, gymnastics and so on) with other outdoor sports (running, swimming, cycling), which will mainly help improve your breathing and endurance. Insufficient training probably represents the major 'subjective' danger: on a particularly difficult stretch of rock or in an emergency, tiredness – and all mountaineers know only too well the feeling of cramp in the hands or trembling in the legs the first time they climb in the season – causes a sense of insecurity and fear which can lead to a loss of that calmness essential to safe climbing.

This sequence shows the phases in rescuing a climber from a narrow crevasse, a fearsome danger which can cause death quite quickly by crushing the rib-cage. Supported by the rescue team, the rescuer lowers himself head first, holding a special 'grip' (shaped like a shark's jaw). With this he grips the injured person around the pelvis, and pulls him from his wedged position. To be effective this type of help must be very prompt. Rescuers must also be able to give on-the-spot emergency medical aid.

Mountaineering also calls for a whole set of moral qualities: strength of mind and character, equilibrium, determination, generosity, openness, maturity and courage – a vital ingredient. A sense of moderation and experience stop these qualities in turn posing a threat. The choice of your fellow-climbers has to be rational: it is not enough to be just good friends, it is vital that everyone can rely on everyone else, if the need arises, and that all the members of a rope have more or less the same capacity and experience. A rope or team is only as strong as its weakest member. An insecure, slow and negligent member of a rope may represent a real danger in tricky situations, just as can an irresponsible leader. What is more, every mountaineer must be careful not to create dangerous conditions for his fellow climber(s) or for other teams further down the mountain; make sure you do not dislodge stones, do not cut across scree or slide-prone slopes, and do not cause cornices to collapse. Solo mountaineering, the most exposed, in absolute terms, to both subjective and objective dangers, calls for deep motivation, long experience, outstanding technical abilities, and perfect self-control: as a broad rule it is not advisable, because of the risks it involves.

The mountain environment is exposed to a number of objective dangers which cannot be eliminated altogether, but which we must nevertheless try to reduce as much as possible by respecting certain rules, choosing the route with great care, keeping to sensible timetables, and only proceeding – up or down – when

conditions are favourable. Rock-falls constitute one of these dangers. On more exposed routes a good first safeguard is to protect the head with a helmet and stay away from dangerous stretches when the rocks and stones above are no longer held together by ice, or have been dislodged by rain. If there is a really serious risk, which cannot be avoided (for example climbing up a landslide-prone gully), it is advisable for climbers to stick close together to stop falling rocks gaining speed as they hurtle downwards.

A similar danger is posed by falling chunks of ice, hanging séracs and cornices. Where this risk is present you must cover the ground involved very early in the morning, when the temperature is at its lowest and before the sun is shining directly on the glacier or rock-face. Very often in these stretches it is advisable to proceed using the light from your lamp, and do not hesitate to turn back if the termperature rises too fast. On glaciers, always proceed roped together, because of the danger of hidden crevasses. Séracs or hanging ice-walls can collapse at any moment, as a result of the continual forward movement of the glacier, which alters the position of any hanging blocks and structures. After heavy falls of snow, even in midsummer, small avalanches and slips can occur on steep snow- or ice-covered slopes. The slips may consist of powdery, inconsistent snow (these occur as soon as the weight of the snow breaks the cohesion of the new layer) or of heavy, wet snow, which tend to occur mainly in the warmest part of the day.

Bad weather gives rise to a number of risks, both direct and indirect: cold, loss of sense of direction because of bad visibility, wind, lightning, black ice and blizzards. The first rule in avoiding the dangers of bad weather is to pay close attention to weather reports before undertaking an ascent, and to be aware of warning signs typical of a given area (for example, the notorious 'fish-shaped' cloud on the Aiguille Verte, near Mont Blanc): the direction of the wind, and atmospheric humidity and pressure. An altimeter can be useful as a barometer too: a drop in atmospheric pressure corresponds to an increase in altitude. Basically speaking, when you are taken by surprise by bad weather, the most important factor is the speed with which you can make a safe retreat, once the decision has been taken – with the 'courage of fear' – to abandon the ascent. During short-lived but violent spring and summer storms, you must be particularly alert to the risk of being directly struck by lightning, or indirectly by the displacement of air caused by it: so leave an exposed summit or ridge at once, keep well away from niches in rock-faces, remain belayed at all times, keep away from routes fitted with metal rails, and from pitons, beware of sudden build-ups of static electricity which occur with humming and buzzing, vibrations in the air, light haloes around the rope or ice-axe, and the impression that someone is pulling you by the hair.

An ascent must be planned on the basis of the time calculated as necessary for the climb up, and the return to base, including stops and any eventualities which might crop up. The technical and other equipment and the food supplies are got ready and worked out on the basis of the difficulty and length of the climb. On very long climbs or ascents it is advisable to be prepared for a possible bivouac. And everything should take second place to principles of safety and caution. In the words of Edward Whymper: 'Always remember that just a split second of negligence or carelessness can destroy the happiness of a whole life. Don't do anything in a rush, take every step with care, and from the outset keep your mind on how the climb will turn out.'

Mountains for everyone

There is more to mountaineering than the sixth grade. Mountains also mean tradition, culture, meadows, flowers, animals, Alpine huts, refuges, paths and tracks, woodland, torrents and mountain streams, snow, silence, and dawns and dusks with incredible hues. Mountains are accessible to one and all, and in fact, especially in the summer months, ever-larger numbers of people elect to roam and hike for days on end from refuge to refuge, using the delicate network of paths and tracks shown on the various maps, clambering up mountain-sides, and down into remote valleys, discovering the marvels of nature which cry out for protection and respect. The upper routes in the Dolomites, the scores of maintained paths, the Alpine Path leading to places made famous in the First World War, the *Via delle Bocchette* in the Brenta group, excursions to the Stelvio, Gran Paradiso National Parks, or to Savoy or the Pyrenees offer justifiably famous itineraries.

Hiking is a healthy sport available to all and sundry (as long as you can assess your own strength and are reasonably fit); it also enables those who do not want to venture too high up to derive just as much enjoyment and pleasure from all the delights of mountains: their skies, blue or stormy, their boundless views from summits and cols, their leaping chamois, the alarmed whistle of a marmot, and the majestic flight of an eagle. Mountain-walking does not require too much heavy or particularly specialized equipment; the basic clothing needed consists only of a pair of comfortable woollen or corduroy trousers, a light shirt, an anorak or windcheater, and a sweater. Your boots should be quite high and sufficiently tough to prevent twisted ankles; they should also be such as to allow you to move nimbly on uneven terrain, or in snow, so they must not be too rigid. Your rucksack must be big enough to hold a tea- or water-flask or Thermos, food, sweets and sugar lumps to suck while you are on the move, spare socks and T-shirt, and a waterproof cloak in case the weather suddenly changes for the worse.

It is very important to keep going at a steady, slow pace as you climb: in this way

From the early years of this century onwards mountain holidays have become a habit for many families. Hiking from refuge to refuge using well-prepared itineraries with maintained paths and tracks is one of the favourite activities of those in search of a mountaineering experience free of problems. Left: a late nineteenth-century photograph showing a woman negotiating the chaotic séracs of one of the glaciers of Mont Blanc, helped by guides. Left below: a group of hikers in the Gran Paradiso National Park in Italy. Right: the Via delle Bochette in the Brenta group is one of the most popular maintained routes in the Dolomites. These itineraries still require a lot of experience, and a watchful eye at all times.

you can proceed without exerting yourself and stopping as little as possible. A good average rate of progress is 300 – 400 metres (1000 – 1300 ft) upward in an hour (this is the Alpine hiker's rate), stopping for a breather for ten minutes after every fifty minutes. Even on an 'easy' path or track you must always have your wits about you, learning how to choose instinctively exactly where best to tread, avoiding slippery stretches or scree, and calculating your own movements with the same concentration as if you were on a climb. In this way you will avoid constantly breaking your rhythm, you will avoid awkward and badly balanced positions, and you will be less tired.

On the whole the weight of your rucksack forces you to walk bent quite well forward, with your legs and knees working with suppleness. It can be helpful to have a walking stick or ski-pole with you. With time, and with experience, you will learn how to walk easily with automatic and instinctive movements. When going uphill it is never a good idea to stray from well-worn paths. But you may have to traverse across steep slopes where there is no evident track. When this is the case concentrate above all on the position of your body, which must be held well clear of the slope and straight above the feet and legs. The closer you get to the slope above you (which can give you the impression of being in a safer position) the greater the risk of slipping. Climbing boots will grip on their edges if the terrain is even, or on projections from the slope. Be especially careful on grassy slopes (especially if wet) and on detritus-covered terrain where there is scree or loose stones. On sloping rock slabs avoid slipping on loose stones. In snow-covered areas, dig in the toes of your boots hard when climbing along the line of the slope, or use the inside edge when traversing a slope diagonally.

The best and least tiring uphill route consists of an upward zigzag pattern. It is advisable to avoid detritus-ridden gullies and slopes covered with scree or boulders; it is better to climb around the edges or on small rocks at the sides. Near glacial 'tongues' the moraine often poses the danger of large unstable blocks of ice or slip-prone walls of stones and earth. If you have to climb up narrow, detritus-strewn gullies, it is a good rule to check that there is no one above you who might dislodge stones, and for the same reason, that there is no one below you.

Ski mountaineering is an increasingly popular sport which enables its fans to venture up to mountain-tops even in the off-season. It entails certain risks, because of the very nature of the environment in which it takes place. The safest snow conditions usually occur in late spring. Right: with skis towards the Gnifetti refuge after climbing up to the Margherita refuge on Monte Rosa (4554 metres/14,940 ft), a classic Alpine goal in May and June. Far right, top: rock-climbing school near the Gardeccia refuge in the Catinaccio group. Far right, below: a training gym in Turin, built in 1980 on English and German models, enabling climbers to keep in trim all year round.

Climbing down a gully can pose more problems than the upward climb. On paths try to keep as supple a gait as possible, absorbing your body-weight and not jarring yourself at every step. If you are not acquainted with short cuts, it is best to avoid them because they are usually steeper, and because there is always the danger that you will send stones crashing down on to the path below.

If you are fit, and experienced, you can descend very fast and athletically leaving the main track and climbing directly down steep slopes, scree, and snow-covered slopes. In such cases the descent becomes a 'controlled fall' and can be effected at very considerable speed. You must keep very alert, remembering that it always takes a few metres to stop; so do not venture down slopes broken by drops, or where you cannot see the bottom. The best descents, which can sometimes be no less than thrilling, are on steep scree-covered slopes, where you can descend considerable distances in just a few minutes. Scree consisting of large stones is more dangerous, both for yourself, and for anyone below. Where there is spring or summer snow, once you have made sure that the snow is not too hard, you can glissade down, using a ski-like technique, covering long stretches with your feet together, using the Christy turning and braking system. On steep descents along the steepest line you must offset the weight of your body, downwards, with the weight of your heels to avoid constantly sitting down backwards. Your legs must be bent, ready to absorb bumps, and your speed can be controlled by taking quick

small steps. To stop, shift the weight from your heels to the edge of your boots, and shift from the position of dynamic forward weight to a static position. But if you have to traverse areas with large boulders you should jump from boulder to boulder in a coordinated way, carefully checking, each time, the best place to land and the best position for your boots; if you fall while doing this it may be quite dangerous, but as a means of progress it is less demanding. To avoid losing your balance, while descending, it is a good idea to adjust your rucksack tightly so it does not swing about as you move.

In the Alps, all the most popular and interesting mountains for the climber or hiker have refuges (or permanent, unsupervised, bivouacs in the more inaccessible areas) and the paths and tracks are signposted. Despite this, it is always a good rule to study and plan your itinerary with great care: if you are suddenly enveloped in mist, or surprised by bad weather, or if you take the wrong path by losing track of the signs, the situation can quickly become difficult. To find your way off the beaten track you will need, in addition to a detailed map, a compass and an altimeter. Life in refuges does not really have precise rules for discipline; it is governed more by rules of courtesy and respect, so do not bother or disturb other climbers who might be resting, do not make a noise, and do not make a mess. In unsupervised bivouacs do not light fires, replace blankets and kitchen equipment, close all the shutters and doors when you leave, and pay the proper fee. The same rules of behaviour also apply to any other circumstances: the mountains are everybody's heritage and they must not become a refuse tip where people throw litter. It is also quite unacceptable for campers or hikers to cause fires in woodland, disturb the animal life and pick rare plant species. These problems have become extremely serious in the most popular mountain areas, and surveillance is not easy, even in national parks. Anyone who ventures into the mountains must respect them above all else: the upbringing and conscience of a climber can be measured not least by the careful way he tidies up after a meal outdoors, and stashes the rubbish in a pocket in his rucksack.

The proper organization of a mountain hike also involves a careful calculation of the times involved, taking into account the climber's own fitness and any changes of fortune which might occur. If you are in a large group, times will obviously be longer. As a general rule it is best to start off early in the morning: when it is cool you can walk better and it is less tiring. The way back down, after a break in a refuge or at the end of a hike, should be started early enough to avoid being overtaken by darkness, which can make any descent a risky business. Even on an ordinary mountain stroll never underestimate the dangers of a mountain. On more demanding hikes (with maintained tracks and paths) abide by all the rules of caution and safety that apply to a proper mountain ascent.

Mountain photography

The figure of the mountain photographer is well known to everyone, and very necessary if anyone not actually present during an ascent, with all its unforgettable experiences, is to be made part of it. The choice of equipment is often based on weight: many mountaineers prefer a pocket model like the well-proven Rollei 35. The modern reflex cameras, with their low weight and compactness, have simplified the photographer's task, enabling him to take along one or more different lenses without weighing himself down. The equipment should be straightforward, practical, tough and always ready at hand even in the most precarious and difficult situations. A mistake made by many people is to keep the camera in the rucksack. This of course restricts your photographic range to panoramic 'views' snapped when you have stopped somewhere, or from the mountain-top, and these photographs are often unfortunately somewhat trite. The most interesting photographs, on the other hand, are those taken of fellow-climbers in action. When you have found a good spot for a picture (a ridge, or an interesting stretch of rock, with good back lighting) it is a good rule to warn the person about to be photographed and if necessary hold him in a secure position by tying off the rope.

As a rule the mountain photographer tends to photograph only himself or his companion during an ascent. For a more complete and effective photographic record, however, it is a good idea to alternate photos taken on the rock-face with more general photos of the surroundings, and even, on other occasions, following teams climbing the same route from below: an average 135 mm telephoto lens is usually adequate. It is also worth remembering that the best, most dramatic and striking photographs come in difficult conditions and situations: in fog or mist, in sleet or fine snow, on a wind-lashed ridge, on more exposed stretches of the climb, in short, in all circumstances where the last thing you are probably thinking about is the camera in your rucksack. In snow, in icy conditions, and at high altitudes, the reflection belies the readings on the exposure-metre, which should be adjusted manually by opening a stop or two. The use of an ultraviolet or 'skylight' filter to compensate for the dominant blue is always helpful. Low temperatures generally make it inadvisable to use automatic electronic cameras, because the batteries are quickly worn out in cold conditions. The mountain world offers an endless variety of themes and emphases to which the presence of people can add meaning. Close-up photographs with a 35 mm or 24 mm wide-angle lens contrast action and environment, with the mountaineer (symbolizing 'man') looming in the foreground in his confrontation with the mountain. Different effects are achieved by following other teams of climbers from below, or from afar.

The greatest disappointment for the mountaineering photographer is the difficulty of re-creating, in a photo, the sense of the steepness of a climb. Taken upwards from below, or vice versa, photos tend to be 'flat', and often hard to comprehend. The most real perspective (even if you use simple tricks to increase the vertical aspect, such as playing with the alignment of the horizon) is the lateral one, which can be most easily taken during a traverse. However, a useful device for giving a picture verticality is to put the rope in the near foreground.

Mountain photography is often bound up with out-of-date 'rules' which sometimes make it over-aesthetic and predictable. On the contrary, in the spirit of the real activity represented by photography, it should, as far as possible, be documentary and uncluttered. Detail can often be extremely expressive: an ice-framed face, a hand outstretched towards a hold, a piton driven into the rock. Photos joined together in sequence can be very interesting, on a technical level as well: for example the stages involved in negotiating an overhanging passage, climbing up a chimney, or proceeding up a snow ridge. The particular nature of the environment in which the mountaineer moves makes it advisable to include, where possible, something indicating the scale of the place, a detail (or a highlight) which indicates the volume and depth of the image: the most grandiose landscapes appear 'flat' in a photograph, and disappointing if there is no contrast between the different planes. The choice of colour or black-and-white is purely personal: colour may be more 'real' or 'truthful', but in some cases black-and-white photographs may have a more dramatic vigour, especially when you know how to juggle with the

Above: *William Henry Jackson at work in the Yosemite Valley. This unrivalled photographer of the real American West used gigantic 50 × 60 cm (20 × 24 in) plates, 'the only ones,' he said, 'capable of interpreting the majesty and grandeur of the mountain'. With his magnificent photographs he successfully urged the American government to set up the first National Park at Yellowstone, in Wyoming, in 1872.*

Above: the mountaineer Vittorio Sella (credited with the first winter ascent of the Matterhorn in 1882) was regarded as the greatest mountain photographer of his day. He recorded all the expeditions made by the Duke of the Abruzzi on St Elias (1897), Ruwenzori (1906) and in the Karakorum range (1909). The thousands of collodium plates (30 × 40 cm/ 12 × 16 in and 18 × 24 cm/ 7 × 10 in) are now in safe keeping in the Institute at Biella named after him.
Right: one of Sella's finest pictures: a team on one of the Barre des Ecrins glaciers, in the Dauphiné.
Below: a modern mountain photographer, whose job is certainly made quite a lot easier by modern technology.

contrast, and when you remember to use a yellow filter to bring out all the nuances of the sky. The mountain photographer must, of course, be able to move freely, and keep his distance from his climbing companions. Their cooperation will always make matters simpler. The commitment of the mountaineering photographer must never detract from the basic safety rules and regulations. Suffice it to mention, by way of a tragic warning, what occurred on the top of Piz Palú, where nine climbers fell to their death because a cornice collapsed while they were posing for a souvenir photograph.

Notable ascents in mountaineering

Europe

Mont Blanc (France)	4807 m	A. Paccard, J. Balmat	1786
Jungfrau (Switzerland)	4158 m	R. & G. Meyer	1811
Bernina (Switzerland)	4049 m	Coaz, Ragut-Tscharner	1850
Monte Rosa (Switzerland)	4634 m	Smyth, Stephenson and guides	1855
Grivola (Italy)	3969 m	Ormsby, Bruce, Dayne Cachat, Tairraz	1859
Barre des Ecrins (France)	4101 m	Moore, Walker, Whymper, Almer, Croz	1864
Marmolada (Italy)	3343 m	P. Grohmann, A. & F. Dimai	1864
Matterhorn (Switzerland)	4478 m	Whymper, Croz, Douglas, Hudson, Hadow, Taugwalder	1865
Cima Toas (Italy)	3173 m	Loss	1865
Grandes Jorasses (Italy)	4208 m	Walker, Anderegg, Jaun, Grange	1868
Cima Grande di Laveredo (Italy)	2999 m	Grohmann, Salcher, Innerkofler	1869
Ailefroide (France)	3954 m	Coolidge, Almer, Gertsch	1870
La Meije (France)	3983 m	Boileau de Castelnau, Gaspard	1877

Asia

Everest (Nepal)	8848 m	E. Hillary, N. Tensing (British expedition)	1953
K2 (Pakistan)	8611 m	L. Lacedelli, A. Compagnoni (Italian expedition)	1954
Kanchenjunga (Sikkim)	8598 m	G. Band, J. Brown (English expedition)	1955
Lhotse (Nepal)	8511 m	E. Reiss, F. Luchsinger (Swiss expedition)	1956
Makalu (Nepal)	8481 m	J. Couzy, L. Terray (French expedition)	1955
Cho Oyu (Nepal)	8153 m	H. Tichy, S. Jöchler, Pasang Dawa Lama (Austrian expedition)	1954
Dhaulagiri (Nepal)	8167 m	A. Schelbert, E. Forrer, K. Diemburger, Nime Dorje, Nawang Dorges (Swiss expedition)	1960
Nanga Parbat (Pakistan)	8125 m	H. Buhl (Austro-German expedition)	1953
Manaslu (Nepal)	8156 m	I. Imanishi, Gyalzen Norbu (Japanese expedition)	1956
Annapurna (Nepal)	8091 m	M. Herzog, L. Lachenal (French expedition)	1950
Hidden Peak (Pakistan)	8068 m	J. Kauffman, P. Schoening (American expedition)	1958
Broad Peak (Pakistan)	8047 m	M. Schmuck, F. Wintersteller, K. Diemburger, H. Buhl (Austrian expedition)	1957
Gasherbrum II (Pakistan)	8035 m	F. Moravec, S. Larch, H. Willenpart (Austrian expedition)	1956
Gasherbrum IV (Pakistan)	7980 m	W. Bonatti, C. Mauri (Italian expedition)	1958
Kanjut-Sar (Pakistan)	7760 m	C. Pellissier (Italian expedition)	1959
Shisha Pangma (Pakistan)	8013 m	(Chinese expedition)	1964
Tirich Mir (Afghanistan)	7750 m	Kwernberg (Norwegian expedition)	1950
Peak of Communism (USSR)	7485 m	Abalakov (Russian expedition)	1933
Elbrus (USSR)	5633 m	(British expedition)	1868
Ararat (Turkey)	5165 m	F. Parrot (German expedition)	1829
Carstensz Massif (New Guinea)	5030 m	(Dutch expedition)	1936

Africa

Kilimanjaro (Tanzania)	5895 m	H. Meyer, L. Purtscheller (German expedition)	1889
Mt. Kenya (Kenya)	5199 m	H. Mackinder (British expedition)	1889
Ruwenzori (Uganda)	5119 m	Luigi Amedeo de Savoia Duca degli Abruzzi Petigax, Ollier, Brocherel (Italian expedition)	1906
Toubkal (Morocco)	4165 m	(French expedition)	1923

North America

McKinley (Alaska)	6194 m	Stuck, Tatum, Harper (American expedition)	1913
Logan (Canada)	6050 m	(American-Canadian expedition)	1925
Whitney (California)	4418 m	(American expedition)	1873
Grand Teton (Wyoming)	4196 m	(American expedition)	1898

South America

Aconcagua (Argentina)	6959 m	E. Fitzgerald (British expedition)	1897
Chimborazo (Ecuador)	6310 m	E. Whymper, J. A. Carrel L. Carrel	1880
Cotopaxi (Ecuador)	5897 m	W. Reiss, A. Stubel A. Escobar	1872
Illimani (Bolivia)	6462 m	M. Conway, A. Maquignaz L. Pellissier	1898
Huascafán - lower summit	6768 m	A. Peck and Swiss guides	1908
Fitz Roy (Argentina)	3375 m	G. Magnone, L. Terray (French expedition)	1952

Index

Bibliography

On the Heights, Walter Bonatti, Hart-Davis 1964
Summits and Secrets, Kurt Diemberger, Allen & Unwin 1971
Big Wall Climbing, Doug Scott, Kaye & Ward 1974
The White Spider, Heinrich Harrer, Hart-Davis 1959
On Snow and Ice and Rock, Gaston Rébuffat, Kaye & Ward 1971
Technique de l'Alpinisme, Bernard Amy, Arthaud 1977
The Day the Rope Broke, Ronald Clark, Secker & Warburg 1965
The Seventh Grade, Reinhold Messner, Kaye & Ward 1974